Faulkner's
Olympian
Laugh 🙷

"Mythology breaks the whole of life into a vast, horrendous Divine Comedy. Its Olympian laugh is not escapist in the least, but hard, with the hardness of life itself."
—Joseph Campbell, *The Hero with a Thousand Faces*

"To Phil Stone
He did half the laughing for thirty years."
—Faulkner, Dedication to *The Town*

Faulkner's Olympian Laugh

MYTH IN THE NOVELS

by *Walter Brylowski*
EASTERN MICHIGAN UNIVERSITY

Wayne State University Press, Detroit 1968

To Anna

Contents

Acknowledgments

I would like to express my gratitude to Professors Russell B. Nye, Hazard Adams, and Bernard Duffey for their guidance and encouragement in this study. My thanks are also due to Mrs. Ursula Christian who typed the manuscript.

For permission to quote, my thanks to the following: The Bollingen Foundation for *The Hero with a Thousand Faces* by Joseph Campbell, Bollingen Series 17, copyright 1949, distributed by Princeton University Press; George Braziller, Inc. for *Myth and Mythmaking*, edited by Henry A. Murray, copyright 1960; Cambridge University Press for *Themis: A Study of the Social Origins of Greek Religion* by Jane Ellen Harrison; Harper & Row for *Cosmos and History* by Mircea Eliade (translated by Willard Trask), and *Worship* by Evelyn Underhill; University of Kentucky Press for *William Faulkner, From Jefferson to the World* by Hyatt Waggoner; Liveright Publishing Corporation for Faulkner's *Mosquitoes* and *Soldiers' Pay*; Louisiana State University Press for *The Novels of William Faulkner* by Olga Vickery; The Macmillan Company for *The Golden Bough* by James G. Frazer; University of North Carolina Press for *The Tragic*

Acknowledgments

Mask by John L. Longley, Jr.; Princeton University Press for *Anatomy of Criticism* by Northrop Frye, copyright 1957; The University of the South for Andrew Lytle's essays, "Regeneration for the Man" and "The Son of Man: He Will Prevail," *Sewanee Review* (Winter, 1949, 1955); University Press of Virginia for *Faulkner in the University*, edited by Frederick L. Gwynn and Joseph L. Blotner; Yale University Press for *William Faulkner, the Yoknapatawpha Country* by Cleanth Brooks, and *The Philosophy of Symbolic Forms, Vol. II* by Ernst Cassirer (translated by Ralph Manheim); Random House, Inc. for *Love in the Western World* by Denis de Rougement, copyright 1940, 1956 and reprinted by permission of Pantheon Books, a division of Random House, and for the following works of Faulkner: *The Unvanquished* (copyright 1934, 1935, 1936, 1938 and renewed 1961, 1962 by William Faulkner and 1964, 1965 by Estelle Faulkner and Jill Faulkner Summers); *Sartoris* (copyright 1929 and renewed 1956 by W. F.); *Absalom, Absalom!* (copyright 1936 and renewed 1964 by E. F. and J. F. S.); *A Fable* (copyright 1950, 1954 by W. F.); *Go Down, Moses* (copyright 1942 by W. F.); *The Hamlet* (copyright 1931 by W. F., 1932 by the Curtis Publishing Company, 1931, 1936, 1940 by Random House); *Intruder in the Dust* (copyright 1948 by W. F.); *The Mansion* (copyright 1955, 1959 by W. F.); *The Reivers* (copyright 1962 by W. F.); *Requiem for a Nun* (copyright 1950, 1951 by W. F.); *The Town* (copyright 1957 by W. F.); *The Wild Palms* (copyright 1939 by Random House and renewed 1966 by E. F. and J. F. S.); *Pylon* (copyright 1935 and renewed 1962 by W .F.); *Light in August* (copyright 1932 and renewed 1959 by W. F.); *As I Lay Dying* (copyright 1930 and renewed 1957 by W. F.); and *The Sound and the Fury* (copyright 1929 and renewed 1956 by W. F.).

1. Faulkner's "Mythology"

*F*_{aulkner} *criticism*, even from the time regarded by his present critics as the dark ages of his fame, has shown an awareness of the quality of myth in his writings. Perhaps this awareness has been stimulated by a renewed attention to the study of myth, which began at about the same time that criticism became aware of Faulkner. While the two areas of study have been developed in parallel periods, they have met only casually. "Myth" appears in many studies of Faulkner, but the meaning of the word is often unclear. At times it may be used to signify a fiction embraced by a culture as a representation of some essential truth of existence, a definition central to the work of the Cambridge School of myth-ritual scholars. Again, it might be used in a more casual sense to denote fictions compounded in the form of a saga and thus serve as a label for the Yoknapatawpha works. Or "myth" might be determined from context to import some large world view for which the critic intends to supply a schematized explanation. In any case, there is usually too much taken for granted in the use of the term with much ambiguity resulting. The word "myth" has come to have sonorous overtones in the modern critical vocabulary and, due to a multitude of possible meanings, has become, like the bearded patriarch, a symbol evoking unexamined respect. It is not my purpose to destroy that respect, but to examine the basis for it and perhaps thereby to enhance its dignity.

To do this, it will be necessary to distinguish between various levels of myth apparent in Faulkner's work. The first and simplest level of myth is that of allusion and analogy. As allusion, the references to classical myths in the earlier work might most kindly be termed naive decoration. Faulkner, however, quickly abandons his excessive attraction to this rhetorical embroidery and by the time of *The Sound and the Fury* the pose of classicism is transferred from the implied author to a character, Mr. Compson, where it serves the function of accenting a debilitating divorcement from action. However, the references to classical myths used in a simple analogical manner do not suffer the same fate. In the early period, before *The Sound and the Fury*, these are found largely as compressed similes, adjectives applied to characters with the facility of stock epithets. These undergo a functional transformation as Faulkner's use of myth becomes thematic, and, as in *Absalom, Absalom!* become integrated with the "myth" in the sense of plot. It is on this level that we might include many of Faulkner's uses of the Christian myth.

What I would term the second level of myth to be found in his works is to be distinguished from the first level in degree rather than in kind, for here too myth functions as analogy. But on this level, myth is not to be considered as a trope integrated with the plot; instead, it *is* plot. Thus, though there are many images which strike analogies between Joe Christmas and Christ, it is the larger mythic pattern of the scapegoat which governs the action and which includes both Christ and Joe Christmas. Myth and theme here are inseparable; myth arises from theme and informs theme. Within the body of Faulkner's work, two such archetypal patterns of mythic action occur: the casting out of the scapegoat and the initiation of the youth.

On the third level of myth there is a sharp distinction in kind. Here we pass from the rhetoric of the first level and the *mythos* of the second level to an examination of the epistemology of the actors and even to a consideration of that of the author. Here I shall use the term "mythic mode of thought" derived from Cassirer's attempt to achieve a philosophic definition of myth as symbolic form:

> To seek a "form" of mythical consciousness in this sense, means to inquire neither after its ultimate metaphysical causes nor after its psychological, historical or social causes: it is solely to seek the unity of the spiritual *principle* by which all its particular configurations, with all their vast empirical diversity, appear to be governed.
>
> A critical phenomenology of the mythical consciousness . . . will seek to apprehend the subject of the cultural process, the human spirit, solely in its pure actuality and diverse configurations, whose immanent norms it will strive to ascertain.[1]

Cassirer's discussion examines the consciousness of the object as "the product of a formative operation effected by the basic instrumentality of consciousness, by intuition and pure thought,"[2] and differentiates between this consciousness as it appears in mythical thought and as it appears in theoretical-scientific or rational-empiric thought. It will be my object to examine the epistemology of some of Faulkner's characters and to demonstrate that their configurations of reality which frustrate analysis attempted in terms of the rational-empiric mode of thought, can be explained more satisfactorily in terms of the mythic mode.

When we begin to consider the nature of some of Faulkner's own thoughts as evidenced by his novels, we raise the problem of the relation of myth to art. Here again there is a problem about the meaning of "myth." Richard Chase, limiting the meaning of "myth" to a formulated story, then equates all myth with art. This is to obscure the problem, for there is the vast area of mythic thought, of myth formation to be considered. When I speak of the mythic mode of thought, I shall mean the spiritual activity of the individual seeking to create a configuration of reality, an activity that is determined by laws other than the rational-empiric, which have received their most coherent analysis in Cassirer's study. This much will suffice for the characters of the novels. However, when we speak of the artist we must remember that in the creation of his work he has already divorced himself from the primary quality of myth, the immediacy with which the mythic mode seizes upon the essential unity of the subject-object relation. The artist's world of the *logos* acknowledges at once a removal into the area of pure forms where this primary unity does not exist.

It is possible, therefore, for a character within a novel to be presented as operating within the mythic mode, a character whose epistemology is governed by the laws of myth formation; but when we speak of the artist's work as myth we are already approaching another realm. The mythic mode of thought, governed by the immediacy and unity of the subject-object relation, is expressed in action. The participant in ritual action *becomes* the subject of his actions. The myth that arises *after* the ritual already admits of the distance between the subject and object. So long as the myth commands complete belief it remains in the area of the mythic mode. However, once this belief disappears, we have a fiction, a residue which now has a new being in the rational-empiric world. The writer of fiction is, then, not a creator of myth. We must grant him the ability to recognize the subject-object distance, the ability to resist the equation of his work with what we call empiric reality. To equate fiction with myth does credit to neither. I believe it *is* possible, however, to speak of the degree to which fiction can approximate the quality of myth. Here we may dignify both myth and the writer of fiction. The artist's recognition of the force of myth in man's spiritual activity and his desire—even necessity—to use this as a tool wherewith to express his own intuitions constitutes a valid area of study.

The artist's intuitions are frequently beyond the ability of language used in its rational-empiric fashion to express, yet the artist must find his expression. *"Intuitive activity possesses intuitions to the extent that it expresses them."* [3] Several critics have remarked the dissatisfaction Faulkner expresses in his early novels with "talk, talk, talk," and I believe it is his felt need to discover a mode of communication which carries an aura of meaning beyond the bounds of what might be recognized as a scientifically rational mode of knowledge that leads him to employ the perceptions of irrational characters, characters whose "truth" is a configuration of the mythic mode of thought. The discovery of this as a tool of his art marks the beginning of that series of books labeled the great middle period.

As Faulkner's thinking centers around an examination of the nature of evil, the experiments in form and structure become almost dominant. The function of his mythic analogues becomes an exploration of evil beyond the bounds of morality. It is a mode allowing him to treat in narrative form his vision of a world permeated with evil and yet to balance this with his faith that evil will, in the long run, consume itself while the "verities"—courage, honor, love—will maintain their static nobility and allow man to "endure." It will be the major work of this book to trace a progression through Faulkner's works of his coming to grips with the problem of evil in terms of this mythic mode of thought. There is ample evidence in the early novels that he was well acquainted with the residual myths of the classical period, but there is little evidence that he had penetrated to the significance that informed them before they had lost their true mythic meaning. There is later evidence that Faulkner was acquainted with the work of the anthropologists in the area of myth studies and, in the middle period, his work begins to employ techniques which result in a movement toward the true force represented

by myth. In the later period, forecast by *The Unvanquished*
and covering the novels from *Go Down, Moses* to *A Fable*,
his work reflects the evolution of the mythic consciousness to
the mythical-religious consciousness, a movement which reveals his own intellectual resolution of the problem of evil
through transcendence.

There is yet another level of myth that must be treated
in the works of Faulkner. Criticism has insisted so much on
the "myth" of Yoknapatawpha that some consideration must
be given to the validity of the term. Henry A. Murray, discussing "The Possible Nature of a 'Mythology' to Come,"
says,

> I would be ready to agree with Schorer's 1946 opinion that
> the definition of myth "must be both broad and loose," had
> not the broadness and looseness of recent usage—partic-
> ularly since 1946 in literary circles—gone so far as to deprive
> the term of cognitive utility. It seems to have lost connec-
> tion with its inherited domain and come to mean almost
> any product of the imagination and hence nothing distin-
> guishable from other things, since the imagination, as we
> now realize, is involved in all but the simplest sensations.
> The question is whether this most notorious semantic hobo
> of our time can ever be persuaded to stick to a few habitats,
> each of them susceptible of definition in a way that will di-
> minish, if not abolish, the confusion that currently exists in
> many circles as to the conceptual places in which it is, or
> should be, its privilege and duty to abide.[4]

Perhaps the ever-present association of the word "myth" with
the history of the South has led to the rather loose trans-
ference of the word to Faulkner's works dealing with his fictional southern county. Nonetheless, there *is* a sense in which
the "myth of the South" does play a role in his vision of a
ruined society. I shall indicate its general nature as I see it in
the introductory exposition of the four levels of myth in *Absalom, Absalom!* but thereafter shall reserve the overall examination of the Yoknapatawpha cycle until Faulkner returns to
his county in his last novels.

These levels of myth are advanced merely as a means of

analysis of myth in Faulkner's work. While the distinctions may at times appear to be artificial, it is necessary to establish some distinctions to avoid the danger that attends the random use of "myth" in such criticism. Before proceeding to the major work of tracing the continuum of Faulkner's involvement with the mythic mode, it might clarify my terms to illustrate them in relation to one of the mature works, *Absalom, Absalom!*

On the first level of myth, that of allusion and analogy, *Absalom, Absalom!* is particularly rich. The title, not reinforced by any allusion in the text itself, establishes the analogy between Henry and Absalom and Charles Bon and Amman and is used thematically in the incest motif and the fratricide. Ilse Dusoir Lind in her study, "The Design and Meaning of *Absalom, Absalom!*" suggests further parallels between these characters and classical and biblical mythology:

> If the characters in the Sutpen story remind us of Greek actors and epic Biblical figures, so does the action itself recall the events of an ancient tragic myth. A synopsis of the Sutpen legend would read like one of the summaries of Greek myths conveniently placed as prologue to modern translations of Greek plays. The continuing (though loose) analogies which exist between Sutpen and Oedipus, Sutpen's sons and Eteocles and Polyneices, Judith and Antigone, suggest that the Oedipus trilogy might have served as a general guide in the drafting of the plot. At the same time, Sutpen's fall and the obliteration of his house bring to mind the great myth of man's original fall from innocence and the visitations of Divine justice upon third and fourth generations. Old Testament violence evoking God's wrath is recaptured here in a legend of father turning against son, son against father, and brother against brother.[5]

In the passage (355–56)* where Henry returns to the campfire and the waiting Bon, she finds the language and allusions

* Page references are to the Modern Library edition of *Absalom, Absalom!* (New York, 1951).

17

by which this "Cain-Abel conflict" are rendered "appropriately Biblical."

There are further biblical analogies in Mr. Compson's structuring of the account of Sutpen's early life. Born in the Edenic mountain life of what was to become West Virginia,

> he didn't listen to the vague and cloudy tales of Tidewater splendor that penetrated even his mountains because then he could not understand what the people who told him about it meant . . . and when he got to be a youth and curiosity itself exhumed the tales which he did not know he had heard and speculated on, he was interested and would have liked to see the places once, but without envy or regret. (222)

Then, after the death of the mother who had been responsible for the family's push into the mountains, "They fell into it, the whole family, returned to the coast from which the first Sutpen had come . . . , tumbled head over heels back to Tidewater by sheer altitude, elevation and gravity, as if whatever slight hold the family had had on the mountain had broken" (222–23). Unlike the biblical fall, however, Sutpen's takes place after the departure from "Eden" and is not a manifestation of the will, but imposed upon him by society. Lind points out that with the loss of innocence before the door of the plantation house where he had been sent upon an errand, Sutpen felt, "like Adam in Paradise, the shameful inadequacy of his natural garb ('his patched overalls and no shoes')." [6] The fall leads to the godlike formulation of Sutpen's design, "creating the Sutpen's Hundred, the *Be Sutpen's Hundred* like the oldentime *Be Light*" (9).

Returned from the war, his "design" fallen in ruins, Sutpen becomes in Shreve's words an Abraham:

> "the old Abraham full of years and weak and incapable now of further harm, caught at last and the captains and collectors saying, 'Old man, we don't want you' and Abraham would say, 'Praise the Lord, I have raised about me sons to bear the

burden of mine iniquities and persecutions' . . . the same old Abraham who was so old and weak now nobody would want him in the flesh on any debt." (325–26)

The Cadmus myth is invoked three times to suggest the nature of the strife bred between Sutpen's "get." Mr. Compson naming over the children first uses the image: "Yes. He named Clytie as he named them all, the one before Clytie and Henry and Judith even, with that same robust and sardonic temerity, naming with his own mouth his own ironic fecundity of dragon's teeth" (62). This is repeated in one of Quentin's silent musings (182) and finally repeated aloud to Shreve (266).

Sutpen might also be associated with the fisher king of myth through the wounds received in the Haitian uprising, " 'one of which, Grandfather said, came pretty near leaving him that virgin for the rest of his life too' " (254). In terms of theme, this might relate the color-line flaw of Sutpen's (and allegorically, the South's) "design" to the social-political sterility of the South, a flaw that could be eliminated (and, in terms of the myth, with resultant "fertility") upon the recognition of Charles Bon as his son. But the recognition does not occur; Henry, who inherits the flaw, kills Bon and the decay increases in tempo.

All of these analogies serve in a general explication of one of the two major themes of the novel, the theme of the myth, or plot, tracing the life of Thomas Sutpen. There are other allusions to myths which are either very minor or which, although used repetitiously, do not reflect this close unity with theme. The constant use of the Agamemnon myth would, if attributable to Faulkner as narrator, constitute grounds for the charge that he had not outgrown the habit of liberally sprinkling his writing with the casual allusions which is evidenced in the early novels. However, in this novel, these allusions, sometimes inadequate in their application, are found in the voices of the characters and their limited value serves to reflect and to heighten these characterizations.

Faulkner, in the person of narrator, first describes Miss Rosa as having "an air Cassandralike and humorless and profoundly and sternly prophetic out of all proportion to the actual years even of a child who had never been young" (22). Later Mr. Compson picks up the image: "In a grim mausoleum air of Puritan righteousness and outraged female vindictiveness Miss Rosa's childhood was passed, that aged and ancient and timeless absence of youth which consisted of a Cassandralike listening beyond closed doors . . ." (60). But Mr. Compson seems to love the sense of doom aroused by the name and a few pages later is applying it to Clytie. "I have always liked to believe that he intended to name Clytie, Cassandra, prompted by some pure dramatic economy not only to beget but to designate the presiding augur of his own disaster . . ." (62). Shreve echoes the image and expands it in several directions:

> ". . . and she was right about the brother-in-law because if he hadn't been a demon and his children wouldn't have needed protection from him and she wouldn't have had to go out there and be betrayed by the old meat and find instead of a widowed Agamemnon to her Cassandra an ancient stiff-jointed Pyramus to her eager though untried Thisbe who could approach her in this unbidden April's compounded demonry and suggest that they breed together for test and sample and if it was a boy they would marry." (177)

Shreve's ranging for allusions to fit the story taking shape makes of the scythe that killed Sutpen " 'that scythe, symbolic laurel of a caesar's triumph,' " and then Sutpen becomes " 'this Faustus, this demon, this Beelzebub' " (177–78). The tone of these images found in these various perspectives will be discussed in terms of the second and third levels of myth as they relate to the characters involved.

It remains only to note some decorative allusions in Mr. Compson's narration and two in Rosa's. Mr. Compson describes Ellen, Sutpen's wife, as "this Niobe without tears who had conceived to the demon in a kind of nightmare" (13), "the woman who had quitted home and kin on a flood of tears and in a shadowy miasmic region something like the bitter purlieus of Styx had produced two children" (69). Charles Bon appeared on the scene as "almost phoenix-like" (74), " 'a man a little older than his actual years and enclosed and surrounded by a sort of Scythian glitter' " (93). The young men leaving for war provide a moving spectacle, " 'far more so than the spectacle of so many virgins going to be sacrificed to some heathen Principle, some Priapus' " (122), and Bon's son becomes a " 'delicate and perverse spirit-symbol, immortal page of the ancient immortal Lilith' " (196). Miss Rosa is given a short flight of allusiveness in her long monologue when Clytie becomes *"the cold Cerberus of his* [Sutpen's] *private hell"* who had watched her approach to the house with a sense of *"that justice whose Moloch's palate-paunch makes no distinction between gristle bone and tender flesh"* (136–37).

So much, then for the first level of myth. From the time of his first novel, Faulkner made much use of such allusions, but in no novel besides *Absalom, Absalom!* is this level so rich and so completely controlled.

The second level of myth in *Absalom, Absalom!* is that of the action and theme. This theme, the rise and fall of Thomas Sutpen in terms of his "design" and, on a larger, allegorical level, the flaw in the design of the antebellum South, includes not only the subject of the narrative, but the narrators as well insofar as they are included in the cycle of history under examination and are, by their drives to tell the story, still attempting to find the flaw in the grand design and thereby to understand their own lives as well as the life of Thomas Sutpen. The flaw is quite apparent: the moral failure of Negro-white relations.

When the young Sutpen was sent to the planter's mansion and turned away from the door by the Negro servant, like Huck Finn he went to the woods to think. The design he conceives to cope with the world is based on simple acceptance of the terms of that world: wealth equals social acceptance and power. But the design is also dynastic and calls for progeny— at least one male child of pure blood. It is the undeviating commitment to his design and the inevitable consequences of this commitment that make Sutpen the tragic figure he is. Like Lord Jim, Sutpen will attempt to live his life in terms of an idea established by society's propaganda, an attempt that can only be accounted for by his innocence, while the rest of society, protected by an ironic sense against too complete acceptance of the very words they mouth, look on puzzled and try to understand this fanaticism. This view of Sutpen is, of course, ironic and emerges only at the end of the novel and in the reader's mind as he puts together the total meaning of the various narratives.

These narratives offer four major viewpoints of Sutpen's life, which can, I think, be best classified by Northrop Frye's theory of modes to illustrate the richness of depth Faulkner has achieved in this novel. Frye, proceeding from Aristotle's *Poetics*, establishes five modes of fiction:

> In literary fiction, the plot consists of somebody doing something. The somebody, if an individual, is the hero, and the something he does or fails to do is what he can do, or could have done, on the level of the postulations made about him by the author and the consequent expectations of the audience. Fictions, therefore, may be classified, not morally, but by the hero's power of action, which may be greater than ours, less, or roughly the same.[7]

Of the modes thus posited, the first involves a hero "superior in *kind* both to other men and to the environment of other men," a divine being, "and the story about him will be a *myth* in the common sense of a story about a god." The second mode posits a hero "superior in *degree* to other men and to his environment . . . whose actions are marvellous but who is himself identified as a human being." This is the hero of romance who "moves in a world in which the ordinary laws of nature are slightly suspended: prodigies of courage and endurance, unnatural to us, are natural to him." The third mode posits a hero "superior in degree to other men but not to his natural environment. . . . He has authority, passions, and powers of expression far greater than ours, but what he does is subject both to social criticism and to the order of nature. This is the hero of the *high mimetic* mode." The hero of the fourth mode is "superior neither to other men nor to his environment," but is one of us. This is the hero of the low mimetic mode. And the hero of the fifth, or ironic, mode is "inferior in power or intelligence to ourselves, so that we have the sense of looking down on a scene of bondage, frustration, or absurdity." [8]

Much of the complexity of the narrative structure of the novel can be explained by examining the perspective each narrator has toward Sutpen. He is obviously not the god of the mythic mode, but in Miss Rosa's demonizing of him, he assumes some of the stature of the hero of the romantic mode with overtones of myth lingering on. As Quentin sits with Miss Rosa in the opening pages of the book, the author establishes the tone of her vision of Sutpen:

> Meanwhile, as though in inverse ratio to the vanishing voice, the invoked ghost of the man whom she could neither forgive nor revenge herself upon began to assume the quality almost of solidity, permanence. Itself circumambient and enclosed by its effluvium of hell, its aura of unregeneration, it mused (mused, thought, seemed to possess sentience, as if, though dispossessed of the peace—who was impervious anyhow to fatigue—which she declined to give it, was still irrevocably outside the scope of her hurt or harm) with that quality peaceful and now harmless and not even very attentive—the ogre-shape which, as Miss Coldfield's voice went on, resolved out of itself before Quentin's eyes the two half-ogre children, the three of them forming a shadowy background for the fourth one. (13)

As the narrative moves into Miss Rosa's own voice, Sutpen becomes a " 'fiend, blackguard and devil, in Virginia fighting, where the chances of the earth's being rid of him were the best anywhere under the sun, yet Ellen and I both knowing that he would return, that every man in our armies would have to fall before bullet or ball found him' " (15). Her imagery evoking the supernatural qualities of Sutpen incorporates the mythic allusions already noted: Clytie is *"the cold Cerberus of his private hell,"* and Sutpen returns from the War to undertake his "Herculean task," while at table *"talking that which sounded like the bombast of a madman who creates within his very coffin walls his fabulous immeasureable Camelots and Carcassonnes"* (160). As her narrative reaches the point of Sutpen's proposition to breed for test, her hysterical note calls forth repeatedly the designations of "demon" and "ogre" that will be picked up in Shreve's ironic part of the narration.

Mr. Compson picks up the narrative in the low mimetic mode. To him, Sutpen partakes of nothing of the supernatural, nor, since he was of the same planter class does he envision him as superior to himself in the high mimetic status of leader. There is a slight tendency for him to regard Sutpen in the ironic mode when he conceives of him as a player in some kind of cosmic drama with "behind him Fate, destiny, retribution, irony—the stage manager, call him what you will—" calling the tune. But his limited knowledge of the facts of the story as finally pieced together by Shreve and Quentin keeps his narration largely on the low mimetic plane, especially since what we know of Mr. Compson as a character indicates that he too regards himself as a kind of player in a controlled drama.

It is when Mr. Compson communicates the vision of Sutpen held by Wash that we see Sutpen in the high mimetic role of leader, a man superior to other men. Mr. Compson imagines Wash watching Sutpen galloping on the black thoroughbred, " 'thinking maybe, . . . *If God Himself was to come down and ride the natural earth, that's what He would aim to look like'* " (282). And when Wash is faced with the idea of Sutpen's seduction of his fifteen-year-old granddaughter, unaware that it is merely breeding "for test," he is able to reconcile himself to it because Sutpen is "different." This attitude persists right up to the moment of the ultimate insult which forces Wash to accept his own dignity as a human being and to kill Sutpen with the scythe. On the morning when the granddaughter is delivered of child, his view is still that

> *"he is bigger than all them Yankees that killed us and ourn, that killed his wife and widowed his daughter and druv his son from home, that stole his niggers and ruined his land; bigger than this whole country that he fit for and in payment for which has brung him to keeping a little country store for his bread and meat; bigger than the scorn and denial which hit helt to his lips like the bitter cup in the Book."* (287)

Quentin's perspective of Sutpen is not so simple. Based as it is on derivative views, it partakes somewhat of each view. Yet it remains toward the center of Frye's spectrum of modes, not following Miss Rosa's hysterical demonizing toward myth and resisting Shreve's use of the same imagery in the ironic mode which, Frye observes, "moves steadily toward myth, . . . dim outlines of sacrificial rituals and dying gods" beginning to reappear in it.[9] Although Shreve's ironic view is at first pronounced, Faulkner insists on a modification of this as he is taken up by and becomes emotionally involved with the story: "This was not flippancy either. It too was just that protective coloring of levity behind which the youthful shame of being moved hid itself [280], that incorrigible unsentimental sentimentality of the young which takes the form of hard and often crass levity" (275). The burden of the final ironic view is transferred to the reader.

The narrative thus moves back and forth through the spectrum of modes as different views of Sutpen are presented. For Miss Rosa he partakes of something of the supernatural, his evil something like Faustus' covenant with the devil, immune to death on the battlefield, spared that his pattern of

evil may fulfill itself. For Wash and for Quentin's moments
of longing for romantic ideals he partakes of the high mimetic
mode with its elevation of the hero to a position superior to
other men. At the same time, Quentin recognizes him with
his father as a man no different than other men and, with
Shreve, witnessing the frustration, bondage, and absurdity of
his quest, partakes somewhat of the ironic vision of the man.
With all the facts of the story as given him, it is finally the
reader, however, who is filled with "the sense of looking down
on a scene of bondage, frustration, or absurdity," not only for
Sutpen but for the narrators of the story.

Whatever overtones of myth surround Sutpen in this
final ironic vision of the novel, he does not take on the garb of
the *pharmakos* unless we force him into the position of a
figure sacrificed to the design of the South. Yet, his full and
active acceptance of this design and his commitment to it
throughout the action, albeit a result of the "innocence"
stressed by General Compson, makes of him the tragic actor,
the agent of his own destruction. The role of *pharmakos* is
filled by his unacknowledged progeny, especially Charles Bon,
the innocent victim of a fraction of Negro blood in his veins.
When Sutpen takes over the design of the planter class of the
South as his own to protect that boy knocking at the front
door of the mansion and commits himself to it irrevocably, he
becomes in a sense the priest of that cult, capable of sacri-
ficing his first born son. As Frye says of the *pharmakos*, "He is
innocent in the sense that what happens to him is far greater
than anything he has done provokes . . . He is guilty in the
sense that he is a member of a guilty society, or living in a
world where such injustices are an inescapable part of existence." [10] Bon partakes of some of the guilt of this society in
taking an octoroon wife whom he is willing to set aside. He is
passive until the moment he writes to Judith, "We have
waited long enough," and sets in motion the inevitability of
his own sacrifice. Henry, who is willing to tolerate the idea of
a morganatic marriage and even incest, cannot brook the idea

of miscegenation and kills his brother. The sequence of choices offered Henry magnifies the moral quality of the one thing the cult will not allow, the one thing that can bring him to fratricide. Bon's death, "Aged 33 years and 5 months," merely repeats Faulkner's device of identifying the scapegoat with the archetypal Christian pattern of the *pharmakos*, not with the person of Christ.

After Charles Bon, the sufferings for the sins of the father are carried unto the fourth generation as the grandson, Charles Etienne Saint-Valery Bon, strikes out in his confusion at a society that is willing to let him pass as white if he will remove himself from the scene. Like Joe Christmas, he forces himself into a series of situations that will bring him violence, flouting his coal black wife at those who would let him pass, " 'treading the thorny and flint-paved path toward the Gethsemane which he had decreed and created for himself, where he had crucified himself and come down from his cross for a moment and now returned to it' " (209). Charles Etienne's son, the "bright-colored" Negro idiot who now passes by the name of Jim Bond, completes the biblical pattern of the four generations.

Viewed in its overall pattern, *Absalom, Absalom!* illustrates Faulkner's habit of probing the moral situation of the South and projecting it against a screen of mythic references where the actions find their analogues. This technique of extending the meaning of a work into the realm of myth is further supplemented by employing as points of view characters whose modes of thought might be termed mythic. As Faulkner sought to construct a fictional world embracing the sum total of his vision, both the rational-empiric and the intuitive, he discovered the necessity of creating characters whose perceptions could communicate these intuitions, for Faulkner's work in this period stands as a demonstration of Croce's axiom that "intuitive activity possesses intuitions to the extent that it expresses them." This brings us to the third level of myth in his work.

Criticism has devoted much of its time to translating, or to an attempt at translating, the reality of some of Faulkner's characters into a scientific-empiric order of reality which will easily communicate the "facts" of that experience to the reader. As an end in itself, the "facts" so translated become dead and the characters, labeled neurotic or moronic, are sent off to join Benjy and Darl at Jackson. As Faulkner began writing the novels of the great middle period, beginning with *The Sound and the Fury,* two of his great discoveries in technique were the use of a narrator disoriented from the scientific-empiric mode of perception and the destruction of empiric time, usually through the mind of the disoriented perceiver. The narrations of Faulkner's neurotics and idiots bear out many of the qualities of the mythic consciousness as outlined by Cassirer in the second volume of *The Philosophy of Symbolic Forms.*

Miss Rosa's narrative, dominated by a passionate reaction to an insult received forty-three years before, presents the story of Sutpen in the immediacy of the fury felt then, a fury that has prevented her from the analysis and abstraction necessary to arrive at an understanding of the events in terms of a scientific epistemology. Instead, the entire life of Sutpen has become equated with a mythic pattern of evil haunted by demons and ogres. It is, indeed, a version of reality which in Cassirer's terms of analysis is a product of the mythical consciousness. "For the mythical consciousness," says Cassirer, "the impression is not merely relative but absolute":

> It manifests and confirms itself by the simple intensity of its presence, by the irresistible force with which it impresses itself upon consciousness. Whereas scientific thought takes an attitude of inquiry and doubt toward the "object" with its claim to objectivity and necessity, myth knows no such opposition. It "has" the object only insofar as it is overpowered by it. . . . It has no will to understand the object by encompassing it logically and articulating it with a complex of causes and effects; it is simply overpowered by the object.[11]

Miss Rosa lives not in a world of " 'things' and their 'attributes' but of mythical potencies and powers, of demons and gods." Sutpen's story is inextricably mixed with the fate of the South in her mind, a part of the whole, and therefore, in the mythic consciousness, equal to the whole. The Coldfield family is but another part in which the workings of the whole are evident and which becomes an identity of the whole:

> ". . . as though there were a fatality and curse on our family and God Himself were seeing to it that it was performed and discharged to the last drop and dreg. Yes, fatality and curse on the South and on our family as though because some ancestor of ours had elected to establish his descent in a land primed for fatality and already cursed with it, even if it had not rather been our family, our father's progenitors, who had incurred the curse long years before and had been coerced by Heaven into establishing itself in the land and the time already cursed." (21)

For Miss Rosa Coldfield, this constitutes the entire meaning of Sutpen's story and with the completion of the "curse," the burning of Sutpen's house and what she believes to be the last of his line, the curse will have fulfilled itself and it is fitting that she dies soon after, evidently with the belief that *her* death completes the spiritual reality with which she has lived so long.

That her narrative is incomplete and filled with errors indicates that her reality does not call for the cause and effect rationale of empiric thought, the pattern that will only be constructed as Quentin and Shreve piece out the story in their rooms. For Miss Rosa it is enough that there is a central "curse" which unifies her reality; beyond that she does not seek. It is for her the pure form of myth. This mode of thought is understood as different by the Compsons, father and son, but is analyzed in terms of a kind of male chauvinism and is tolerated in terms of a kind of chivalry:

> "Ah," Mr. Compson said. "Years ago we in the South made our women into ladies. Then the War came and made the

ladies into ghosts. So what else can we do, being gentlemen, but listen to them being ghosts?" (12)

"Yes. They lead beautiful lives—women. Lives not only divorced from, but irrevocably excommunicated from, all reality." (191)

Which in Quentin's elaboration becomes:

> *Beautiful lives women live—women do. In very breathing they draw meat and drink from some beautiful attenuation of unreality in which the shades and shapes of facts—of birth and bereavement, of suffering and bewilderment and despair—move with the substanceless decorum of lawn party charades, perfect in gesture and without significance or any ability to hurt.* (211)

Mr. Compson creates for Quentin an image of the young Rosa sitting at Sutpen's table

> with still and curious and profound intensity as though she actually had some intimation gained from that rapport with the fluid cradle of events (time) which she had acquired or cultivated by listening beyond closed doors not to what she heard there, but by becoming supine and receptive, incapable of either discrimination or opinion or incredulity, listening to the prefever's temperature of disaster, which makes soothsayers and sometimes makes them right. (66)

"To seek a 'form' of mythical consciousness," says Cassirer, "is solely to seek the unity of the spiritual *principle* by which all its particular configurations, with all their vast empirical diversity, appear to be governed." [12] The principle which governs Miss Rosa's reality unifying her sensory impressions of an empirical diversity embracing her strange childhood, the War, the suffering of the South, and her forty-three year fury is a complex of the sacredness of the South in terms of its mythic status engendered by the War and the biblical idea of an evil rooted out over the generations. Add to this a feminine mystique of love and we have the core of her thought.

As independent agent of action, her first gestures are to offer her housekeeping knowledge to Judith upon her betrothal and next, upon being rejected in this, to steal cloth from her father's store to sew articles for Judith's trousseau. When the War begins and her father boards himself up in the attic of their house, it is on that night she begins the composition of the odes and elegies on the Confederates which will reach more than a thousand in number. Her ambivalence toward Sutpen who was the "ogre" of her youth but becomes the accepted suitor after the War, partakes also of the sacredness of the cause which he has come to represent through his courageous action in the field:

> . . . there was a shape which rode away beneath a flag and (demon or no) courageously suffered—and I did more than just forgive: I slew it [the image of the ogre], because the body, the blood, the memory which that ogre had dwelt in returned five years later and held out its hand and said 'Come' as you might say it to a dog, and I came. (167)

Then after the insult, she seeks to find an image to express his nature in the typical mythic opposition of light to darkness:

> Because he was not articulated in this world. He was a walking shadow. He was the light-blinded bat-like image of his own torment cast by the fierce demoniac lantern up from beneath the earth's crust and hence in retrograde, reverse; from abysmal and chaotic dark to eternal and abysmal dark completing his descending (do you mark the gradation?) ellipsis, clinging, trying to cling with vain unsubstantial hands to what he hoped would help him, save him, arrest him—(176)

Her romantic evocation of Bon which calls forth that bit of incredible rhetoric, "I became all polymath love's androgynous advocate," is punctuated by the refrain, "I never saw him." Of Bon, Mr. Compson admits,

> "He is the curious one to me. . . . He seems to hover, shadowy, almost substanceless, a little behind and above all the other straightforward and logical, even though (to him) incomprehensible, ultimatums and affirmations and defiances and challenges and repudiations, with an air of sar-

donic and indolent detachment. . . . with that sardonic and surprised distaste which seems to have been the ordinary manifestation of the impenetrable and shadowy character. Yes, shadowy: a myth, a phantom: something which they engendered and created whole themselves; some effluvium of Sutpen blood and character, as though as a man he did not exist at all." (93, 104)

Mr. Compson can identify the product of her configuration, but it is Miss Rosa herself who must attempt to communicate something of the mode of that configuration to Quentin:

> *There are some things which happen to us which the intelligence and the senses refuse just as the stomach sometimes refuses what the palate has accepted but which digestion cannot compass—occurrences which stop us dead as though by some impalpable intervention, like a sheet of glass through which we watch all subsequent events transpire as though in a soundless vacuum, and fade, vanish; are gone, leaving us immobile, impotent, helpless; fixed, until we can die.* (151–52)

> *That is the substance of remembering—sense, sight, smell: the muscles with which we see and hear and feel—not mind, not thought: there is no such thing as memory: the brain recalls just what the muscles grope for: no more, no less: and its resultant sum is usually incorrect and false and worthy only of the name of dream.* (143)

Or, one might suggest, worthy of the name of myth.

Faulkner relies upon the mythic mode of perception manifested by Miss Rosa to fill out that part of expression and meaning which has always eluded words used in a theoretical-empirical manner, a failure of language behind the many complaints Faulkner voices about words throughout his works. Mr. Compson, Quentin, and Shreve as narrators remain largely within this latter mode of thought, and, restricted to their narratives, we would miss much of the moral pattern which Miss Rosa's narrative supplies. Their mode of thought governs the search for the "facts" of Sutpen's story, but it is Miss Rosa who posits and makes explicit the concept of an evil rising beyond the lives of the actors into a symbolic and allegorical level of meaning embracing the history of the South. In this sense, she is adequately called the Cassandra figure in that her frenzied half-knowledge fixes upon a larger moral order, the "curse," and enables her to explain cryptically the moral truth of the action.

As it is illuminating in an analysis of Miss Rosa's forms of reality to counterpoint quotations from Faulkner's text with quotations from Cassirer's study of mythic thought, so it is helpful to note other aspects of this symbolic mode functioning in Sutpen's vision of the world. Sutpen's actions are those of a figure operating within the magical world view. His struggles against social traditions, nature, and time may be seen as a struggle to achieve a concept of the I or the soul. It is a feature of myth, Cassirer tells us, that it does not start from a finished concept of the I or the soul, but achieves this concept, forms this picture, out of itself.[13] Sutpen's grand scheme admits of no external force that he cannot conquer through his will and desire. It is this *desire* which Cassirer calls the first energy by which man achieves an independent being in opposition to things; he is no longer content to accept the world and the reality of things, but, in terms of this desire, gives a new form to reality, a form to which everything else must submit. In this magical world view, the I has almost unlimited power over reality and "through the magical omnipotence of the will . . . seeks to seize upon all things and bend them to its purpose." [14]

> The soul itself appears as a demonic power which acts upon man's body from outside and possesses it—and hence possesses the man himself with all his vital functions. Thus precisely the increased intensity of the I-feeling and the resulting hypertrophy of action produce a mere illusion of activity.[15]

However, it is precisely at this point in the evolution of his soul concept that Sutpen falters. As empirical reality forces more and more upon him the distinction between the objects of his desire and the I, as these two spheres gain independent reality, he gives up and walks out to meet Wash and his death. It is in the fullest Aristotelian sense that we may look upon Sutpen as a tragic character, his action charting a quest for a concept of self which he cannot cope with when he faces it.

Although Quentin's mind is dominated by the scientific-empiric mode of thought and must pursue the story of Sutpen with an objective logic, there is one aspect of his participation in the story that is primarily mythic in mode: the disintegration of empiric time. "For myth," Cassirer tells us,

> there is no time "as such," no perpetual duration and no regular recurrence or succession; there are only configurations of particular content which in turn reveal a certain temporal *gestalt*, a coming and going, a rhythmical being and becoming.[16]
>
> The stages of time—past, present, future—do not remain distinct; over and over again the mythical consciousness succumbs to the tendency and temptation to level the differences and ultimately transform them into pure identity. . . . The magical "now" is by no means a *mere* now, a simple, differentiated present, but is . . . laden with the past and pregnant with the future.[17]

Faulkner as narrator sets out at once to establish the timelessness of the tale in Quentin's mind and to pose one of the theoretical problems of his technique:

> It (the talking, the telling) seemed (to him, to Quentin) to partake of that logic- and reason-flouting quality of a dream which the sleeper knows must have occurred, stillborn and complete, in a second, yet the very quality upon which it must depend to move the dreamer (verisimilitude) to credulity—horror or pleasure or amazement—depends as completely upon a formal recognition of and acceptance of elapsed and yet-elapsing time as music or a printed tale. (22)

When Quentin is challenged in the course of his narrative by Shreve's " 'Don't say it's just me that sounds like your old

34

man,'" his musing on time that follows is primarily in terms of biological rhythms, a feature belonging to the earliest configurations of the mythic consciousness:

> *Maybe we are both Father. Maybe nothing ever happens once and is finished. Maybe happen is never once but like ripples maybe on water after the pebble sinks, the ripples moving on, spreading, the pool attached by a narrow umbilical water-cord to the next pool which the first pool feeds, has fed, did feed, let this second pool contain a different temperature of water, a different molecularity of having seen, felt, remembered, reflect in a different tone the infinite unchanging sky, it doesn't matter: that pebble's watery echo whose fall it did not even see moves across its surface too at the original ripple-space, to the old ineradicable rhythm* thinking Yes, we are both Father. *Or maybe Father and I are both Shreve, maybe it took Father and me both to make Shreve or Shreve and me both to make Father or maybe Thomas Sutpen to make all of us.* (261–62)

And finally as the rhythm of the story reaches its crescendo, the emotional quality of timeless identity is fully achieved in the minds of both Quentin and Shreve.

> So that now it was not two but four of them riding the two horses through the dark over the frozen December ruts of that Christmas Eve: four of them and then just two—Charles-Shreve and Quentin-Henry. (334)

> Four of them there, in that room in New Orleans in 1860, just as in a sense there were four of them here in this tomb-like room in Massachusetts in 1910. (336)

Miss Rosa's vision of Sutpen is completely mythic in orientation. We have seen that her vision "begins with the intuition of purposive action" common to myth—the "curse" already upon the land to which her ancestors came like actors to a stage to play the roles directed by Mr. Compson's cosmic stage manager. It is her vision that reaches back through layers of time to find the definite beginning, positing a genesis of forces that later find their definite forms in the persons of the story, forms which are elevated to the sphere of the sacred (not necessarily morally "good") with the stature of demons, romantic gods, or Jobs suffering under an enormous evil. In her mythic sense of time the past has no "why"—it *is* the why of things. Her consciousness singles out only those things in time that have the sacred quality of being a part and therefore equivalent to the whole of the mythic pattern of evil seeking its end through the sufferings of its chosen actors; all else is relegated to the sphere of the profane and elided from her consciousness. It is her vision that primarily lends to the novel its mythic tone.

But this tone could not be sustained without some reinforcement in the other narratives. Miss Rosa's monologue is rather short and cannot bear the burden for the entire novel. We have already seen that mythic allusions in the other narratives help to sustain this tone as does the disintegration of time for Quentin and Shreve. Mr. Compson, although primarily given to the rational-empiric mode, contributes, besides his many classical allusions, images and ideas that strike a mythic chord. Ellen's change of character in the middle life is a "metamorphosis, emerging into her next lustrum with the finality of actual rebirth" (64); the octoroon mistress-wife of Bon dies a death that is but another such metamorphosis removed from the empiric understanding of death (196); Bon is a shadowy creation belonging to the realm of myth; and the entire tale is " 'just incredible. It just does not explain. Or perhaps that's it: they don't explain and we are not supposed to know' " (100).

There is no evidence to support the idea that Faulkner was conscious of a mythic mode as such. There is, I believe, enough evidence in the works that Faulkner by this time had penetrated to the true force of mythic thought underlying the residual fictions with which he was so familiar. His intuitive readings in classical and Christian mythology provided him with a knowledge necessary to reconcile poles of a vision of life, poles essentially incompatible on the level of theoretical-empirical thought: the pervasiveness of evil and suffering, and the optimistic faith in man's ability to prevail over this fact of his existence. Throughout his writings, this basic opposition resists synthesis. In the middle period to which *Absalom, Absalom!* belongs, Faulkner gains the presence of these two poles on his scene by comic contrast or by structural juxtaposition; in the later novels there is some attempt to deal with this problem through the initiation of a character into the experience of a society that embraces them in a kind of equilibrium; then, after the heroic attempt at transcendence represented by *A Fable*, there is an attempt to demonstrate the general impotence of evil.

Absalom, Absalom! offers us neither the comic contrast of *As I Lay Dying* nor the structural juxtaposition of his two views as found in *Light in August*. Instead we have the ambiguous and highly dramatic close of the novel, Shreve's question:

> "Now I want you to tell me just one thing more. Why do you hate the South?"
> "I dont hate it," Quentin said, quickly, at once, immediately; "I dont hate it," he said. *I dont hate it* he thought, panting in the cold air, the iron New England dark; *I dont. I dont! I dont hate it! I dont hate it!* (378)

This acceptance by negation is as close as we come to Faulkner's optimism in this novel. In the sense that this acceptance is almost entirely without empiric justification, we might label it irrational and dismiss the whole question by attributing it completely to the character of Quentin. But if we hear Faulkner in this, the problem remains. Among the critics, Hoffman, Slatoff, and Waggoner have attempted to come to grips with Faulkner's pronouncements about the endurance of man and his faith that man will prevail. Their approach has been in terms of "What do the words *exactly* mean?" and their conclusions are generally frustration. I believe that instead of labeling these pronouncements irrational with all of that word's derogatory connotations we might better accept them as a statement of a mythic configuration of man's condition, something of the same sort that we might find in the better of those beliefs we accept with that irrational quality, "faith."

On the fourth level of myth, that equated with a quasi-historical saga, our examination must work in two directions: toward the historical "reality" which the saga reflects and toward the explanation of that history which Faulkner seeks to make in his works. The idea evoked by the cliché "the myth of the South" is strictly a fabulous projection a short way back in time to a golden age, an age when peace and manners reigned, when romances flourished in jasmine-scented gardens, and every woman was a lady and every man a gentleman committed to the highest standards of chivalry. All well and good, but rather inadequate to counterpoint a study of Faulkner's use of the southern history in his works. Even a cursory reading of Faulkner will establish the fact that this cliché of fiction does not occupy his attention.

The golden age does have a position in Faulkner's work, but it is there as part of a larger mythic reading of history. It presupposes and focuses upon an actual presence which is understood to be decadent and inadequate by comparison with that time in the past which is termed golden; it accepts the suffering and apparent chaos of the present and places upon it a moral evaluation in terms of some mythic "fall" which occurred in a definite historical moment. The golden age serves primarily as a norm against which the present is to be judged, but it is the *present* which is the focal point of attention.

This reading of a cyclical theory of history in terms of myth has been studied by Mircea Eliade who contrasts the empiric view of history with that held by "archaic man" —man operating in terms of the mythic consciousness:

> Archaic man . . . tends to set himself in opposition, by every means in his power, to history, regarded as a succession of events that are irreversible, unforeseeable, possessed of autonomous value. He refuses to accept it and to grant it value as such, as *history*—without, however, always being able to exorcise it; for example, he is powerless against cos-

mic catastrophes, military disasters, social injustices bound
up with the very structure of society, personal misfortunes,
and so forth.[18]

Archaic man opposes the empiric-scientific view of history through ritual action which "guarantees" the cyclical re-
juvenation of life in harmony with the rhythms of nature. As
the sufferings of the dead season are contrasted with the
memory of the ease of the fertile period of the year, so the social catastrophes of the present are contrasted with the order
of the golden past. And as ritual action secures the return of
the fecundity of the earth, so ritual action can restore cosmos
to the chaos of the present. The key to this theory in Eliade's
view is the acceptance on the part of archaic man of the "nor-
mality of suffering" and the insistence upon a moral reading
of history:

> What could suffering and pain signify? Certainly not a
> meaningless experience that man can only "tolerate" insofar
> as it is inevitable, as, for example, he tolerates the rigors of
> climate. Whatever its nature and whatever its apparent
> cause, his suffering had a meaning; it corresponded, if not
> always to a prototype, at least to an order whose value was
> not contested.
> If it was possible to tolerate such sufferings, it is precisely
> because they seemed neither gratuitous nor arbitrary. . . .
> The archaic mind cannot conceive of an unprovoked suffer-
> ing; it arises from a personal fault . . . or from his neigh-
> bor's malevolence . . . ; but there is always a fault at the
> bottom of it, or at the very least a cause, recognized in the
> will of the forgotten Supreme God, to whom man is finally
> forced to address himself. In each case the suffering be-
> comes intelligible and hence tolerable.[19]

It is this reading of history that is found in many of
Faulkner's characters and which, I believe, informs Faulkner's
own understanding of the history of the South. The moral
guilt is equated with the exploitation of the land and of the
Negro. The apparent cosmos of the antebellum period, the
golden age, was wiped out in the chaos of the War and the

suffering compounded by the Reconstruction. The suffering persists into Faulkner's historical present and the moral searching for culpability remains. This is not a complex, intellectual reading of the history of the South, but Faulkner is not an intellectual writer. It is an emotional and mythic reading of history, not unlike that offered by the southern agrarians in their manifesto *I'll Take My Stand* where the inertia and decay of the South is posited against an assumed golden age which can be restored if only the scapegoat of industrialism can be driven out of the land.

Throughout Faulkner's work we find the attempt to deal with the immediacy of suffering, the desire to annul time, and the pressing need to understand the cause of chaos, of suffering. In *Absalom, Absalom!* this necessity of understanding the suffering of the South as it is embodied in the tale of Sutpen provides the structural framework. Through the minds of the various narrators a tale is eventually constructed that in part reflects what is termed the myth of the Old South: the taking of the virgin land, the construction of the great plantation, and by deft touches, the period of social grandeur with its Wedgwood, crystal, gowns and balls—the period of cosmos. But how little this is the object of Faulkner's tale can be seen by the economy with which he presents it. Cosmos became chaos in the War. It is through the narrators' examinations of the prototype Sutpen that the moral flaw which brought down this chaos will become apparent.

Upon being summoned by Miss Rosa, Quentin,

the Quentin Compson preparing for Harvard in the South, the deep South dead since 1865 and peopled with garrulous outraged baffled ghosts, listening, having to listen, to one of the ghosts which had refused to lie still even longer than most had, telling him about old ghost-times (9),

thinks at first,

It's because she wants it told . . . so that people whom she will never see and whose names she will never hear and who have never heard her name nor seen her face will read it and know at last why God let us lose the War: that only through the blood of our men and the tears of our women could He stay this demon and efface his name and lineage from the earth. (11)

Within Quentin's heritage, a South filled with "garrulous outraged baffled ghosts" each with a moral solution to the problem of the South's history, this is the normal initial reaction to a summons from such a "ghost" of the past.

The suffering of the South in the War is pervasive. Bon's letter to Judith, preserved by the Compsons, tells of the ironic capture of the Union stove polish by the starving soldiers. The scarcity of food and clothing is like a refrain throughout both Miss Rosa's narration and the other parts concerned with her history. Although accustomed to a life of penury, she makes much of the weed gathering and the remaking of handed-down clothing. Judith's wedding gown is made of " 'scraps—perhaps scraps intended for, which should have gone for, lint and did not' " (132). In this respect, Sutpen's mansion becomes a central symbol of the ravages of war and continuing decay after the War. Once the showpiece of the county, at War's end it is

> "the huge house where a young girl waited in a wedding dress made from stolen scraps, the house partaking too of that air of scaling desolation, not having suffered from invasion but a shell marooned and forgotten in a backwater of catastrophe—a skeleton giving of itself in slow driblets of furniture and carpet, linen and silver, to help to die torn and anguished men who knew, even while dying, that for months now the sacrifice and the anguish were in vain."
> (132–33)

The house waits to play its final role in the cycle of the myth, the final and ultimate catastrophe, the conflagration that should mark an end to Sutpen's world. But Faulkner's vision is not the limited vision of Miss Rosa. Sutpen's idiot great grandson haunts the scene at the close and the moral guilt remains, not wiped out by the gothic flames.

Faulkner's reading of the "myth of the South'" does not

dwell on an antebellum golden age but posits a deeper historical view. The golden age can be defined only morally and that in relation to the land. In *Go Down, Moses*, Ike postulates the end of that golden age as the moment the Indian assumed the illusory sense of ownership for the purposes of trade. The guilt which the white man brought, slavery, merely compounded a fallen state. There is no immediate solution to this problem. With Ike of *Go Down, Moses*, Shreve posits a period of years in the thousands before the problem can be solved:

> "I think that in time the Jim Bonds are going to conquer the Western hemisphere. Of course it won't quite be in our time and of course as they spread toward the poles they will bleach out again like the rabbits and the birds do, so they won't show up so sharp against the snow. But it will still be Jim Bond; and so in a few thousand years, I who regard you will also have sprung from the loins of African kings." (378)

Within the context of the body of works built up around Yoknapatawpha County, *Absalom, Absalom!* presents yet another version of this search for a moral reading of history.

It is in terms of these four levels of myth that I intend to examine the novels of Faulkner. They are not all to be found in all his works, for his search for a subject and a form began in a derivative waste land through which we must go.

2. The Early Novels

Faulkner's first novel, Soldiers' Pay, is usually passed over lightly by the critics. Only Mrs. Vickery has given it adequate attention as a germinal work in the Faulkner corpus. Her approach to the novels is centered in Faulkner's "fascination with the multiplicity of responses which mankind makes to a common experience, with time, with language and action, and with man's endeavor to define himself." [1] Her work explores the multiple ironies inherent in his vision, but stops short of an explicit formulation of that ironic sense, a study still to be desired.

The central irony of the book, not considered by Mrs. Vickery, is that of the dying soldier returning to the society which had sent him off to war, a society set in the physical environment of the luxurious natural fecundity of a southern spring. Throughout Faulkner's work we find imagery demonstrating an acute consciousness of the mythic earth mother, from these earliest passages celebrating the reawakened fecundity of the cyclic seasons to Mink Snopes' burrowing return to the womb of the earth at the close of The Mansion. In the later novels this takes on the magnitude of the farm fields and the woods with the natural analogies between human procreation and the fertility of the earth, but in the early novels it is present in the images of flower gardens of which Faulkner had more than a passing knowledge.

Januarius Jones, appearing at the rectory, is invited into the garden:

> The garden was worth seeing. An avenue of roses bordered a graveled path which passed from sunlight beneath two over-arching oaks. Beyond the oaks, against a wall of poplars in a restless formal row were columns of a Greek temple, yet the poplars themselves in slim, vague green were poised and vain as girls in a frieze. Against a privet hedge would soon be lilies like nuns in a cloister and blue hyacinths swung soundless bells, dreaming of Lesbos. Upon a lattice wall wistaria would soon burn in slow inverted lilac flame, and following it they came lastly upon a single rose bush. The branches were huge and knotted with age, heavy and dark as a bronze pedestal, crowned with pale impermanent gold. (16)*

The Rector tells Jones of the crisis this rose once occasioned when its covering was removed too early in March and the Rector, in a neighboring town for a conference, made a dramatic return in time to cover it before the snow fell. Jones is bored. "Januarius Jones was not particularly interested in flowers" (62). For Faulkner, who *is* interested in flowers, this helps to establish a rather unpleasant character. A few pages later, Cecily, Donald's fiancée, receives a similar negative characterization in that she arrives too late in the morning for the Rector to pick the hyacinths he had intended to give her. Cecily couldn't care less; and not many authors would be aware of such a simple touch of garden lore to establish a point of characterization. Faulkner is never at a loss for a particular flower in season. At times a character's stream of consciousness is triggered by the scent of flowers as Miss Rosa's is

---

* Page references are to the Horace Liveright edition of *Soldiers' Pay* (New York, 1926).

by the scent of wistaria which carries her back to the "vintage year of wistaria," or as Quentin's is by the overpowering odor of honeysuckle.

The garden described above illustrates one pole of the ironic contrast between life and death in the novel. Its over-lush imagery carries throughout the book in opposition to the images of death and sterile sophistication. The romance of Greek columns and hyacinths dreaming of Lesbos perhaps makes the reader a bit uncomfortable today, but Faulkner had evidently come to this novel fresh from a reading of Ovid, and, as little as we might like to admit it, regarded this kind of writing as sophisticated. This liberal scattering of Ovidian allusions throughout the book illustrates his early adherence to what I have called the first level of myth.

The Rector, continuing the story of the rose bush to Jones, says, "In this bush is imprisoned a part of my youth, as wine is imprisoned in a wine jar. But with this difference: my wine jar always renews itself" (62). And the reader, who has already been conditioned into an awareness of myth, catches the allusion to the story of Baucis and Philemon. I say already conditioned, for in the first chapter the reader was introduced to Cadet Lowe as knowing "all the old sorrows of the Jasons of the world who see their vessels sink ere the harbor is left behind"(31), and then to Jones who bears the improbable name Januarius and whose "face was a round mirror before which fauns and nymphs might have wantoned when the world was young" (58). Jones accidentally steps into a bucket of water and "rose a sodden Venus" (65). And Jones, meeting Cecily, seeks an image for her: "At last he had her classified in the animal kingdom. Hamadryad, a slim jeweled one" (77). In the Rector's garden, Faulkner had already employed an image equating poplars with girls and now Cecily is equated with a hamadryad as will be Patricia, the young virgin in *Mosquitoes*. The image will gain significance when Benjy equates the virginal Caddie with the smell of trees in *The Sound and the Fury*.

Atalanta seems to have impressed herself on Faulkner, for he uses the myth three times in *Soldiers' Pay* without achieving any relationship between the images. Once it is Cecily's legs "like Atalanta's reft of running" (78), and again, after Jones has engaged in a running pursuit of Emmy, he joins Margaret Mahon and Gilligan on the veranda and is asked for an explanation of his panting:

> "Perhaps Mr. Jones was merely preparing to write a poem. Living it first, you know," Mrs. Mahon offered.
> Jones looked at her sharply. "Atalanta," she suggested in the dark.
> "Atalanta?" repeated Gilligan, "what—"
> "Try an apple next time, Mr. Jones," she advised. (287)

A few pages later a poplar tree is equated with what we might assume to be the still virginal girl: ". . . and here was the evening star bloomed miraculously at the poplar's tip and the slender tree was a leafed and passionate Atalanta, poising her golden apple" (292).

Jove is used three times also. The Rector in the shadows becomes a "'laureled Jove" (60); Cecily's suitor, George Farr, is described ironically as exhibiting "Jove-like calm" (147); and again, "Jove would have said, How virginal her [Cecily's] legs are" (200). Jones is both Narcissus (92) and a fat satyr (286). Niobe (203), Mercury (135), the Gorgon (236), Cerberus (250), and the sybils (304) all find their places in Faulkner's rhetoric. That most of these references come from a fresh reading of Ovid might be attested by the allusion to Atthis, another name Jones finds for Cecily (227). This is most probably the Athis who appears briefly in Book 5 as a victim of Perseus:

> There was a youngster there, Athis, from India,
> Whose mother was a river-nymph, Limnaee,
> And he was beautiful, with beauty doubled
> By the rich robes he wore, the purple mantle
> With fringe of gold, and a golden chain adorning

His throat, and a golden circlet holding in
His hair, and perfumed with myrrh.[2]

If this be the source of the allusion, its obscurity argues either great or immediate familiarity with the text.

These myth allusions, self-conscious as they are, may serve only as evidence that in his first novel Faulkner *was* interested in one area of myth. In addition to these, I might cite an allusion, howsoever faint, to the *Agamemnon*. As the question of Cecily's marriage to Donald rises to a resolution, Faulkner inserts a chapter of "Voices" in which "The Town" as chorus remarks:

> I wonder what that woman that came home with him thinks about it, now he's taken another one. If I were that Saunders girl I wouldn't take a man that brought another woman right up to my door, you might say. (261)

This, however, functions in no more important manner in the novel as a whole than do the other allusions already noted. Perhaps the only mythic allusion which *is* successfully integrated with the action of the story is the Christian burial service which is used to counterpoint the finally achieved seduction of Emmy by Jones. With everyone else attending the funeral of Donald, Emmy is left alone with Jones, and in her preocccupation with her sorrow she passively accepts him. Parenthetically inserted between the flat description of the seduction are the phrases "(I am the Resurrection and the Life, saith the Lord. . . . Whosoever believeth in Me, though he were dead. . . . yet shall he live. And whosoever liveth and believeth in Me shall never die)" (297). At the end of this passage "afternoon became abruptly rain." Faulkner probably intended this to signify a rebirth of life-in-life now that death-in-life has been removed from the scene. The novel then ends on a vague note of Christian resolution with Gilligan and the Rector walking past a Negro church:

> The singing drew nearer and nearer . . . then it swelled to an ecstasy, taking the white man's words as readily as it took

his remote God and made a personal Father of Him.

Feed Thy Sheep, O Jesus. All the longing of mankind for a Oneness with Something, somewhere . . . .

Feed Thy Sheep, O Jesus. The voices rose full and soft. . . . Then the singing died, fading away along the mooned land inevitable with to-morrow and sweat, with sex and death and damnation; and they turned townward under the moon, feeling dust in their shoes. (319)

There is a tension in this passage which points up the failure of the book as a whole. The 318 pages of floundering sophistication are suddenly brought into focus through the Negroes' ritual breathing life into the Christian myth. Man blunders through his life seeking a "oneness with something," aware of the dust of death like the blackness creeping up the legs of Joe Christmas.

Whatever personal criticism Faulkner might have received about his first novel, it is to be hoped that it included a comment about the excessive "myth dropping." Whether it was his own observation or someone else's, these superficial allusions drop markedly in *Mosquitoes*.

We have in *Mosquitoes* the image of the nymph and the tree in its median stage between the direct identification of hamadryad and Caddy in Benjy's consciousness when Talliaferro meets Patricia, the niece of Mrs. Maurier, who is organizing the yachting party which constitutes the major action of the novel. He is aware of "the clean young odor of her, like that of young trees" * (21).**

---

* There is another image associated with Patricia which will find its way into Benjy's consciousness of Caddy. The young steward David, returned from the mosquito-aborted attempt to run away with Patricia, sits alone on the deck at night. "When Fairchild stopped beside him David raised his head slowly into the moonlight and gazed at the older man, making no effort to conceal that which he held. Fairchild leaned nearer to see. It was a slipper, a single slipper, cracked and stained with dried mud and disreputable, yet seeming still to hold in its mute shape something of that hard and sexless graveness of hers." (235)

** Page references are to the Horace Liveright edition of *Mosquitoes* (New York, 1927).

There is yet a "Maecenas" (18), a "Phillida" (129), a "Venus" (133), a "Philomel" (247), a "Hermaphroditus" (252), and a "Leda" (318) gracing the rhetoric. Gordon, the sculptor, the only character to whom Faulkner does not take a superior position, would seem to bear the burden of leading this society out of its Prufrockian aimlessness. In his musings he becomes "crowned with stars christ by his own hand an autogethsemane carved darkly out of pure space" (47–48). And twice he is equated with Israfel, the angel of Islam who will blow the trumpet on the day of the resurrection (48, 187). Again, when he has been presumed drowned and reappears, another character suggests he celebrate his resurrection (267).

Among the critics, certainly Mrs. Vickery has been the kindest toward this novel. Looking back over thirty years of Faulkner's work to *Mosquitoes* she finds that "Faulkner's enduring interests and preoccupations stand out in bold, though sketchy, relief":

> One of the basic attitudes running throughout all his work is the view that language and logic act to obscure truth rather than to reveal it. Accordingly, a primary concern is to demonstrate the barrenness that attends all discussion. . . .
> The separation of words and deeds is occasioned or at least paralleled by a distinction between living and consciousness of living. . . . The state of "just being" and of instinctively knowing, which precedes self-consciousness and verbalization, is one of the constant sources of value and strength in Faulkner's novels.[3]

I shall return to this interesting observation later in connection with the transition to *The Sound and the Fury*.

I think, however, that we can dismiss *Mosquitoes* quite easily. The book, like *Soldiers' Pay*, is an exercise in irony, easily the most dominant feature of Faulkner's early work. Irony by definition posits an intelligence that arrogates to itself a superior position in relation to those about it. I believe this simple fact can explain the failure of Faulkner's first

novels. They are the work of an immature and arrogant mind.
For Faulkner at this stage of development to retain the ironic
position necessitates consideration of characters holding
values which even the immature author can contain ironically
within his own limited vision. Thus we get such blatant
ironies as the characterizations of Cadet Lowe and George
Farr in *Soldiers' Pay*, such callous youths that we cringe for
the author enjoying his superiority to them. The same holds
true for the whole of *Mosquitoes*. Here we have a boatload of
characters talking about sex, art, religion, education, etc. For
Faulkner to maintain his ironic pose, these characters must
hold ideas inferior to his own (or, in the case of the sculptor
Gordon whom Faulkner holds as his equal, ideas equal to his
own). The simple fact is that Faulkner's own ideas are immature and crudely Romantic as in Gordon's pseudo-Shel-
leyan musings about the true artist effecting some kind of
resurrection. And, of necessity, any ideas he can attribute to
his characters as contained within his own self-conscious
ironic vision are cruder still. The reader is faced with the almost incredible gaucherie of this arrogant young author placing his own adolescent Bohemianism in a superior position
through the perspective of Jenny, the shop girl whimsically introduced to the cruise by Patricia:

> "I was waiting for them, and I got to talking to a funny
> man. A little kind of black man—"
> "A nigger?"
> "No. He was a white man, except he was awful sun-
> burned and kind of shabby dressed—no necktie and hat.
> Say, he said some funny things to me. He said I had the
> best digestion he ever saw, and he said if the straps of my
> dress was to break I'd devastate the country. He said he was
> a liar by profession, and he made good money at it, enough
> to own a Ford as soon as he got it paid out. I think he was
> crazy. Not dangerous: just crazy. . . ."
> "I remembered it [his name] because he was such a funny
> kind of man. It was . . . Walker or Foster or some-
> thing. . . ."

"Wait . . . Oh, yes: I remember—Faulkner, that was it."
(144–45)

Mosquitoes must be written off as an unqualified disaster, yet in its badness it brings to sharp focus many of the inadequacies that haunt the later Faulkner, foremost among them the inability to establish and maintain a coherent system of values for the narrator who functions as the norm of values within the novel. The ironic mode is used with greater success in *Soldiers' Pay* where the juxtaposition of the dying Mahon to the fructifying spring, the false joys of homecoming felt by the Rector, the empty marriage of Mahon and Mrs. Powers (with death rather than life in the immediate future) are woven into a coherent pattern against a norm of accepted values. Behind all the criticisms of a shallow society stands the idea of the death-in-life figure of Mahon as a sacrificial victim offered up to preserve this very society. The scarred hero is returned to society unable to communicate, an ironic adumbration of the journey of the hero who ideally should return to his society with the essence of his new knowledge. Throughout Faulkner's works we will find this emphasis on the sacrifice of the victim, meaningless in this ironic phase but growing to a fully transcendent meaning in *A Fable*.

Faulkner's citation of *Sartoris* as marking a turning point in his writing, together with the fact that it introduces the personnel of Yoknapatawpha County, accounts for the fact that this novel has received more critical attention than the first two. Richer in characterizations and setting, it yet remains an apprentice work lacking true focus and without any major changes in techniques or patterns of thought.

John Sartoris and the Civil War are legends kept alive by Will Falls and Aunt Jenny:

She had told the story many times since . . . and as she grew older the tale itself grew richer and richer, taking on a mellow splendor like wine; until what had been a harebrained prank of two heedless and reckless boys wild with their own youth had become a gallant and finely tragical focal point to which the history of the race had been raised from out of the old miasmic swamps of spiritual sloth by two angels valiantly fallen and strayed, altering the course of human events and purging the souls of men. (9)*

Some critics see Bayard's course of action as dominated by this legend of the first Bayard and of the first John Sartoris. His erratic actions are thus explained as a drive to live up to these family legends. While this is true to some extent, I believe the novel focuses primarily on two contrasting societies —the bucolic, backward-looking society symbolized by the horse, and the new machine society symbolized by the airplane and Bayard's automobile.

Any attempt to deal with Bayard's psychology that leaves out the involved relationship with his twin brother cannot hope to offer an explanation of his actions. We can perhaps gain some insight into his character by examining the allusions to the various ritualistic initiations he has undergone in the past. His initiation into the old society we learn of through the burning of Johnnie's things when Bayard returns from the first accident with his broken ribs. This was the rite of the hunt which is so fully developed in *Go Down, Moses*. However, we have reason to believe that this was an ineffective initiation when Bayard later returns to the scene, the Mac. Cullum's farm. His initiation into the new society of the machine bears Faulkner's ironic stamp: the only thing we know of it is the drunken statement, "Taught us in ground-school never seduce a fool nor hit a cripple" (129).

Bayard's first act upon returning home is to go to Memphis to buy the high powered automobile with which he can fight against the old society, frightening horses and trying to free the traces of the mules hauling country wagons by striking the whiffle tree with the bumper at high speed.

* Page references are to the Harcourt, Brace and Co. edition of *Sartoris* (New York, 1951).

Faulkner emphasizes derision and arrogance in these attacks on the old society. Old Simon is severely frightened by his first automobile ride, "and when Bayard glanced the cruel derision of his teeth at him presently, Simon knelt on the floor, his old disreputable hat under his arm and his hand clutching a fold of his shirt on his breast" (116). When Simon succeeds in turning off the ignition and stopping the car, he insists on walking back the several miles. Bayard drives on alone. "Just outside of town he came upon another wagon and he held the car upon it until the mules reared, tilting the wagon; then he swerved and whipped past with not an inch to spare, so close that the yelling negro in the wagon could see the lipless and savage derision of his teeth" (119). At the dinner table, Bayard hits out at the legend of the old society: "Little two-bit war . . . and on a horse. Anybody can go to war on a horse. No chance for him to do much of anything" (230).

The horse will be linked constantly with the legends of the War, frequently in the image of the centaur. Here it is General Stuart who "whirled, roweling his bay, and with the thunderous coordination of a single centaur they [the raiding party] swept down the knoll and crashed into the forest" (13–14). The centaur image will be used again for Colonel John Sartoris in *The Unvanquished,* and the horse as a symbol of natural power is often used later with the mythic force of a mana symbol unifying man with an elemental power of nature.

Bayard, however, has little enough justification for his arrogance toward the old society in terms of the new. The old roads designed for wagons and horses turn his driving into anything but a mastery of the machine. When Bayard meets Rafe MacCallum in town and gets drunk on Henry's "cawn," his attention is drawn from the possibility of a fight only by mention of a horse. He attempts to ride the stallion but is thrown. It seems he is master in neither society. After the final automobile accident which results in the death of old Bayard, young Bayard sends a Negro for his horse and, in effect, runs away from his deed to the scene of his adolescent initiation into the old society, the MacCallum farm. It is here that we gain the greatest insights into Bayard.

Virginius MacCallum, the patriarch ruling over his six sons—Jackson, Lee, and Stuart among them—is the one character who goes beyond the degree of merely keeping a legend alive in his dedication to the myth of the Old South. The myth is sustained with a passion that dominates his thought and actions. His household, however, does not seem to offer an idyllic solution to the conflict between the old and new societies in that, governed by an adherence to the old ways, there is a marked sterility, five sons confirmed bachelors with only the hope of a marriage for Buddy held out to perpetuate the line. Bayard immediately violates the honor of the household with a lie about his grandfather's health. The lie is sustained by the failure of the two sons going into town for supplies to reach their destination due to a broken axle tree, and Bayard is thus given a week's respite.

It soon becomes evident that of the twins, it was John who achieved a successful initiation into the hunt. When Bayard burned some of John's effects earlier there had been "a shotgun shell to which was attached by a bit of wire a withered bear's paw. It was John's first bear, and the shell with which he had killed it in the river bottom near MacCallum's when he was twelve years old" (214). No mention is made of any kill of any ritualistic significance by Bayard. Mandy, the Negro cook, greets Bayard with her expectation of a gift which Bayard glibly says he has not forgot. "But he had. Money, to Mandy, did not compensate for some trinket of no value which John never forgot to bring her when he came" (314). This attention to the amenities by John is again mentioned while the party is on the hunt:

> "Too bad Johnny ain't here," Stuart said quietly. "He'd enjoy this race."
> "He was a feller for huntin', now," Jackson agreed. "He'd keep up with Buddy, even."

"John was a fine boy," the old man said.

"Yes, suh," Jackson repeated, "a right warm-hearted boy. Henry says he never come out hyer withouten he brung Mandy and the boys a little sto'-bought somethin'" (332).

The eulogy continues with some pointed contrasts between Bayard's behavior and that of Johnny, contrasts that are especially meaningful to Bayard with his guilty conscience.

Mrs. Vickery points out that Narcissa's mind wandering back to her youthful encounters with the twins always fastens with emotion on Johnny and that her acceptance of Bayard "is an echo of her response to Johnny's balloon flight." [4] What we get through this is a picture of Bayard as second best in a sibling rivalry and the heavy burden of guilt which he bears in relation to Johnny's death, which he obviously could not avert, might be explained by an unconscious wish for this very thing to happen.

His week's respite up, Bayard leaves, accepting a jug of "cawn" for his grandfather. As he rides away from town on a bleak Christmas Eve, he is completely alone; two ways of life have been presented in relation to him and he has failed to master either. His bedding down for the night in a stable is not very effective irony and any symbol hunting is forestalled by Faulkner's description of the shared meal the next morning:

> The negroes drank with him, amicably, a little diffidently—two opposed concepts antipathetic by race, blood, nature and environment, touching for a moment and fused within an *illusion* [italics added]—humankind forgetting its lust and greed for a day. (347)

I believe that the critics who deal with this book as an exposition of a myth and a legend do so in terms of Faulkner's later works and impose upon it a burden it cannot bear. It remains a novel of his apprenticeship dominated by an ironic balancing of two ways of life: the old and the unassimilated new. To inflate the presence of a family legend into a dominating myth does no service to an understanding of the novel nor to an understanding of myth. Faulkner adequately characterized his own efforts in this novel when he said that he had discovered "that writing was a mighty fine thing. You could make people stand on their hind legs and cast a shadow." [5] The strength of the book lies just in those achieved characterizations which are only incidentally related to a legend. More pertinent to the story of these characters is the ghost of Johnny Sartoris rather than that of Colonel Sartoris. Bayard is able to deride the legend of the Colonel, but he is driven toward death by his guilt relation to his brother, who like most of Faulkner's dead in World War I occupies the role of a gratuitous sacrifice.

That the old people—Will Falls, old Bayard, Aunt Jenny, and Simon—are dominated by their memories of the Colonel, functions largely as one way to characterize the old way of life. For them, Colonel John Sartoris is less a living, vital myth than a focus for their wandering minds in what approaches senility. Will Falls is ninety-three years old and his visits to old Bayard focus about the figure of the Colonel. *For them* "He was far more palpable than the two old men cemented by a common deafness to a dead period and so drawn thin by the slow attenuation of days" (1). Aunt Jenny is dominated not by the memory of John Sartoris but of the "Carolina Bayard" and Jeb Stuart with whom she had once danced a valse in Baltimore in '58, and though her mind seems as sharp as her tongue, within the year we find her moving closer and closer to senility. Old Bayard, who is a comparative youngster in his late sixties, moves into the past when he opens the chest containing the family relics, but this passage focuses not just on his father John, but on all the past Sartorises from the earliest one in Virginia to the most recently dead, young Bayard's wife and son who died in 1918. Simon, who seems to be old Bayard's contemporary, invokes the ghost of John Sartoris in his senile musings over the conflict between the old and the new symbolized by the carriage and the car. The accent here is always on the diminishing effectiveness of the past, the *loss* of an empiric configuration of reality rather than upon the *construction* of a reality that would lead us into an attempt to discuss the mythic mode of thought in these characters.

It is in conflict with the old way of life that we are given Bayard's year, beginning in the early spring and ending the following late spring when his death and the birth of the new Sartoris come within a day of each other, suggesting dimly the tenure of the king who reigns for a year and then is deposed or replaced by a new king.

If we are to talk of *Sartoris* in terms of myth, it must be by examining the mythic mode of thought in terms of this very senility which moves the characters' consciousness away from empiric reality to a focus in the past which creates its own reality. This is in no way the dominant mode of the novel, but it does help to prepare us for Faulkner's next work in which we are introduced to the history of the Compsons through the distorted vision of Benjy.

In reviewing the three first novels we find a great deal of mythic allusion in *Soldiers' Pay* and a sharp focus on the fructifying earth in contrast to the dying figure of Mahon. As Frye observes about the ironic mode, dim images of the dying god have crept in. With the death of Mahon, Faulkner brings in the idea of a resurrection, an idea he repeats in *Mosquitoes* through the allusions to Israfel associated with Gordon and through the suggestion that the returned Gordon celebrate his own resurrection. The heavy-handed mythic allusions decrease in number through the progression of these novels, but the cyclic nature of life with its suggestion of resurrection is again found in *Sartoris*.

The dominant mode of these novels is ironic. Both in *Soldiers' Pay* and *Mosquitoes* Faulkner gives us an implied contrast between the behavior of his characters and a standard of behavior he holds to be better. However, since the contrasting value systems are relatively naive, the resultant satire is rather broad, although there is little doubt that the young author regarded them as sophisticated. Perhaps as the ironic mode moves toward true sophistication it accounts for those mythic patterns that Frye finds creeping into the works of this mode. As the author finds himself at an ironic distance from the sufferings of his characters, so the sophisticated student of myth finds himself at an increasing distance from the sufferings of the dying god and the meaning of myth disappears as he attempts his empiric explanation of the historical grounds of the myth as Frazer attempts his own redefinition of the death of Christ. This detachment from both the meaning of myth and the sufferings of his characters might well lead the young author to equate the two in just the manner described by Frye.

Sartoris represents a movement away from this broad ironic contrast between systems of values as Faulkner refuses to identify himself clearly with either the values of the new society or the old. Instead, we see the characters allowed to occupy the forefront of the novelist's stage, to become realized acting within a world of their own. With Faulkner's next published work, *The Sound and the Fury*, the technique is carried to an experimental extreme.

3. The Dark Vision

What happened to Faulkner between *Mosquitoes* and the
novel following it in composition, *The Sound and the Fury?*
What element of personal or literary experience can account
for such a leap? At the door of this mystery there is no use
pretending entry.[1]

*H*owever *true* Howe's observation may be, it is
nonetheless also true that a closed door will always arouse
curious hypotheses and at least a few tentative knocks. That
the leap between the early novels and *The Sound and the
Fury* is great, no one will dispute. However, it is equally true
that there is much continuity.

Carvel Collins cites four sketches that provide material
later reworked in *The Sound and the Fury*, the most obvious
being "in 'The Kingdom of God' the cornflower blue eyes of
the idiot, his broken narcissus, his bellowing, and his silent
departure from the final furious scene which anticipate the
extended and effective treatment of Benjy." [2] There is also in
Mosquitoes the image already noted of the steward David
huddled over the soiled slipper which becomes part of Benjy's

characterization. Benjy's perception of Caddy, "Caddy smelled like trees," has also been long in the works. In *Soldiers' Pay* it appears as the allusive image of the hamadryad and in the equation of trees and young virginal girls; in *Mosquitoes*, Talliaferro is aware of "the clean young odor" of Patricia, "like that of young trees." The history of this image suggests that long before *The Sound and the Fury* Faulkner's imagination had fixed upon an equation between virginity and straight, slim trees, an image further extended to include the odor of each as the identifying principle, the sense of smell being labeled by Faulkner as "one of my sharper senses." [3] The image originally taken from classical mythology has grown into a complicated focal image moving toward the biblical realm of Eden, containing within itself an emotional center for a new and more mature examination of the problem of evil. Whereas the early novels focused upon a problem of evil that was merely social and called forth a rather shallow evaluation, the novels of the middle period are centered on a more metaphysical concept of evil, essentially mythic in that it is emotionally centered and given formulation through the narrative mode rather than centered in any objective quest for knowledge through an explicitly philosophical mode. The glib handling of a misguided society operating in terms of an inadequate value system with the author conspicuously present as the representative of a norm of values is forsaken for a direct presentation of a personal, emotional vision of man's estate.

In his exposition of the novel, Faulkner constantly returns to the image of Caddy as a child climbing the tree to look in the window:

> . . . the explanation of that whole book is in that. It began with the picture of the little girl's muddy drawers, climbing that tree to look in the parlor window with her brothers that didn't have the courage to climb the tree waiting to see what she saw. And I tried first to tell it with one brother, and that wasn't enough. That was Section One. I tried with

another brother, and that wasn't enough. That was Section Two. I tried the third brother, because Caddy was still to me too beautiful and too moving to reduce her to telling what was going on, that it would be more passionate to see her through somebody else's eyes I thought. And that failed and I tried myself—the fourth section—to tell what happened, and I still failed.[4]

When questioned again about this "impression," Faulkner elaborated his explanation:

Well, impression is the wrong word. It's more an image, a very moving image to me was of the children. 'Course, we didn't know at the time that one was an idiot, but they were three boys, one was a girl and the girl was the only one that was brave enough to climb that tree to look in the forbidden window to see what was going on. And that's what the book—and it took the rest of the four hundred pages to explain why she was brave enough to climb that tree to look in the window. It was an image, a picture to me, a very moving one, which was symbolized by the muddy bottom of her drawers as her brothers looked up into the apple tree that she had climbed to look at the window. And the symbolism of the muddy bottom of the drawers became the lost Caddy. . . .[5]

The central image, as it has been designated by Faulkner, reveals the mythic approach to the problem of evil. The satiric pose of the first two novels is explicitly brushed aside in a comment before the Department of Psychiatry at the University of Virginia:

I think the writer is not really interested in bettering man's condition. He really doesn't care a damn about man's condition. He's interested in all man's behavior with no judgement whatever. That it's motion, it's life, the only alternative is nothingness, death. And so to the writer, anything man does is fine because it's motion. . . . Maybe the writer has no concept of morality at all, only an integrity to hold always to what he believes to be the facts and truths of human behavior, not moral standards at all.[6]

But while abjuring "moral standards," it is evident that his avowed objectivity (expressed as hindsight and certainly not including the first two novels) does not extend itself to dismiss the abstract problem of evil in conflict with good, or more specifically, the problem of sustaining optimistic faith in man's ability to subscribe to ideals or "verities" in the immediate and almost overwhelming presence of physical and moral decay. The problem of sustaining such a faith is more a problem for Faulkner, the artist and the man, than for any of his characters, and it is a struggle that informs his work from this point on.

The image of Caddy suggests the inevitability of loss of innocence through the muddied drawers, but Faulkner's emphasis in reviewing the novel is on the courage—one of his "verities"—embodied in the climb to look in the "forbidden window" upon the presence of death. When Dilsey comes out to put an end to the scene it is " 'You, Satan.' Dilsey said. 'Come down from there' " (54).* It would seem that for Faulkner, Caddy in this crucial scene shares a role similar to Milton's Satan in the Romantics' eyes—the courage of defiance.

From Faulkner's comments it would appear that *The Sound and the Fury* was intended to be Caddy's story and was probably to be dominated by the image of Eden and the courage to claim forbidden knowledge. This comes to focus in his later comments in Virginia where even the tree Caddy climbed becomes specifically an apple tree, that in the novel is mentioned only in Quentin's musings on his sister. The oblique narrative method intended to exempt her from any involvement in the telling results, however, in a much larger story with her moving out of the reader's range of vision almost entirely. The image which ostensibly gave impetus to the story does not dominate it. The equation of virgin with tree or smell of trees does not carry with it any moral value of

* Page references are to the Jonathan Cape and Harrison Smith edition of *The Sound and the Fury* (New York, 1929).

good: the drawers are muddied as a foreshadowing of what is for Faulkner the inevitable *natural* fallen state. Caddy's courage in climbing the tree for forbidden knowledge is the same courage which allows her to accept life and the forbidden knowledge of sex. This is contrasted to the neurotic rejection of sex by Quentin who symbolically drops the knife held at Caddy's throat after she has refused to put her hand on it, an act that would have constituted a symbolic consummation of incest. Earlier, employing another phallic symbol, Quentin rejects the gun offered him by Dalton Ames after Ames has demonstrated its effectiveness. Quentin's mind wanders over the pressures of sex which he cannot cope with in any natural manner:

> Versh told me about a man mutilated himself. He went into the woods and did it with a razor, sitting in a ditch. A broken razor flinging them backward over his shoulder the same motion complete the jerked skin of blood backward not looping. But that's not it. It's not not having them. It's never to have had them then I could say O That That's Chinese I dont know Chinese. And Father said it's because you are a virgin: don't you see? Women are never virgins. Purity is a negative state and therefore contrary to nature. It's nature is hurting you not Caddy and I said That's just words and he said So is virginity and I said you dont know. (143)

Of the other two brothers, one is a gelding and the other resorts to sex without love. But if sex and a kind of Shavian life force were to be the center of values, Caddy's daughter Quentin would have to share equally with her mother the honor of courage. However, there is no apple tree for Quentin: her prosaic promiscuous rendezvous are via the pear tree. The reader almost feels cheated when Quentin, who has become a fully realized character, triumphs over Jason but is immediately and forever dismissed by Faulkner who continues to cling to Caddy, even fabricating her continued existence among the Nazis in his later comments on the characters of the novel in the appendix provided for *The Portable Faulkner*.

If morality in terms of sex does not provide the rationale of evil, where does it lie? Its center is in the absence of Christian love, *agape,* and the novel is successful not in its exploitation of the fall through knowledge, but in its unremitting examination of various eccentricities which throw the ego in upon itself to the exclusion of any ability to love. Once Caddy, who had this ability to love, is exiled, the scene is a waste land of activity signifying nothing until the final chapter when Dilsey's pilgrimage to the church with Frony, Luster, and Benjy is offered as an action of endurance. The novel ends with Jason restoring the world of the idiot "each in its ordered place," and we are left with the sense that the "order" is the stasis and sterility of the waste land.

The informing myth of the novel is not, then, that of the fall but of the god of love crucified. Its theme is an examination of an Emersonian evil: the absence of good. It is on the second level of myth, as theme, the total integration with plot, that this is most apparent, and here the allusions are all to the Christian myth of crucifixion and resurrection. But before proceeding to this, I might cite the few allusions on the first level of myth. Shreve alludes to Mrs. Bland as a Semiramis (125) and Quentin, brooding upon Caddy's sexual experiences with Dalton Ames, alludes to the swine of Euboeleus, the mythical swineherd who saw the rape of Persephone on the way to the underworld and passed the information on to the searching Demeter (184). Karl Zink, writing of "Faulkner's Garden: Woman and the Immemorial Earth," generalizes about Faulkner's pregnant women:

> Despite the fact that so many of these women are unmarried, they are good women; they have an integrity that conventionally respectable women in the novels consistently do not have. These women, more than their men, are akin to the "fecund" earth, like the earth itself potential sources for renewal and development, for physical continuity within the continuous process of Nature.[7]

In speaking of Eula Varner, he advances the image of Persephone. "Only with Eula's return, like Persephone, the following spring, does the dessicated land know release and respond normally to the plow." [8] Although he does not cite the Euboeleus allusion in connection with Caddy, the image functions in much the same way, reinforcing the sterility of the Compson world when Caddy's fruitful promiscuity relegates her to the "underworld" of Mrs. Compson. Unlike Eula, she does not return bringing with her the fructifying spring.

Shreve, trying to explain why Quentin began the fight with Gerald Bland which has resulted in his thorough beating, brings in an allusion to Leda and the swan (206–7). And in the amazing compression of the last few pages of his monologue, as he is preparing ritually for his death by drowning, Quentin's mind wanders over images of water which associate with sleep, the sleep of death he is seeking. Going from his room to the bathroom becomes associated with the child's journey for a late night drink, the fixtures with "less than Moses rod" (216). There is one passing allusion to Cupid, 'the blind immortal boy" (217) in association with Uncle Maury, the philanderer.

On the second level, the integration of the Christian myth demonstrates more of the continuity of imagery from the earlier novels with a radical shift in emphasis. The hopeful image of the resurrection loosely tacked on the end of *Soldiers' Pay* and glibly dropped throughout *Mosquitoes* in relation to the Gordon-Israfel character is now superimposed on the total action of the novel through a structural device which forces it to carry a great burden of meaning. What began in the early novels as a debate between a cloddish society and a cocky, sophomoric young man has become a dialogue between a highly verbal, aggressive awareness of evil and a mute, indomitable, and perhaps sentimental faith in "verities." The "mute" participant in this dialogue makes itself known largely through the structure of the novel until in the last section, the attempt by Faulkner himself to tell the story, Dilsey is brought forward as an almost sentimental antidote to the large doses of corruption and decay which have made up the major part of the story. It is Faulkner's strength as an artist that he communicates evil well—"it's easier to conceive of evil than of good . . . easier to make believable, credible, than good" [9]—and his weakness that in portraying the struggle between good and evil, the powers of light appear to have been grossly mismatched. His vision of evil lies completely within the rational-empiric realm. When he attempts to communicate his intuition of the sustaining verities, he seems to be aware of the danger of falling off into sentimentality as in the portrayal of Dilsey. I believe it is the need to communicate the positive element of his vision by some means other than direct statement or characterization that leads to his highly experimental forms that suggest more obliquely, that communicate indirectly the positive pole of his vision as a counterbalance to the direct dramatic presentation of evil.

The structural device of the dates of the three parts focused around Easter seems to suggest the lost soul (Benjy) in hell on Saturday, the killing of the god of love (through Jason's characterization) on Friday, and the resurrection with its *potential* hope on Sunday. This antithesis between a realistic portrayal of moral and social corruption and the inclusion of hopeful idealistic elements which are so vague and amorphous that they must be suggested by structural juxtaposition or by allusion to the myths which embody man's greatest hopes, constitutes the most unifying element in Faulkner's work. His oft-repeated sense of failure in *The Sound and the Fury* might have been due to the shift from the Eden myth to the killing of the god of love, but this failure can easily be dismissed as a product of the intentional fallacy and not justified by the work. What cannot be dismissed, however, is the mistake in the choice of the analogue which calls for a thoroughly triumphant denouement which Faulkner is obviously unable to accept. The myth of the resurrection is too strong and too concrete in its connotations for his faith, which at this point in his intellectual history must content itself with vague abstractions that cannot triumph over the vital and concrete expressions of evil.

The Christian myth is used explicitly in the text as a norm for the values of love missing from the lives of the characters. Mrs. Compson, in her maudlin egocentricity, complains, " 'Nobody knows how I dread Christmas. Nobody knows' " (7). And when, in the last section, she explains to Jason about letting the servants go to special Easter services, her whining justification is: " 'I know it's my fault. . . . I know you blame me.' 'For what?' Jason said. 'You never resurrected Christ, did you?' " (348). Mrs. Compson, one of Faulkner's most brilliantly realized characters, stands at the core of the novel as she stands at the core of the family, the decay and disintegration of the Compsons effected largely by her failure—that passes through Quentin's mind as: "*My little sister had no. If I could say Mother. Mother*" (117) and "*. . . if I'd just had a mother so I could say Mother Mother*" (213).

The similarities between Mrs. Compson and her son Jason are made explicit by her constant avowals that he is her only true child, a true Bascomb. On Good Friday, perhaps his most symbolic action is dropping the free passes for the tent show into the fire as Luster watches, a dramatic indication of the absence of human feeling. His monologue is punctuated by the repetitious use of *hell* as the only mythic reference, and in view of the novel's tight structure it must be viewed as having that significance.

Jason's characterization, however, is most interesting in another respect. Here we find Faulkner's first attempt at a dramatic presentation of the solution to the problem of evil. For those who suffer under evil, endurance is the only answer: the solution is that evil will create its own destruction.* In Jason we find this pattern offered for the first time. The evil

* Later Faulkner modifies this position in accordance with a more positive view of the power of man's spirit.

which is found in the egocentricity of the Bascombs (and against which the Compson blood has no defense to offer) finally outwits itself. Jason, whose only symbol of success is money (his name designates the pursuit of the golden, and for fleece Faulkner provides the speculation in cotton) is outmaneuvered in his cotton speculations and by the niece from whom he has been stealing money over the years. Uncle Job, the Negro worker at the store, sums up the point:

> "I wont try to fool you," he says. "You too smart fer me. Yes, suh," he says, looking busy as hell, putting five or six little packages into the wagon, "You's too smart fer me. Aint a man in dis town kin keep up wid you fer smartness. You fools a man whut so smart he cant even keep up wid hisself," he says, getting in the wagon and unwrapping the reins.
>
> "Who's that?" I says.
>
> "Dat's Mr. Jason Compson," he says. (311–12)

For Faulkner there is no "just retribution" for evil which would imply an abstract moral scheme; there is only the irony of events. With Jason and with Flem Snopes, the actions they have set in motion merely turn back on them. With Popeye, it is the irony of happenstance. Nor do these setbacks result in the triumph of any abstract "good." It is merely man in motion, which for Faulkner is the meaning of life: "That it's motion, it's life, the only alternative is nothingness, death."

The greatest concentration of allusions to myths is found in Quentin's monologue, reinforcing the nature of his perception of reality which I should like to examine as the mythic mode. Carvel Collins has suggested that the three brothers might be studied as Faulkner's conscious fragmentation of the mind according to Freud's theory.[10] I too should like to advance a scheme of sorts, not far removed from Professor Collins' Freudian analysis but in terms of Cassirer's analysis of the mythic mode.* Benjy's monologue may be viewed as a

---

* Susanne Langer has pointed out the closeness of Cassirer's theory of mind to Freud's. But Cassirer refused to explore the "fund of corroborative

pre-mythic apprehension of the world, Quentin's as an example of the mythic configuration of the world, and Jason's as an example of the rational empirical mode.

Benjy's monologue does not reveal any coherent configuration of reality. His perceptions are chaotic, disoriented in any time-space relationship; his world remains a chaos of impressions.* At the other extreme, Jason's configuration of the world is best characterized by Faulkner's later comments in his appendix: "The first sane Compson since before Culloden and (a childless bachelor) hence the last. Logical rational contained and even a philosopher in the old stoic tradition." It remains to examine Quentin's mode of perception as the intermediary stage in this epistemological progression.

"It is one of the first essential insights of critical philosophy," says Cassirer,

> that objects are "given" to consciousness in a rigid, finished state, in their naked "as suchness," but that the relation of representation to object presupposes an independent, spontaneous act of consciousness. The object does not exist prior to and outside of synthetic unity but is constituted only by this synthetic unity. . . . *The Philosophy of Symbolic Forms* . . . seeks the categories of the consciousness of objects in the theoretical, intellectual sphere, and starts from the assumption that such categories must be at work wherever a cosmos, a characteristic and typical world view, takes form out of the chaos of impressions. All such world views are made possible only by specific acts of objectivization, in which mere impressions are reworked into specific, formed representations.[11]

evidence" offered by the field of "dynamic psychology" because he felt that Freud considered all cultural achievements to be mere by-products of the libido; "whereas to him they were the consummation of a spiritual process which merely took its rise from the blind excitement of the animal 'libido,' but received its importance and meanings from the phenomena of awareness and creativity, the envisagement, reason, and cognition it produced"—"On Cassirer's Theory of Language and Myth," *The Philosophy of Ernst Cassirer*, ed. P. A. Schilpp (Evanston, 1949), p. 395.

* Philip Wheelwright mentions Benjy in this manner in *The Burning Fountain* (Bloomington, 1954), p. 160.

It is this "cosmos" that is missing from the world view of Benjy. A synthetic unity is given the disordered impressions by the reader in terms of his later knowledge of these events, but taken alone Benjy's section would remain largely unintelligible to the reader. It is the reader who must perform the act of objectivization and rework the material into a formed representation.

It is Cassirer's methodology in his study of the mythical consciousness to work backward through the strata of the consciousness of the object preceding the "theoretical object-consciousness of our experience" to determine the possible variants "the *direction* and *means* of this process of objectivization" may have. It is here that he makes the distinction between the mythic mode and the scientific-empiric mode. Empirical reality, he says, is distinguished from the mere world of representation or imagination in that "the permanent is more clearly differentiated from the fluid, the constant from the variable." Sense impressions gain the status of determinate objective existence only if they can be confirmed by experience as a whole, and this constant testing of experience results in the changes in that which we call objective reality.[12]

The aim of this scientific-empiric mode of thought is to achieve a universal synthesis; but to achieve this order presupposes a corresponding analysis. "Where the sensory world view sees only peaceable coexistence, . . . empirical-theoretical thinking finds an interpenetration, a complex of 'conditions.' " The sensory world view is content to establish the mere "what" of the given, whereas the scientific-empiric mode transforms the "what" into "because" and replaces the mere coexistence of the contents of apprehension in space and time with an ideal dependency. Since this ideal dependency is not a factor of sensory perception, its prominence tends to displace the sensory perception from the center of objectivity. "The objective significance of an element of experience depends no longer on the sensuous force with which it individually strikes consciousness, but on the clarity with which the form, the law of the whole, is expressed and reflected in it" [13] This process of analysis and synthesis by which theoretical knowledge arrives at a concept of objectivity involves the constant differentiation between the "accidental" and the "essential."

> Myth too lives in a world of pure forms which it looks upon as thoroughly objective . . . . But its relation to this world discloses no sign of that decisive "crisis" with which empirical and conceptual knowledge begin. Its contents, to be sure, are given in an objective form, as "real contents," but this form of reality is still completely homogeneous and undifferentiated. Here the nuances of significance and value which knowledge creates in its concept of the object, which enable it to distinguish different spheres of objects and to draw a line between the world of truth and the world of appearance, are utterly lacking. Myth lives entirely by the presence of its object—by the intensity with which it seizes and takes possession of consciousness in a specific moment . . . . Consciousness is bound by its mere facticity; it possesses neither the impulsion nor the means to correct or criticize what is given here and now, to limit its objectivity by *measuring* it against something not given, something past or future. And if this mediate criterion is absent, all "truth" and reality dissolve into the mere presence of the content, all phenomena are situated on a single plane. Here there are no different *degrees* of reality, no contrasting degrees of objective certainty. The resultant picture of reality lacks the dimension of depth.[14]

This distinction between modes of object-consciousness provides us with a means of distinguishing between various characters in Faulkner's work, and, I believe, with a means of closer analysis of the many characters usually labeled simply "neurotic"—among them, Quentin Compson.

Quentin's reality is homogeneous and undifferentiated. Central to his entire neurosis (I am using the term to indicate an orientation to a reality other than the scientific-empiric reality by which it is judged) is the fixation upon his sister as what amounts to a sacred vessel of chastity or purity. The

mythic force of the sacred as opposed to the profane dominates his consciousness of Caddy's sexual character. The contents of his consciousness are ordered by the mythic principle.
This principle, says Cassirer,

> is of an entirely different kind and origin from the universal
> principle of the logical concept. For precisely through their
> special character all the contents of the mythical conscious-
> ness are rejoined into a whole. They form a self-enclosed
> realm and possess a common tonality, by which they are dis-
> tinguished from the contents of common, everyday, empir-
> ical existence. . . . In their mere immediate existence they
> . . . contain a revelation and at the same time retain a kind
> of mystery; it is this interpenetration, this revelation which
> both reveals and conceals, that gives the mythical-religious
> content its basic trait, its character of the "sacred." [15]

While the defiled sanctity of Caddy dominates his mind,
images of another sacred character crop up frequently, the allusions to the Christian myth.

Quentin's day begins in time. "When the shadow of the
sash appeared on the curtains it was between seven and eight
o'clock and then I was in time again, hearing the watch"
(93). He has already determined his suicide and his problem
is to live this last day. His first act is to break the crystal of his
watch and twist the hands off as if to remove himself from the
empirical sequence of time. "I turned the face up, the blank
dial with little wheels clicking and clicking behind it, not
knowing any better" (99). Later he cannot look at the
watches in the jeweler's window until he has satisfied himself
by asking the jeweler that none of them tells the "correct"
time. Although he cannot stop time or turn it back, he can
refuse to acknowledge it and can accept the mockery of confusion the various wrong timepieces display. It is, in a sense,
an act of regression signaling his total rejection of a world
that is now ruled by the profane element of his private vision,
a vision which on this last day flows through his mind in terms
of its destruction through Caddy's loss of virginity. His rejec-

72

tion of measured time becomes a part of the mythic construct of his consciousness. "It lies in the essence of mythical thinking," says Cassirer, "that wherever it posits a relation, it causes the members of this relation to flow together and merge. . . . The stages of time—past, present, future —do not remain distinct; over and over again the mythical consciousness succumbs to the tendency and temptation to level the differences and ultimately transform them into pure identity." [16] Time or the attempt to avoid time is the dominant feature of this particular day of his life and merges with the other ideas flowing through his mind:

> You can be oblivious to the sound [of a watch] for a long while, then in a second of ticking it can create in the mind unbroken the long diminishing parade of time you didn't hear. Like Father said down the long and lonely light-rays you might see Jesus walking, like. And the good Saint Francis that said Little Sister Death, that never had a sister. (94)

The allusion to Christ and St. Francis is repeated almost at once as the chimes strike the hour and then leads into Quentin's obsession with Caddy's sin:

> Like all the bells that ever rang still ringing in the long dying light-rays and Jesus and Saint Francis talking about his sister. Because if it were just to hell; if that were all of it. Finished. If things just finished themselves. (97)

Faulkner's inclusion of Saint Francis is obviously to gain the easy relation provided by the mystic's habitual form of address, in this case especially, "little sister death." Coupled with Jesus here, the allusions may be meant to suggest an ideal—unattainable or destroyed, as in Mr. Compson's words recalled by the working of the watch: "Father said that. That Christ was not crucified: he was worn away by a minute clicking of little wheels. That had no sister" (94). The watch again calls forth an allusion, this time evidently pointing to the absurdities of these ideal images:

The watch ticked on. I turned the face up, the blank dial with little wheels clicking and clicking behind it, not knowing any better. Jesus walking on Galilee and Washington not telling lies. (98–99)

Quentin's allusions to the resurrection also reject the promise offered. His body will not rise, only the flatirons he intends to use for weights (98 and 139).

It is the myth of Eden he seems to accept for its suggestions about the nature of women. And it is his father, Mr. Compson, who acts as the voice of the scientific empiric mode, attempting to make Quentin "correct or criticize what is given here and now, to limit its objectivity by *measuring* it against something not given, something past or future." As Quentin attempts to recreate the "homogeneity" of his objective world by fitting in the fact of Caddy's pregnancy, he attempts to substitute himself for Dalton Ames in an incest fantasy. "I said I have committed incest, Father I said" (95).

In the South you are ashamed of being a virgin. Boys. Men. They lie about it. Because it means less to women, Father said. He said it was men invented virginity not women. Father said it's like death: only a state in which the others are left and I said, but to believe it doesn't matter, and he said, That's what's so sad about anything: not only virginity, and I said, Why couldn't it have been me and not her who is unvirgin and he said, That's why that's sad too; nothing is even worth the changing of it. (96)

. . . you are confusing sin and morality women dont do that your Mother is thinking of morality whether it be sin or not has not occurred to her. (126)

But Quentin's mind remains fastened on Caddy and her "sin":

. . . *the curtains leaning in on the twilight upon the odour of the apple tree her head against the twilight her arms behind her head kimono-winged the voice that breathed o'er eden clothes upon the bed by the nose seen above the apple.* (130)

74

> *The chair-arm flat cool smooth under my forehead*
> *shaping the chair the apple tree leaning on my hair above*
> *the eden clothes by the nose seen.* (139)

He remembers the confrontations of Caddy, his attempts to preserve the sacred world in which they would be alone together, bridging the two of them into a supernatural world of hell where the fantasy of incest would guarantee their eternal immolation in a substitute purity replacing the purity of nature Benjy found in the smell of trees equated with Caddy and now lost.

The incest motif as it appears in Quentin's monologue is, strangely enough, best explained in another southern novelist's rationale of his own mythmaking as Andrew Lytle discusses the incest motif in his novel *The Velvet Horn*. In a society such as the defeated South, he says, the induced self-consciousness led to a heightened contemplation of self with a consequent withdrawal of the life force. The mythic analogue he cites is that of Adam and Eve experiencing the worlds of cosmos and chaos:

> Their expulsion from the earthly paradise seemed to put them into the disorder of chaos. Actually, they were confronted by a natural order which was a multiplicity of the conflict of opposites. This is not chaos but life as we suffer it and we fall into it as the child falls into the world. Continuance depended upon the exercise of the will and especially the crafts, not only to survive but to try to restore, to bring together the two halves which make a whole . . . .
> It was some years after I had been working on the as yet untitled *The Velvet Horn* that I realized I was treating an aspect of this ancient drama. The brothers and sister, under the guidance of the eldest, withdrew from the stresses of formal society in an effort to return to the preternatural equilibrium of innocence and wholeness. This is an habitual impulse, the refusal to engage in the cooperating opposites that make life. It is also as illusory as any Golden Age, and forbidden by divine and human law. Therefore it is the grounds for one of the oldest forms of search and conflict.

75

The symbol for this is incest. It need not be fact; but it is symbol . . . . But the actual union between close kin was not my interest. It was the incest of the spirit which seemed my subject, a spiritual condition which inhered within the family itself . . . .

And I had the controlling image well fixed in the top part of my head: incest, the act of symbolic wholeness, not the wholeness of innocence but the strain toward a return to this state of being.[17]

In *The Sound and the Fury* we find the same society, the same family conditions. The Compsons, as a family, have lost the life force, perhaps a condition symbolized by the dead end of Benjy and his sterilization and the bachelorhood of Jason. But long before this, Quentin has withdrawn from "the stresses of formal society" and the acceptance of the life force made by Caddy. One of the major themes of his part of the novel is Quentin's desire to return to "the preternatural equilibrium of innocence and wholeness," and his symbol for this is incest, a symbolic incest that will allow him to escape the fallen condition of his world. For Faulkner too there is the understanding that this search is also a search for a removal from time, and Quentin, rejecting the clocks and watches around him, seeks this "understanding." But Faulkner does not accept this symbolic incest as the only possible way to achieve this condition. In the final section, we are presented with Dilsey whose clock rotates its one false hand in a wild mockery of formal time and in Dilsey we find an acceptable compromise with the search for a rejoined, coherent world, a world not of primal innocence, but one in which man can at least endure.

Quentin's nearest encounter with sex has been the interlude with Natalie in the barn when she undertakes to teach him how to "dance sitting down," a lesson which is cut short when Quentin sees Caddy standing in the doorway. His first reaction is to translate his psychic reaction to this sex play into an objective equivalent:

76

> I jumped hard as I could into the hogwallow the mud yellowed up to my waist stinking I kept on plunging until I fell down and rolled over in it . . . . mud was warmer than the rain it smelled awful. (169–70)

Having smeared Caddy with the mud too, they then go to the branch to wash it off, a ritual washing away of sin that Faulkner employs again in the story "There Was A Queen" where Narcissa, having prostituted herself to gain possession of the Snopes letters, returns home and goes down to the branch to let the water flow over her.

The negation of sex finds an objective parallel in the story Versh once told about the man who mutilated himself, but again his father's words attempting to give it all perspective obtrude:

> It's nature is hurting you not Caddy and I said That's just words and he said So is virginity and I said you dont know. (143)

> Because women so delicate so mysterious Father said. Delicate equilibrium of periodical filth between two moons balanced. Moons he said full and yellow as harvest moons her hips thighs. (159)

His father's words dissolve into his own as the impurity seizes upon his thoughts: "Liquid putrefaction like drowned things floating like pale rubber flabbily filled getting the odour of honeysuckle all mixed up" (159). The odor of honeysuckle is the point where the two worlds meet—the purity associated with nature and the heavy fecundity which destroys the purity.

In his preparations for suicide, Quentin has come upon some boys watching a large trout from the bridge he intends to jump from. The trout suggests the Ichthus of Christian symbolism by its juxtaposition to Quentin's remark, "And maybe when He says Rise the eyes will come floating up too, out of the deep quiet and the sleep, to look on glory. And after awhile the flat irons would come floating up. I hid them [the

77

irons] under the end of the bridge and went back and leaned on the rail" (144). It is then he first sees the shadow which is the trout and muses:

> *If it could just be a hell beyond that: the clean flame the two of us more than dead. Then you will have only me then only me then the two of us amid the pointing and the horror beyond the clean flame.* (144)

The fish rises to the surface to lip some Mayflies and the fantasy continues: "*Only you and me then amid the pointing and the horror walled by the clean flame*" (144). Three boys come on to the bridge and explain that the fish cannot be caught; a prize is offered for it, but only "Boston folks" still come out to try. The old trout has become a neighborhood character and has driven all the other fish from the pond. This is where Quentin will die at midnight and if the trout has any symbolic value it would again be the futility and impossibility of Quentin's embracing another myth, a myth that reconciles the discordant elements of his experience by transcending them.

In his aimless wanderings to fill out the day, Quentin picks up in the bread shop the little Italian girl who follows him around. The comic, ironic interlude during which he attempts to rid himself of the girl whom, like Saint Francis, he addresses in the country fashion as "sister" represents the closest Quentin comes on this day to a normal handling of his objective world. But this world misunderstands the relationship as Julio, her brother, chases them down, thinking Quentin is some sexual pervert attempting a relationship with the girl. Quentin's reaction is a rather logical burst of hysteria as he dissolves in laughter.

His wanderings on this sunny day have had him constantly relating his progress in terms of his shadow. The shadow in mythical thought is equated with the object casting it. "A man's shadow," says Cassirer, "plays the same role as his image or picture. It is a real part of him and subject to injury; every injury to the shadow affects the man himself. One must not step on a man's shadow for fear of bringing sickness upon him." [18] Leaning over the bridge, Quentin sees his shadow on the water:

> The shadow of the bridge, the tiers of the railing, my shadow leaning flat upon the water, so easily had I tricked it that it would not quit me. At least fifty feet it was, and if I only had something to blot it into the water, holding it until it was drowned, the shadow of the package [with the flat irons] like two shoes wrapped up lying on the water. Niggers say a drowned man's shadow was watching for him in the water all the time. (110–11)

> When I can see my shadow again if not careful that I tricked into the water shall tread again upon my impervious shadow. (118)

> Trampling my shadow's bones into the concrete with hard heels . . . I walked upon the belly of my shadow. (118–19)

The image is repeated many times suggesting in mythic terms the self destruction he has already determined upon as his means of meeting a world where

> all men are just accumulations dolls stuffed with sawdust swept up from the trash heaps where all previous dolls had been thrown away the sawdust flowing from what wound in what side that not for me died not. (218)

At a quarter to midnight, he reviews his rationale for suicide which he had discussed with his father, denying the possibility of his world vision existing and rejecting the one posited by his father:

> The three quarters began. The first note sounded, measured and tranquil, serenely peremptory, emptying the unhurried silence for the next one and that's it if people could only change one another forever that way merge like a flame swirling up for an instant then blown cleanly out along the cool eternal dark instead of lying there trying not to think of the swing [where Caddy's lovemaking began] until all cedars came to have that vivid dead smell of perfume that

Benjy hated so . . . and he we must just stay awake and see
evil done for a little while its not always and i it doesn't
have to be even that long for a man of courage . . . and he
you wanted to sublimate a piece of natural human folly into
a horror and then exorcise it with truth and i it was to iso-
late her out of the loud world so that it would have to flee
us of necessity and then the sound of it would be as though
it had never been and he did you try to make her do it
[commit incest] and i i was afraid to i was afraid she might
and then it wouldnt have done any good but if i could tell
you we did it would have been so and then the others
wouldnt be so and then the world would roar away and he
and now this other [the contemplated suicide] you are not
lying now either but you are still blind to what is in yourself
to that part of general truth the sequence of natural events
and their causes which shadows every mans brow even ben-
jys you are not thinking of finitude you are contemplating
an apotheosis in which a temporary state of mind will become symmetrical above the flesh and aware both of itself
and of the flesh it will not quite discard. (219–20)

This attempt to force the scientific-empiric mode of thought
upon Quentin has failed and he goes to his death. On June 2,
1910, Quentin rejects not only the empiric-scientific view of
the world but the Christian myth that men employ to endure
it. Eighteen years later, that myth can only offer the quality of
endurance. The celebration of the resurrection does not effect
a millennial state; Dilsey may exemplify endurance in terms of
the promise held forth by the preacher who has seen the
"power en de glory" but hell is not harrowed and the most we
find is the world of the lost soul restored to an endurable
state, "each in its ordered place."

The original question, What happened to Faulkner
when he came to write *The Sound and the Fury?* will probably continue to interest Faulkner critics and occasion other
hypotheses. I suggest that his original, if superficial, interest in
mythology received some impetus that caused him to incorpo-
rate in his style elements that belong to the theory of myth
and, in his matter, elements that are taken from the vast body

of anthropological speculations on myths and myth formation.

In the search for a style, I have already quoted Mrs. Vickery's comment about Faulkner's distrust of the potentialities of language: "One of the basic attitudes running throughout all his work is the view that language and logic act to obscure truth rather than to reveal it." [19] Florence Leaver, in her study of the relation of diction to myth in Faulkner's works, also remarks this distrust:

> Faulkner is extremely conscious of words as tools, although he does not trust them . . . . Perhaps it is this distance between the deed and the word, the idea without form and the form which it must take, however imperfectly, which accounts for Faulkner's intensity, his attempt to make words do more than they can do—to find *logos* for *mythos*.[20]

Faulkner's distrust of the word is as it is used as a tool of scientific-empiric thought restricted by tradition to the creation or communication of a limited world vision, which neither he nor many of his characters share either exclusively or at all. In experimenting with "distorted" visions of objective reality, he has worked forward from Benjy's merely sensuous perception of objective reality to Quentin's mythic configuration with its own coherence, to a configuration such as Jason's which, while reprehensible, would still be considered "sane" in terms of a scientific-empiric mode of thought. In his appendix to *The Portable Faulkner*, Faulkner calls Jason "The first sane Compson since before Culloden" (16) but at Nagano he spoke of him as "the most vicious character in my opinion I ever thought of." [21] Evidently "sane" has a somewhat pejorative meaning for Faulkner.

In regard to matter, *The Sound and the Fury* represents a further departure from the early novels in that myth allusion is coherently employed as *mythos* in Aristotle's sense of the term. There is also a wider range of mythic reference. While there are fewer allusions to literary myths and the story seems to be dominated by the Christian myth of the resurrection and the older myth of Eden, many details suggest that Faulkner may have been reading some of the anthropological treatises on myth. It is not unlikely, for instance, that in his bookstore experience he would have come across the one volume abridgement of Frazer's *The Golden Bough* which was published in 1922 and reprinted eight times through 1927.* Here he might have found the relation between the goddess and the tree inherent in his hamadryad images, tree worship and its association with life forces (109 ff.), the crime of incest related to the waste land and punishable by death (141), the requirement that a goddess of fertility be supplied with a mate (which might apply to Eula of *The Hamlet*) (141), and citations of the deaths of servants when the king dies (as in the short story "Red Leaves"). The mythic significance of the shadow is given several pages:

> Often the savage regards his shadow or reflection as his soul or at all events as a vital part of himself, and as such it is necessarily a source of danger to him. For if it is trampled upon, struck, or stabbed, he will feel the injury as if it were done to his person. (189)
>
> We can now understand why it was a maxim both in ancient India and ancient Greece not to look at one's reflection in water, and why the Greeks regarded it as an omen of death if a man dreamed of seeing himself so reflected. They feared that the water-spirits would drag the person's reflection or soul under water, leaving him soulless to perish. (192)

The castration image in *The Sound and the Fury* is much like the description of the self castration of the eunuch priests of Attis (347–48) and the prostitution of Temple Drake might find some significance in the accounts of religious prostitution of various cults.

> In Armenia the noblest families dedicated their daughters to the service of the goddess Anaitis in her temple of Acilisena, where the damsels acted as prostitutes for a long time before they were given in marriage. Nobody scrupled to take one of

* Page references are to this edition.

82

these girls to wife when her period of service was over. (331)

There might even be the possibility that the Atthis allusion in *Soldiers' Pay* is to the god Attis who was equated with a tree rather than to the Athis of Ovid's *Metamorphoses*.

The various discussions of resurrection are many, especially in relation to Adonis and the reviving vegetation his resurrection signifies. The killing of the sacred bear is the most obvious parallel that can be found in Faulkner's work; it occurs in Frazer on pages 505–18, 522, 524, and 532–33. The sacred snake that is also found in *Go Down, Moses* is found in Frazer on page 520. And the ceremonies associated with the scapegoat, significant to *Light in August*, are found in pages 542–79.

It is not impossible that Faulkner might have looked into the unabridged edition with its much greater detail. There he might have found Frazer quoting a Catholic missionary in support of the absence of the fear of death among natives:

> On entering the house I found a woman seated at his bedside sewing the mourning dresses of the family. Moreover, the carpenter was fitting together the boards of the coffin quite close to the door of the house, so that the dying man could observe the whole proceeding from his bed.[22]

This source is closer to the scene in *As I Lay Dying* than is the already noted source in *Adam Bede*, if indeed a source need be cited.

When questioned about his reading, Faulkner always defended the author's right to make use of anything he had read, but when questioned about specific books he had read, he left no public record of ever having read *The Golden Bough*. This in itself would not rule out the possibility, for his answers to this question were always rather vague, ending in his repeated favor for the Old Testament.

That Faulkner was familiar with the methods of Frazer and his fellows might be inferred from a passage in "Impressions of Japan" which he read to a group at Nagano. He is speaking of the likenesses he has observed in the farming economy:

> And the names are the same names too: Jonathan and Winesap and Delicious; the heavy August foliage is blue gray with the same spray which we use. But there the resemblance ceases: every single apple enclosed in this twist of paper until that whole tree to this western eye becomes significant and festive and ceremonial like the symbolical tree of the western rite of Christmas. Only it is more significant here: where in the West there is one small often artificial tree to a family, wrested from the living dirt to be decked in ritual tinsel and then to die as though the tree were not the protagonist of a rite but the victim of a sacrifice, here not one tree to a family but every tree of all is dressed and decked to proclaim and salute older gods than Christ: Demeter and Ceres.[23]

It would seem that in considering the question of Faulkner's sources and their influence upon him in the important period of the late twenties, consideration must be given to his travels in the realms of *The Golden Bough* and similar works.*

Faulkner's new-found powers result in what must be regarded as pessimistic expression in *The Sound and the Fury*. Although built around two major mythic images, the novel does not accept the promise inherent in the Christian myth of the fall and the resurrection. On the one hand, he is fully aware of man's potential for making his life a hell; it is the documentation of this activity which constitutes his pessimistic naturalism. It might, in terms of the antithesis I have been using, be equated with a scientific-empiric view of the world. On the other hand, Faulkner has a very optimistic emotional

---

* Carvel Collins, speaking before the American Literature Section of the Modern Language Association, December 28, 1967, referred to facts of Faulkner's life contained in private papers to which he had been granted access. Among these was the fact that Faulkner did read Sherwood Anderson's one volume edition of *The Golden Bough* while he was living in Anderson's apartment in New Orleans in 1925. I should like to thank Professor Collins for permission to cite this.

vision of man's estate. After the pronouncements attendant upon the reception of the Nobel prize, there was a critical rush to prove that this positive part of his vision entitled him to the accolade of "traditional moralist," and to fit him into the Christian tradition. Soon after, the publication of A *Fable* wrought consternation among the critics who, examining the theology they found in the novel, found that it was not orthodox Christianity and blamed Faulkner for this "defect." *The Sound and the Fury* illustrates very early that although Faulkner makes much use of the images associated with Christianity he offers no great allegiance to their mythic content. The Christian myths are useful tools, he admits, but they are subordinated in his overall vision to larger mythic ideas, such as the scapegoat and the earth mother images. It is around such vast mythic patterns and not around the narrow, limited myths of any specific culture that his positive ideas of man's estate are organized.

In this middle period of his career, Faulkner seems to be trying to reconcile these two poles of his vision with little success. The negative tone of *The Sound and the Fury* is balanced by a comic, positive reading of life in *As I Lay Dying*. *Sanctuary* again gives a dark reading of life, a reading which he obviously could not let stand alone even many years later and which *necessitated* the attempt at balance found in *Requiem for a Nun*. In *Light in August*, Faulkner attempts to reconcile the two poles of his vision by the juxtaposition of two stories, an experiment repeated in *The Wild Palms*. It is in terms of his attempt to reconcile the two poles of an empiric reality and a mythic hopefulness that I would like to examine his middle period, in which he was able to demonstrate what C. S. Lewis's character Dr. Ransom learned about mythology: that it is "gleams of celestial strength and beauty falling on a jungle of filth and imbecility." [24]

4. The Comic Vision

As Faulkner has told us, The Sound and the Fury was, in form, an attempt to tell the same story from four different points of view. No single part of the novel contains the whole and no single point of view could communicate what Faulkner was attempting, for indeed words are insufficient to his aim. The author, like Addie Bundren, has learned "that words are no good," at least not beyond a certain point. That point for Faulkner becomes the point between words as symbols and form as symbol. In his next novel, he once again demonstrates this distrust for a straight narrative communication and forces the reader into a consideration of form as meaning. I believe the unifying principle of *As I Lay Dying* is not to be found in Addie Bundren or any one of the characters. Instead, it is to be found in the rhythm of the cyclic process of death to life, an affirmation of life in the face of death and the forces of nature which deal out both life and death.

Criticism has pointed frequently to Addie's monologue, probably because it is the only part of the book to deal explicitly with an abstract idea:

That was when I learned that words are no good; that words don't ever fit even what they are trying to say at . . . . I knew that fear was invented by someone that had never had the fear; pride, who never had the pride. I knew that it had been, not that they [her students] had dirty noses, but that we had had to use one another by words like spiders dangling by their mouths from a beam, swinging and twisting and never touching . . . .

He [Anse] had a word, too. Love, he called it. But I had been used to words for a long time. I knew that that word was like the others; just a shape to fill a lack; that when the right time came, you wouldn't need a word for that any more than for pride or fear . . . .

And so when Cora Tull would tell me I was not a true mother, I would think how words go straight up in a thin line, quick and harmless, and how terribly doing goes along the earth, clinging to it, so that after a while the two lines are too far apart for the same person to straddle from one to the other; and that sin and love and fear are just sounds that people who have never sinned nor loved nor feared have for what they never had and cannot have until they forget the words. (162–65) *

Anse has used similar imagery in his denial of the road:

. . . I told her it wasn't no luck in it, because the Lord put roads for travelling: why He laid them down flat on the earth. When He aims for something to be always a-moving, He makes it long ways, like a road or a horse or a wagon, but when He aims for something to stay put, He makes it up-and-down ways, like a tree or a man . . . . Because if He'd a aimed for man to be always a-moving and going somewheres else, wouldn't He a put him longways on his belly, like a snake? It stands to reason He would. (31–32)

Here the upward line of the futility of words is similar to Anse's conception of man as a static, non-doing being. "Doing goes along the earth" like the road. It is ironic that Addie, who could not make Anse a "doer," a *man* in her estimation, must employ the words she has despaired of to effect an ac-

* Page references are to the Jonathan Cape and Harrison Smith edition of *As I Lay Dying* (New York, 1930).

tion on his part after her death. Anse has been seen on the road only once before—when he came down the road past the schoolhouse in his courting ritual. Now he is forced by his oath to take the road again through flood and fire and the aura of decaying flesh, the terrible "doing." The result of this mock perilous journey is, of course, a reaffirmation of life, symbolized by his new teeth wherewith to enjoy God's vittles and by a duckshaped woman to wife. Much of the humor of the novel depends on the absolute innocence on the part of the players of the terrors, real and implied, of the "perilous" journey.

There is almost no direct mythic allusion in any of the monologues; even most of the Christian allusions are without any significant mythic content, but used in the direct ironic sense of words, words, words. The element of myth most dominant is that of mythic thought in Vardaman's perception of the world and in some of Darl's perceptions as he sinks beneath the terrors of the journey into insanity.

Vardaman, the youngest of the children, comes into the circle of Addie's dying from the river where he has caught an enormous fish. Dr. Peabody arrives shortly thereafter and Addie dies. Vardaman, associating Peabody's presence with the moment of death believes he has killed her and he takes a stick to beat the doctor's horses, driving them off. At about midnight, Vernon Tull discovers the runaway team and at the same time, Vardaman appears at his door in the rain and is asked in:

> But he hung back, dripping, watching me with them eyes. "You was there. You seen it laying there. Cash is fixing to nail her up, and it was a-laying right there on the ground. You seen it." (65)

Tull returns from harnessing the team to get his wife and Vardaman. "I can't get nothing outen him except about a fish," she complains (66). Arrived at the Bundrens, Tull helps to finish the building of the coffin.

It was nigh toward daybreak when we drove the last nail
and toted it in the house, where she was laying on the bed
with the window open and the rain blowing on her again.
Twice he did it, and him so dead for sleep that Cora says
his face looked like one of these here Christmas masts that
had done been buried a while and then dug up, until at last
they put her into it and nailed it down so he couldn't open
the window on her no more. And the next morning they
found him in his shirt-tail laying asleep on the floor like a
felled steer, and the top of the box bored clean full of holes
and Cash's new auger broke off in the last one. When they
taken the lid off they found that two of them had bored on
into her face. (68)

Vardaman's confusion of his mother with the fish may be
likened to an example Frazer cites of the ceremony of bringing back the soul:

They go to the bank of a river, call aloud the name of the
deceased, and entering the water catch a fish or an insect.
This creature they then take home and place among the
sainted dead of the family, supposing that in this manner
the spirit of the departed has been brought back to the
house. Sometimes the fish or insect is eaten in the belief
that it will be thus reborn as a child.[1]

There will, of course, be a birth in the house before too long
since Dewey Dell will not succeed in having her child aborted
in Jefferson. But it is in Cassirer's discussion of the mythic
mode of thought that we again find the clearest analysis of
this kind of behavior:

The analytical discretion which advanced empirical thought
exercises in distinguishing between the manifestations of life
and death and between their empirical presuppositions is
here replaced by an undifferentiated intuition of "existence"
as such. In this intuition *physical* existence does not suddenly break off in the moment of death but merely changes
its scene. All cults of the dead rest essentially on the belief
that the dead also require physical means of preserving their
existence, that they require their food, clothing, and pos-
sessions.[2]

And, in Vardaman's case, we might add *air*. The various objects present at the traumatic moment of his mother's death become merged in a new configuration. In mythical thought,

> every simultaneity, every spatial coexistence and contact, provide a real causal "sequence." It has even been called a principle of mythical causality and of the "physics" based on it that one take every contact in time and space as an immediate relation of cause and effect.[3]

Mother becomes equated in this new homogeneous whole with fish and the concept moves toward totemism and a new outlook toward his brother Jewel whom he regards as an alien to the family, assigning him the totem of the horse. This begins in the barn where he has run after beating away Peabody's horses:

> "Then hit want. Hit hadn't happened then. Hit was a-layin right there on the ground. And now she's gettin ready to cook hit."
> It is dark. I can hear wood, silence: I know them. But not living sounds, not even him [the horse]. It is as though the dark were resolving him out of his integrity, into an unrelated scattering of components—snuffings and stampings; smells of cooling flesh and ammoniac hair; an illusion of a coordinated whole of splotched hide and strong bones within which, detached and secret and familiar, an *is* different from my *is*. (52)

The entirety of "chapter" 19 given to Vardaman is: "My mother is a fish" (78). It is Darl who sets Jewel apart from the rest of the children and confirms Vardaman's "totem."

> But my mother is a fish. Vernon seen it. He was there.
> "Jewel's mother is a horse," Darl said.
> "Then mine can be a fish, cant it, Darl?" I said.
> Jewel is my brother.
> "Then mine will have to be a horse, too," I said.
> "Why?" Darl said. "If pa is your pa, why does your ma have to be a horse just because Jewel's is?" (93)

Darl is, of course, speaking from the intuited knowledge that Anse is not the father of Jewel and seems to be establishing a concept of two Addies, one wife to Anse and the other totally outside of the clan.

Vardaman's totemistic thinking would place his configuration of the world among what Cassirer calls "the truly primordial mythical forms" (86):

> Long before man had knowledge of himself as a separate species distinguished by some specific power and singled out from nature as a whole by a specific primacy of value he knew hmself to be a link in the chain of life as a whole, within which each individual creature and thing is magically connected with the whole, so that a continuous transition, a metamorphosis of one being into another, appears not only as possible but as necessary, as the "natural" form of life itself.[4]

There is no indication in Vardaman's thought that totemism is carried to its ultimate form, "the belief that the members of the different clans not only are descended from different animal ancestors, but really *are* these varieties of animals." [5]

Hyatt Waggoner, whose approach to Faulkner's novels is primarily to relate them to an orthodox Christianity and to express regret when Faulkner's "Christianity" fails to meet the requirements of orthodoxy, finds much in Vardaman and his fish:

> Not to labor the point: the fish which Vardaman pictures "all chopped up . . . laying in the kitchen in the bleeding pan, waiting to be cooked and et" parallels Christ killed and ritualistically eaten and drunk to prevent the death of the believer. Vardaman does not accept his mother's "change" as final; or does not mean the same by "dead" as the others do.[6]

He is, perhaps, more correct in finding a Christian allusion in the behavior of Vardaman when the party comes to the flooded river which has now risen a few inches above the bridge and cross over in what would appear to be a walking "on" the waters. Here he parallels Vardaman's lack of fear as he offers his hand to Tull to Christ's quieting words to the disciples. The effect of this approach is to make Vardaman a true communicant, but it ignores the fact that presumably the others have also partaken of the fish and that Anse and Dewey Dell also "walk upon the waters." The crucial point is obviously that it is Vardaman's "delusion" that constitutes the symbolic value Waggoner finds here and unless this is satisfactorily explained, the rest of the symbolic pattern suffers.

In "The Janus Symbol in *As I Lay Dying*," Roma King, Jr. unites the fish with Jewel's horse to explicate a compound symbol which he finds at the core of the book.

> The most significant symbols are the *horse* and the *fish*, both of which occur in many mythologies. The horse generally denotes the sub-human, the animal state of man's nature, his virility, his instinctive passions. As a means of locomotion, the horse represents the surge of passion that carries man away; as a beast of burden it is related to the mother archetype. The fish, too, is traditionally a symbol of life. It represents the woman, the mother, the primitive sources of life; as a phallic symbol it indicates fertility and life renewal; in Christian symbolism, it stands for Christ and for the life giving Sacraments, Holy Baptism and Holy Communion.[7]

However, he points out, this particular fish is dead and therefore becomes a symbol of death, one face of the "Janus symbol," the other being the horse which is a symbol of life. Vardaman's references to the fish and the horse consequently become his attempts to establish meaningful relations with the other characters in the book, and, since this fails, the theme of the book becomes a kind of frustration suffered by Vardaman.

This ingenious symbol fails to explain the novel. It is representative of an approach taken all too often to Faulkner's work: that he is writing novels united by coherent symbol patterns which, if they can be discovered, will constitute the critics' "open sesame" to the work. It has the advantage of being concrete and offering simple one-to-one relationships, but it ignores all parts of the novels that do not fit and consequently does not explain. In this case, it offers Vardaman as the single quester of the novel and ignores the rest of the party, something the novel itself does not do.

Of the other children, Darl's configuration of reality is the farthest removed from the empiric mode. The spokesman for about one-third of the novel, he is presented as a sensitive clairvoyant cut off in some way from the other members of the family except Vardaman. He is able to intuit that Jewel is only a half brother and that Dewey Dell is pregnant. There is nothing beyond this in the earlier monologues to indicate that he is insane at that time. He is evidently aware that he has not shared as fully in his mother's love as have Jewel and Cash, and the fact of her death seems to call for a revaluation of his relationships to the other members of the family. While he shares some of the mythical elements of Vardaman's perceptions, it is not possible to schematize the disintegration of his mind in terms of a downward passage through the levels of perception to the chaos of another Benjy.

Dewey Dell is the first of Faulkner's mammalian fertility emblems; while picking cotton through the fields toward the trees, she decides that if her bag is full when she reaches the trees it will be a sign and she and Lafe will go into the woods. Her total preoccupation during the death rituals for Addie is the fact that she must get to Jefferson to buy the pills that will effect an abortion. Knowing that Darl knows her secret, she wishes him dead and acts out this wish in a fantasy or dream that incorporates Vardaman and his fish. "I rose and took the knife from the streaming fish still hissing and I killed Darl" (111). Symbolically, she will use her mother's death to rid herself of Darl and his knowledge. Addie herself had demonstrated this power of mind in her prophecy that Jewel would save her from fire and flood.

Even Cash, the most empiric of the lot, seems to have a moment of extrasensory communication. Darl is speaking to Cash, easing his concern about Jewel:

"He can swim," I say. "If he'll just give the horse time, anyhow . . ." When he was born, he had a bad time of it. Ma would sit in the lamplight, holding him on a pillow on her lap. We would wake and find her so. There would be no sound from them.

"That pillow was longer than him," Cash says. (134)

Of Cash's five monologues, the first three are extremely short disquisitions on the carpenter's art of the coffin. The fourth is a rationalization for sending Darl to the state asylum, and the fifth ends the novel with general satisfaction at the way everything has turned out. Jewel is allowed only a page in the novel. However, as the others see him, he is the personification of Addie's "doing goes along the earth," a compact bundle of energy directed at action. His central action recapitulated by Darl is the nightly labors aimed at buying the horse.

While Faulkner has employed the horse in a mythical-symbolic manner before, he has not developed it to this degree. In *Sartoris*, Aunt Jenny told of the horsemen of the Civil War, employing the image of the centaur by which man and beast became fused in one whole, powerful and glorious in relation to the cause. (Faulkner later repeated the same image in *The Unvanquished*.) The stallion is again used as a symbol of a power that the last Bayard cannot control when he attempts his drunken ride and is thrown. Jewel's horse is given much greater development, and I believe may be regarded as a symbol of mana as used by Faulkner. Mana and taboo, says Cassirer,

> represent the characteristic accent which the magical-mythical consciousness places on objects. This accent divides the whole of reality and action into a mythically significant and mythically irrelevant sphere, into what arouses mythical interest and what leaves it relatively indifferent . . . . Both concepts represent, as it were, primary interjections of the mythical consciousness. They still have no independent function of signification and representation but resemble cries of mythical emotion.[8]

Faulkner's frequent use of powerful, dangerous, or noble horses has this air of mythic significance; their symbolic development is never clearly organized and they remain a kind of primary interjection of a natural force that in some mystic way can be communicated to man. Jewel's horse, especially, signifies the wild and untamable powers which evoke the desire of possession and control by the hill people. It is a descendant of the wild spotted horses Faulkner incorporated in *The Hamlet*. Ownership of the horse with its murderous energies gives Jewel a complement to his existence. The horse is not an economic asset; it is merely completion of his energies, his psyche, and its efficacy is in this mystical relation to him.

Darl taunts Jewel about the horse as they ride back to the house where Addie now lies dead, a fact Darl has announced to Jewel from his clairvoyance. " 'It's not your horse that's dead, Jewel,' I say. . . . I cannot love my mother because I have no mother. Jewel's mother is a horse' " (88). And somehow Darl has penetrated to the knowledge that Jewel's fierce desire for the horse is a displacement of his emotional desires for his mother, a fact that Addie herself seemed to apprehend when Jewel first brought the horse home, the reward for his Herculean labors clearing the land. When Anse trades off the horse to replace the team of mules drowned in the river, it is Jewel who voluntarily takes the horse off in the morning to consummate the deal, giving up a part of himself that the journey may continue.

When Darl is turned over to the authorities in what appears to be a vicious conspiracy on the part of Dewey Dell (who has informed upon him as the barn burner in his attempt to burn the putrifying corpse) and Jewel, it is Cash who offers the rationalization for the act:

> But I thought more than once before we crossed the river and after, how it would be God's blessing if He did take her outen our hands and get shut of her in some clean way, and it seemed to me that when Jewel worked so to get her outen the river, he was going against God in a way, and then when Darl seen that it looked like one of us would have to do something, I can almost believe he done right in

a way. But I don't reckon nothing excuses setting fire to a man's barn and endangering his stock and destroying his property. That's how I reckon a man is crazy. That's how he can't see eye to eye with other folks. And I reckon they ain't nothing else to do with him but what most folks says is right. (226)

The Bundren family has rid itself of the corpse of Addie and the penetrating insights of Darl who could not survive the tests of the journey. Anse has his new teeth and a new wife and Dewey Dell remains pregnant. Somehow through all of this blundering, the stasis of death and the malignant powers of nature have been overcome and the forces of life have reasserted themselves.

At Nagano Faulkner labeled the book a *tour de force* and, by his criteria, ranked the book as the least of his favorites. It is probably the most ambiguous of his novels but is certainly a comic affirmation when compared to the waste land of *The Sound and the Fury* and the "jungle of filth and imbecility" which we find in the demonic world of *Sanctuary*.

While Faulkner is given to a good many comic moments in his writings, they are only part of a larger pattern of vacillation between the poles of acceptance and despair. The coupling of *The Sound and the Fury* and *As I Lay Dying* in one volume in the Modern Library edition illustrates by juxtaposition the larger totality of his vision. In *Light in August* this juxtaposition of tragic and comic will achieve a balance within the form of one work. But before that comes *Sanctuary*, an unremitting presentation of despair.

5. A Demonic World

Sanctuary, because of its shock value, occupies a unique place in the history of Faulkner's reputation. First written, according to him, after *Sartoris*, the novel continues the examination of a decaying society taken over by criminals, callow youth, and the entrenched hypocrisy of the privileged class to which Narcissa Benbow Sartoris has committed herself. The dedication of *Sartoris* to Sherwood Anderson, "through whose kindness I was first published, with the belief that this book will give him no reason to regret the fact," and the nature of the follow-up volume suggests that Faulkner had set himself to a fictional representation of Anderson's vision of a race descending into degradation and impotence under the influence of the machine.[1] Perhaps it is in *A Story Teller's Story* that Faulkner even found the guiding image of opposition between horses and machines, for Anderson's epigraph deals with the nature of a thoroughbred and ends, " 'Remember that horses are not machines.' " Later Anderson characterizes the prostitute artist as one who seeks respectability and a Ford and who, on holidays, will seek out the races at Indianapolis. "Not for them the flashing thoroughbreds or the sturdy trotters and pacers. Not for them freedom, laughter. For them machines."

I have repeatedly suggested a polarity in Faulkner's vision, a mystique that attempts to reconcile an empiric observation of life which is largely negative and despairing with an optimism that can be regarded as mythic in mode. In *Soldiers' Pay* there is the vague archetypal motif of the dying Mahon as scapegoat sacrificed to a generally unknowing and undeserving society. The book ends with an attempt at reconciliation through the sustaining myth of resurrection and redemption suggested by the Negroes' singing about Jesus and through the cyclical nature of life suggested by the dust in the shoes of Gilligan and the Rector. In *Mosquitoes*, there is again a static, foolish society stranded on a sand bar in the sea of life. The young people who would break out of this society are not strong enough to withstand the rigors (mosquitoes) of the world they encounter and return to the boat. There is again use of the resurrection motif, this time to suggest that only the artist can break away from this stagnation and create a new world. *Sartoris* gives us a "hero" who cannnot cope with a new machine-dominated society but again suggests an archetypal optimism in the cyclical nature of life, one Sartoris dying as another is born. *The Sound and the Fury* chronicles the defeat of the Compson family and again attempts to suggest that the myth of the resurrection offers the sustenance necessary to "endure." *As I Lay Dying* pits a family against their own ignorance and foolishness on an archetypal quest, testing them with fire and flood as they seek to rid themselves of death (and even new life) and leaves them at the end comically in control of life forces.

Only in *Sanctuary* did Faulkner fail to offer the optimistic counterpoint to his negative vision of life, a failure that he attempted to rectify years later with the writing of *Requiem for a Nun*. *Sanctuary* is indeed Faulkner's dark night of the soul, a demonic expression of pessimism. I should like to examine the novel in terms of the theory of myths offered by Northrop Frye.

I have already referred to Frye's theory of modes which traces five stages in western literature: the mythic mode, the romantic mode, the high mimetic mode, the low mimetic mode, and the ironic mode which tends in a cyclical manner to revert to myth. The relationship of myth to the other modes depends on his key insight, the theory of *displacement*: "As the modes of fiction move from the mythical to the low mimetic and ironic," says Frye, "they approach a point of extreme 'realism' or representative likeness to life. It follows that the mythical mode, the stories about gods, in which characters have the greatest possible power of action, is the most abstract and conventionalized of all literary modes." [2]

At one end of Frye's spectrum of modes is myth. In undisplaced myth the form is that of "two contrasting worlds of total metaphorical identification, one desireable and the other undesircable," the one apocalyptic, the other demonic. Next to myth on this spectrum of modes is the area of romance, by which term Frye means "the tendency . . . to displace myth in a human direction and yet, in contrast to 'realism,' to conventionalize content in an idealized direction." Here the tendency is "to suggest implicit mythical patterns in a world more closely associated with human experience." And finally, at the other end from myth is naturalism where we have a realistic emphasis "on content and representation rather than on the shape of the story." The tendency of ironic literature toward myth is marked, as a rule, by mythical patterns more suggestive of the demonic than of the apocalyptic. The author of such a work must somehow solve certain technical problems created by the presence of a mythical structure in an essentially realistic presentation.[3] The general name given to the devices used to solve these problems is *displacement*. "The central principle of displacement is that what can be metaphorically identified in a myth can only be linked in romance by some form of simile: analogy, significant association, incidental accompanying imagery, and the like." [4]

In the naturalistic world of *Sanctuary* the ironic vision

strains toward the world of myth through the presentation of a demonic world, "the world that desire totally rejects: the world of the nightmare and the scapegoat, of bondage and pain and confusion; . . . the world also of perverted or wasted work, ruins and catacombs, instruments of torture and monuments of folly." [5]

As the apocalyptic symbolism of the vegetable world is the ordered garden, so the displaced demonic world of *Sanctuary* is introduced by the unnatural man Popeye spitting in the spring from which Horace Benbow has just drunk. This begins Horace's initiation into a demonic world. Running away from the stupid world of his marriage he returns to the hill country of Jefferson, wanting just a hill to lie on after the flat delta country, a hill that might suggest to the archetype-hunting psychologist the omphalos, the center of a stable world. His pilgrimage in this sense will be quite ironic. Horace is a lawyer for whom the law represents an idealistic order; human folly, he seems to believe, could be legislated out of existence. His first stop in his quest for "a hill to lie on" is ironically the lawless domain of the Old Frenchman place. Horace goes on to his sister's home outside of Jefferson where Narcissa (her name symbolic in this novel as it was not in *Sartoris*) is entertaining Gowan "in her customary white dress."

Temple and Gowan next intrude on the Old Frenchman place where the drunk Gowan behaves in a literally demonic fashion while Temple becomes little less than a sex bomb among the bootleggers. "'The demonic erotic relation," says Frye,

> becomes a fierce destructive passion that works against loyalty or frustrates the one who possesses it. It is generally symbolized by a harlot, witch, siren, or other tantalizing female, a physical object of desire which is sought as a possession and therefore can never be possessed.[6]

As the various men make their moves toward Temple, it is Popeye who finally shoots Tommy and, impotent himself, rapes Temple with the cob in the crib, seeking to possess that which he cannot possess. This action, too shocking to be accepted as merely shocking, leads the critic to searching for the symbolic values in what must be allegory. Since I, however, am only concerned at the moment with what Frye would call the "tonality" of the piece, I would cite the analogy to the myth of Persephone, Temple raped and spirited away to the underworld of Memphis. But it is not the world of vegetation that dies, it is the world of legal-moral order, and for Horace, whose pilgrimage to Jefferson was originally a search for a personal order, the quest now becomes a search for a larger moral order in terms of justice and the law to which he has committed his idealism. Like Demeter, Horace searches for Temple who, by identifying the true murderer, can save Goodwin, the scapegoat, and restore the order of justice.

Horace's singular mistake is that of believing that his world exists. The novel sets out to prove that society's reality is merely a demonic parody of the apocalyptic world in which justice *does* exist. Thus it is Narcissa, the real agent of society, concerned not with justice at all but only with appearances, who takes on the role of the searching Demeter when she goes to the district attorney to inform him about Temple. The district attorney is not interested in justice either, but in advancing his own ends.

"The demonic human world," says Frye "is a society held together by a kind of molecular tension of egos, a loyalty to the group or the leader which diminishes the individual, or, at best, contrasts his pleasure with his duty or honor." [7] And the world of *Sanctuary* is not of the best. It is not justice this world seeks, but the appearance of justice, and for this a scapegoat is sufficient.

Goodwin, who has decided to put his faith in the law rather than name Popeye as the killer and thereby suffer certain death, waits in the jail with the heaven tree, the tree of life, outside. When Temple appears at the trial, returned from the underworld to society, she is under the guard of her father and four brothers. The father is a judge and two of the brothers are lawyers; another is a newspaper man and the fourth is a Yale student, evidently all bastions of the society Narcissa represents. Temple falsely accuses Goodwin of Tommy's murder and the stage is set for killing the scapegoat. The social relation of the demonic world "is that of the mob, which is essentially human society looking for a *pharmakos*." [8] The "justice" of the demonic world has named Goodwin to this position and the mob executes him in a blaze of gasoline, the burning pyre a displacement of death at the stake, the demonic parody of the tree of life which has appeared as the tree of heaven outside of the jail. A false "order" is once again restored to this demonic world with the sacrifice of the scapegoat and Horace, whose quest has been frustrated returns to his wife. Appearances are restored on all sides.

From start to finish, the ironic vision in *Sanctuary* relies upon the demonic antithesis to the ideal order of the apocalyptic world; it remains a presentation of the world that desire totally rejects. Here Faulkner has reached what Frye would call "a point of demonic epiphany, where we see or glimpse the undisplaced demonic vision, the vision of the *Inferno*." [9] At no other point in his career does Faulkner offer us such an unremitting view of a thoroughly naturalistic world. Here there is no divided stream, as C. C. Walcutt would put it to indicate the opposition between despair and idealism; there is only the single current of despair. For the rest of his work, however, Walcutt's metaphor of the divided stream would hold true in a sense, and if we may view *Requiem for a Nun* as a continuation of this novel, it is eventually true for *Sanctuary* as well.

Faulkner continues his portrayal of a demonic society in the background of *Light in August*. Here, however, he makes one of his strongest affirmations through the juxtaposition of the story of Lena Grove to that of the sacrificial scapegoat, Joe Christmas. Both stories are centered on quests: Lena's comic search for the father of her child and Joe's more complicated tragic quest.

The primary myth held here in counterpoint is that of Christ as the crucified scapegoat. Stated in its simplest form, the myth as used by Faulkner holds Christ, the god, to have achieved his ultimate identification with humanity only through the suffering of his death. It is only in this broad outline that Joe Christmas is to be thought of as a Christ figure. Both Christmas and Christ are examples of an archetypal pattern with the Christ "legend" used as one of Faulkner's oft explained "tools":

> Remember, the writer must write out of his background. He must write out of what he knows and the Christian legend is part of any Christian's background, especially the background of a country boy, a Southern boy. My life was passed, my childhood, in a very small Mississippi town, and that was a part of my background. I grew up with that. I assimilated that, took that in without even knowing it. It's just there. It has nothing to do with how much of it I might believe or disbelieve—it's just there.[10]

Joe Christmas, like the hero of the romantic quest, has origins that are shrouded in mystery. It is only at the end of the novel that Faulkner attempts to solve the "technical problems for making it plausible," the displacement which offers the parentage of Milly and the shadowy circus worker who might have been Mexican or part Negro. Found on the steps of the orphanage on Christmas eve, Joe receives his name. His early youth is spent under the watchful eye of an ogre-like "protector," Doc Hines, his maternal grandfather, who subtly insinuates in the minds of everyone the belief that Joe is part Negro.

Doc Hines, in his madness, partakes of a rabid Calvinist theology that causes him to talk of himself as God's appointed instrument; indeed, he would appear at times to be the figure of god-the-father, a father role he shares toward Joe with McEachern.

It is Hines who establishes the relative values of the Negro-white blood lines:

"I know evil. Aint I made evil to get up and walk God's world? A walking pollution in God's own face I made it. Out of the mouths of little children He never concealed it. You have heard them. I never told them to say it, to call him in his rightful nature, by the name of his damnation. I never told them." (119) *

The name of his damnation is "nigger." In the Calvinist framework of the novel, a framework transposed to the South, the Negro is damned; the white is of the elect. Joe's search for identity can in one sense be likened to the introspection of the Puritan seeking signs of grace.

The center of evil in the novel is in this doubleness of race and religion, the one dividing mankind into black and white, the other into the damned and the elect. In Faulkner's "theology" it is neither *eros*, symbolized by Joe's sexual adventures, nor *agape*, symbolized by the many food offerings, which can overcome this division of mankind; it is only in death that man's essential humanity can be recognized. In the order of society, an order based on the acceptance of this division of mankind, Joe, whose role is ambiguous, who can "pass" for white, represents a threat to the artificial stability. As a social being, Joe must determine his role in society, determine whether he is black or white, determine an identity for himself.

After an adolescent "captivity" under McEachern who attempts to impose an identity on Joe, Joe begins to assert himself first through the knowledge of sex. This becomes a mode of self definition, a symbolic means of differentiating himself from a large part of the world, the female part, that would seek to impose an identity—*any* identity upon him. In true Calvinistic fashion, Joe must achieve his own identity. The ultimate rejection of this "'enclosement" threatened by the female world is, of course, the murder of Joanna Burden when she attempts to force upon him her relation to the Fa-

* Page references are to the Harrison Smith and Robert Haas, Inc. edition of *Light in August* (New York, 1932).

ther with the command, "Kneel with me." His initiation is twice postponed, the first time when he kicks out at the Negro girl in the barn, rejecting the containment threatened, "enclosed by the womanshenegro and the haste . . ." (147). There is a sense of freedom in the male world of McEachern, "as if the whole situation were perfectly logical and reasonable and inescapable. Perhaps he was thinking then how he and the man could always count upon one another, depend upon one another; that it was the woman alone who was unpredictable" (149). But this is a false sense of freedom, a sense equated for Joe with the hard, clean male body, as when he is fighting with the four other boys over the Negro girl in the barn: "There was no She at all now. They just fought; it was as if a wind had blown among them, hard and clean" (147). That night he is late for his chores and McEachern beats him:

> The boy's body might have been wood or stone: a post or a tower upon which the sentient part of him mused like a hermit, contemplative and remote with ecstasy and self-crucifixion . . . .
> When he went to bed that night his mind was made up to run away. He felt like an eagle: hard, sufficient, potent, remorseless, strong. But that passed, though he did not then know that, like the eagle, his own flesh as well as all space was still a cage. (150–51)

The only true freedom for Joe can come when the body that creates chains through its appetites is left behind.

Joe's second attempt at sexual initiation is postponed because the whore Bobby had forgotten her menstrual cycle. The accent on the demonic imagery of sex throughout the book creates a naturalistic equivalent to the damnations of sin and Negro in the religious and racial images. Along with food which is constantly rejected as an offering but sought out in animal necessity, these motifs create a picture of a world in which no metaphysical truth of the spirit can be realized. When Joe had first learned about menstruation through the juvenile grapevine, he had stalked a sheep, killed it, and washed himself in its blood. Evidently this ritual "blood of the lamb" is an attempt on the level of mythical thought to wash away the "sin" of man's animal nature, to expiate.

> Then he knelt, his hands in the yet warm blood of the dying beast, trembling, drymouthed, backglaring. Then he got over it, recovered. He did not forget what the boy had told him. He just accepted it. He found that he could live with it side by side with it. It was as if he said, illogical and desperately calm *All right. It is so then. But not to me. Not in my life and my love.* (174)

But again this sense of security or "immunity" is proved false. When Bobby is trying to tell him about her mistake in making a date for this night,

> He just stood there, with a still downspeaking voice dying somewhere about his ears. He had forgot about the shot sheep. He had lived with the fact which the older boy had told him too long now. With the slain sheep he had bought immunity from it for too long now for it to be alive. (175–76)

His attainment to maturity symbolized by his moral break with the teachings of McEachern is followed by the archetypal break with the father: Joe braining McEachern with a chair, Zeus defeating Cronus, or even Oedipus killing Laius. The Oedipus parallel is fully developed in the excellent essay by Longley:

> Consider another hero. About his birth there is mystery also. He too is spirited away as an infant because dreadful things are whispered about him, and he too is brought up by foster-parents whom he leaves hurriedly for fear he may have killed his foster-father. In a very direct way, it can be said that his very begetting caused the death of his real father. He brings terrible shame, agony, and death to his real mother. After a great deal of wandering, he returns to that part of the world which, unknown to him, was the scene of his begetting and birth. Early in life he was given a free choice of two lines of conduct, one of which will remove

106

him from all danger to himself. He persists in the other because it is necessary to the terms of his own definition of himself. He lives connubially with an older woman, who as a result of his drive toward self-definition dies a horrible death. The fearful rumors break out afresh. There is an old, mad visionary who claims to have special insight into the truth about him, and as a result, his fellowmen are convinced he is a ritual pollution in the community. Pursued by them, he is harried for days and is eventually sacrificed in a particularly horrible ritual murder. He was saddled with an incredibly horrible, inevitable curse; he had not asked for it and had done nothing to deserve it; it was all "decided" before he was born. The second hero is, of course, Joe Christmas.[11]

Frye suggests in his work that the image of the street may serve as a displacement for the hero's maze. It is in just this way that Faulkner compresses the next fifteen years of Joe's life:

He thought that it was loneliness which he was trying to escape and not himself. But the street ran on: catlike, one place was the same as another to him. But in none of them could he be quiet. But the street ran on in its moods and phases, always empty: he might have seen himself as in numberless avatars, in silence, doomed with motion, driven by the courage of flagged and spurred despair. (213)

Early in the novel, the first presentation of Joe has him moving toward the still center of his "maze." The night before he is to murder Joanna Burden he wanders the town and countryside, a journey which leads him into the underworld:

Then he found himself. Without his being aware the street had begun to slope and before he knew it he was in Freedman Town, surrounded by the summer smell and the summer voices of invisible negroes. They seemed to enclose him like bodiless voices murmuring, talking, laughing, in a language not his. As from the bottom of a thick black pit he saw himself enclosed by cabinshapes, vague, kerosenelit, so that the street lamps themselves seemed to be further spaced, as if the black life, the black breathing had compounded the substance of breath so that not only voices but

moving bodies and light itself must become fluid and ac-
crete slowly from particle to particle, of and with the now
ponderable night inseparable and one. (106–7)

This accidental descent into the underworld frightens him:

> He began to run, glaring, his teeth glaring, his inbreath cold
> on his dry teeth and lips, toward the next street lamp. Be-
> neath it a narrow and rutted lane turned and mounted to
> the parallel street, out of the black hollow. He turned into it
> running and plunged up the sharp ascent, his heart ham-
> mering, and into the higher street. He stopped here, pant-
> ing, glaring, his heart thudding as if it could not or would
> not yet believe that the air now was the cold hard air of
> white people. (107)

He passes out of the town and into the surrounding hills:

> But he did not look back until he reached the crest of the
> hill. Then he could see the town, the glare, the individual
> lights where streets radiated from the square. He could see
> the street down which he had come, and the other street,
> the one which had almost betrayed him; and further away
> and at right angels, the far bright rampart of the town itself,
> and in the angle between the black pit from which he had
> fled with drumming heart and glaring lips. No light came
> from it, from here no breath, no odor. It just lay there,
> black impenetrable, in its garland of Augusttremulous lights.
> It might have been the original quarry, abyss itself. (108)

Here again the damnation of "Negro" is established, a damnation Joe still seeks to escape. In the white section of town
he had looked about at the whites on their porches. " 'That's
all I wanted,' he thought. That dont seem like a whole lot to
ask' " (108). But it *is* this society's equivalent of election.

After having killed Joanna Burden (whose function
within the framework of the romance is the rather minor one
of a sexual obstacle in the search of the hero, and within the
framework of damnation and election a force attempting to
enclose and define Joe's nature), Joe eludes his pursuers, once
by trading shoes with a Negro woman to throw off the dogs
set on him, thereby symbolically determining his damnation:

It seemed to him that he could see himself being hunted by white men at last into the black abyss which had been waiting, trying, for thirty years to drown him and into which now and at last he had actually entered, bearing now upon his ankles the definite and ineradicable gauge of its upward moving. (313)

Tired of running, he goes into Mottstown to walk the streets until recognized and apprehended:

Looking [down at Mottstown], he can see the smoke low on the sky, beyond an imperceptible corner; he is entering it again, the street which ran for thirty years. It had been a paved street, where going should be fast. It had made a circle and he is still inside of it. Though during the last seven days he has had no paved street, yet he has travelled further than in all the thirty years before. And yet he is still inside the circle. (321)

At the center of his maze lies not the truth of Negro but the truth of his membership in humanity. There is left but the ritual murder and castration to complete this pact with humanity and to place him in the ironic role of scapegoat to this society, a society which insists on black-white, damned-saved demarkations to assure its own stability. "The adventure of the hero," says Joseph Campbell, represents the moment in his life when he achieved illumination—the nuclear moment when, while still alive, he found and opened the road to the light beyond the dark walls of our living death." [12] Campbell's description of the hero's quest posits an end in which the truth is symbolized as the release of the waters of life and Joe's gushing black blood after his castration might be remarked as a particularly demonic displacement of this symbol.

The use of the Christ figure as a counterpoint to the life and death of Joe Christmas has raised some question about Faulkner's Christianity. The objections are based on Joe's moral and ethical existence: he is a fornicator, bootlegger, and murderer. How then can Faulkner expect the reader to take seriously the parallels to the Christ figure and expect him to regard Joe's death in the realm of the sacred? Such questions directed at Faulkner's "Christianity" demonstrate the level at which the myth of Christianity operates in our society, the level, paradoxically enough, of rational empiricism. "Whereas scientific thought," says Cassirer,

> takes an attitude of inquiry and doubt toward the "object" with its claim to objectivity and necessity, myth knows no such opposition. It "has" the object only insofar as it is overpowered by it; it does not possess the object by progressively building it but is simply possessed by it. It has no will to understand the object by encompassing it logically and articulating it with a complex of causes and effects; it is simply overpowered by the object . . . . The contents of the mythical consciousness form a self-enclosed realm and possess a common tonality, by which they are distinguished from the contents of common, everyday, empirical existence . . . . It is this characteristic *transcendence* which links the contents of the mythical and the religious consciousness. In their mere immediate existence they all contain a revelation and at the same time retain a kind of mystery; it is this interpenetration, this revelation which both reveals and conceals, that gives the mythical-religious content its basic trait, its character of the "sacred." [13]

If we could modify our "scientific" expectations of Faulkner to allow for some of the mythic force of his thinking, I believe there would be much less critical frustration in the attempts to explain his "religion." The same ethical objections which are made to Joe's character are made toward Lena Grove, who as an earth-goddess figure seemingly does not fulfill expectations because of her mammalian stupidity, but her role, after all, does not call for any intelligence and we have no vested interest in earth goddesses, so these complaints are not especially loud.

"The basic principle of all mythology," says Campbell,

> is . . . of the beginning in the end. Creation myths are pervaded with a sense of the doom that is continually recalling all created shapes to the imperishable out of which they first emerged. The forms go forth powerfully, but inevitably

reach their apogee, break, and return. Mythology, in this sense, is tragic in its view. But in the sense that it places our true being not in the forms that shatter but in the imperishable out of which they again immediately bubble forth, mythology is eminently untragical. Indeed, wherever the mythological mood prevails, tragedy is impossible . . . . Herein lies the basic paradox of the dual focus . . . . One breaks into the many, destiny "happens," but at the same time "is brought about." From the perspective of the source, the world is a majestic harmony of forms pouring into being, exploding, and dissolving. But what the swiftly passing creatures experience is a terrible cacophony of battle cries and pain. The myths do not deny this agony (the crucifixion); they reveal within, behind, and around it essential peace (the heavenly rose).[14]

This "basic paradox of the dual focus" lies at the center of my claim for Faulkner's consideration as a writer in the mythic mode. In *Light In August,* he achieves one of the finest resolutions of his "dual focus" in the structural complement to the story of Joe Christmas: the story of Lena Grove which contains the "essential peace" surrounding the crucifixion.

Lena's progress from Alabama to Mississippi "is a peaceful corridor paved with unflagging and tranquil faith and peopled with kind and nameless faces and voices" (4). Pregnant, placid, her role is that of the earth mother. "We still find it said," says Cassirer, "that it is not the earth which imitates women in conceiving and giving birth but women who imitate the earth. But for the original mythical intuition there is here no before or after, no first or second, only the complete and indissoluble involvement of the two processes."[15] Lena's relationship to the story of Joe is somewhat artificial at first. It might be looked upon as a product of displacement, providing us with a credible history of that moment when her giving new birth is required as a mythological counterpart to the death of Joe Christmas.

When Joe is finally caught in Mottstown, on the scene are Doc Hines and his wife who have made this their home for the last thirty years. Mrs. Hines recognizes Joe as her grandson. Dressed in purple suitable to the passion, she takes the old madman in tow and follows Joe to Jefferson where that compound of good Samaritan and St. Christopher, Byron Bunch, takes them under his wing and introduces them to Hightower and then into Lena's cabin. Faulkner was willing to dare much of his craft to achieve the necessary coincidences to support the cyclic idea of life which is to soften the passion of the crucifixion. On that Sunday night, Mrs. Hines tells the story of Joe's origins to Hightower, leading to her one impossible request:

> I am not saying he never did what they say he did. Ought not to suffer for it like he made them that loved and lost suffer. But if folks could maybe just let him for one day. Like it hadn't happened yet. (367)

In the sense that Joe is already dead, she is asking for nothing less than a resurrection. On Monday morning Lena's baby is born with Mrs. Hines in attendance and, as the old woman's mind wavers, the birth is equivalent to the resurrection in that time disappears and Joe's life is somehow revived. At first Lena becomes her dead daughter Milly and the child becomes Joe; then " 'She keeps on talking about him like his pa was that . . . the one in jail, that Mr. Christmas' " (387–88), talk Lena fears because it threatens to mix *her* up as well.

Gavin Stevens, who puts the old couple on the train for Mottstown, promising to send the body along after them, attempts to summarize this:

> "Very likely that was the first time she had ever told it. And very likely she learned it herself then for the first time, actually saw it whole and real at the same time with Hightower. So I don't think it is so strange that for the time she got not only the child but his parentage as well mixed up, since in that cabin those thirty years did not exist—the child and its father whom she had never seen, and her grandson whom she had not seen since he was a baby like the other, and whose father likewise to her had never existed, all con-

fused. And that, when hope did begin to move in her, she should have turned at once, with the sublime and boundless faith of her kind in those who are the voluntary slaves and the sworn bondsmen of prayer, to the minister."(422–23)

The minister. The last phase of romance, the literary form of the quest, is, according to Frye, marked by the movement from active to contemplative adventure. "A central image of this phase, a favorite of Yeats, is that of the old man in the tower, the lonely hermit absorbed in occult or magical studies." [16] Hightower, who is introduced in the chronology of the novel after Joe's murder of Joanna Burden, provides this contemplative depth of the passion and its optimistic mythical counterpart, Lena's perpetuation of the cycle of life. While Gavin Stevens has been introduced to the novels for the first time to provide the scientific-empiric rationale just quoted, Faulkner is not yet ready to forego the mythical thinker.

Hightower is the antithesis of Lena Grove, denying the movement of life for a sterile regression. We are told that he suffered a psychic arrest at the age of eight when he discovered his father's patched coat worn during the War and that from that time "That son grew to manhood among phantoms, and side by side with a ghost" (449), the ghost of his grandfather killed by "a fowling piece, in a henhouse" (459). Hightower's only aim in life becomes the desire to go to the scene of that foolish escapade in Jefferson:

> While at the seminary, after he first came there, he often thought how he would tell them, the elders, the high and sanctified men who were the destiny of the church to which he had willingly surrendered. How he would go to them and say, "Listen. God must call me to Jefferson because my life died there, was shot from the saddle of a galloping horse in a Jefferson street one night twenty years before it was ever born." (452)

He had thought that the seminary would afford him a haven, a place where "truth could walk naked and without shame or fear" (453). But his truth is that of an unrecognized myth, the myth of a moment of time in his timeless consciousness. "In the concrete mythical-religious consciousness of time there always lives a specific dynamic of feeling—a varying intensity with which the I devotes itself to the present, past, or future and so places them in a definite relation of affinity to or dependence on one another." [17]

Married to a daughter of one of the ministers in the seminary, Hightower wins his post at Jefferson and on the train going there tries to communicate his truth to her. With his entire psyche funneled into this private myth, his wife turns away toward her own destruction.

Hightower's career in his Jefferson church was as a

> figure antic as a showman, a little wild: a charlatan preaching worse than heresy, in utter disregard of that whose very stage he preempted, offering instead of the crucified shape of pity and love, a swaggering and unchastened bravo killed with a shotgun in a peaceful henhouse, in a temporary hiatus of his own avocation of killing. (462)

Turned out from his church and refusing to leave the town, he suffered a beating at the hands of the Klan, a beating he regarded as purchasing his immunity, the price of his refusal to involve himself with mankind in time. Hightower's ultimate error has been the belief that "It is any man's privilege to destroy himself, so long as he does not injure anyone else, so long as he lives to and of himself" (464). Having destroyed himself and his wife, it is his involvement in the birth of Lena's child that gives him the momentary illusion that he is once again alive in a kind of biological and therefore mythic time:

> He moves like a man with a purpose now, who for twenty-five years has been doing nothing at all between the time to wake and the time to sleep again . . . . [Thinking,] *More of them. Many more. That will be her life, her destiny. The good stock peopling in tranquil obedience to it the good earth; from these hearty loins without hurry or haste descending mother and daughter.* (383–84)

But this is a false sense of rebirth on his part. Having refused the night before to lie about Joe's whereabouts at the time of the murder in one last attempt to save him, and now having assisted at the birth of Lena's child, "There is one thing more reserved for him" (392). Joe Christmas, pursued by Percy Grimm, runs into Hightower's house where the old man now attempts the lie:

> "Men!" he cried. "Listen to me. He was here that night. He was with me the night of the murder. I swear to God—"
>
> "Jesus Christ!" Grimm cried, his young voice clear and outraged like that of a young priest. "Has every preacher and old maid in Jefferson taken their pants down to the yellowbellied son of a bitch?" He flung the old man aside and ran on. (439)

Joe, dying and castrated, the blood rushing "like a released breath," achieves his apotheosis as victim:

> . . . upon that black blast the man seemed to rise soaring into their memories forever and ever. They are not to lose it, in whatever peaceful valleys, beside whatever placid and reassuring streams of old age, in the mirroring faces of whatever children they will contemplate old disasters and newer hopes. It will be there, musing, quiet, steadfast, not fading and not particularly threatful, but of itself alone serene, of itself alone triumphant. (440)

Grimm is the tyrant-leader Frye remarks in the sacrifice of the *pharmakos*:

> In the sinister human world one individual pole is the tyrant-leader, inscrutable, ruthless, melancholy, and with an insatiable will, who commands loyalty only if he is egocentric enough to represent the collective ego of his followers. The other pole is represented by the *pharmakos* or sacrificed victim, who has to be killed to strengthen the others. In the most concentrated form of the demonic parody, the two become the same.[18]

This most concentrated form of the demonic parody, the identification of slayer and slain is offered through Hightower's reflections:

Byron Bunch's; the woman with the child; and that of the man called Christmas. This face alone is not clear. It is confused more than any other, as though in the now peaceful throes of a more recent, a more inextricable, compositeness. Then he can see that it is two faces which seem to strive (but not of themselves striving or desiring it: he knows that, but because of the motion and desire of the wheel itself) in turn to free themselves one from the other, then fade and blend again. But he has seen now, the other face, the one that is not Christmas. 'Why, it's . . .' he thinks. 'I have seen it, recently . . . . Why, it's that . . . boy. With that black pistol, automatic they call them. The one who . . . into the kitchen where . . . killed, who fired the . . .' Then it seems to him that some ultimate dammed flood within him breaks and rushes away. (465–66)

But Hightower is not the only agent of this movement from active to contemplative adventure which marks the last phase of romance:

On a more popular and social level it takes in what might be called cuddle fiction: the romance that is physically associated with comfortable beds or chairs around fireplaces or warm and cosy spots generally. A characteristic feature of this phase is the tale in quotation marks, where we have an opening setting with a small group of congenial people, and then the real story told by one of the members . . . . The effect of such devices is to present the story through a relaxed and contemplative haze as something that entertains us without, so to speak, confronting us, as direct tragedy confronts us.[19]

And this is the way Faulkner ends *Light in August* for us. "There lives in the eastern part of the state a furniture repairer and dealer who recently made a trip into Tennessee to get some old pieces of furniture which he had bought by correspondence" (468). Lying in bed with his wife, he recounts the final comic adventure of Lena, her child, and Byron Bunch "just travelling."

Light in August may be viewed as a romance, a quest on the part of Joe Christmas for identity in a society that denies identity, setting up various schema of division in opposition to this quest. The central myth is that of the scapegoat and its archetypal representative the Christ who, part divine and part human, achieved his identity with humanity only through the sacrifice of his death. It is the most successful artistic embodiment of Faulkner's dual focus, his rational empiric view of life with its tragic implications and his optimistic, mythic faith with its essentially comic implications. Perhaps because of this success he was able, after the "breather" represented by *Pylon*, to concentrate on the largely historical myth presented in *Absalom! Absalom!* without the necessity of insisting on some kind of apocalyptic resolution to the lingering defeat of the South.

Pylon finds Faulkner reverting to the conscious manipulation of ironies found in the earlier novels. The novel appears to be attempting an ironic contrast between "normal" humans and the flyers, those dedicated to a superhuman mode of life. The contrast is further embodied in "news" as opposed to some kind of essential truth which the reporter, as bridge between the two worlds, is trying to grasp and communicate to his editor, Hagood (half-good?); the "news" is constantly presented in the fragmented form of partial headlines while in the truth lies some essential unity which we are trying to sense, but without appreciable help from Faulkner.

This truth fails to find any unification in the mythical imagery scattered throughout the novel, although there is enough of it to awake the reader's expectations for a meaningful pattern. First, the reporter who physically resembles a skeleton in that he is very tall and so skinny as to appear emaciated, is Lazarus to one of the characters and abroad in the world only because he failed to return to the graveyard before it closed:

> He collapsed upon the chair with a loose dry scarecrowlike clatter as though of his own skeleton and the wooden chair's in contact, and leaned forward across the desk, eager, appar-

ently not only on the verge of the grave itself but in actual sight of the other side of Styx. (43) *

Later he is the guide of the covey of flyers in another image of the underworld, passing over Grandlieu Street with its "tinseldung of Momus' Nilebarge clatterfalque" (77),

> the four of them hurrying quietly after the hurrying reporter as though Grandlieu Street and its light and movement were Lethe itself just behind them and they four shades this moment out of the living world and being hurried, grave, quiet and unalarmed, on toward complete oblivion by one not only apparently long enough in residence to have become a citizen of the shadows, but one who from all outward appearances had been born there too. (80)

But then he also becomes a Christ figure of sorts in that the jumper, who opposes his kindness, asks, "What has this guy done to you? give you a dose of faith in mankind?" (155) and more specifically, "Does the race committee think he is Jesus too, the same as the rest of you do?" (188). Jiggs, the mechanic, hearing the reporter's tale of how he and Schumann flew the dangerous plane which is to lead to Schumann's death, begins to exclaim "Sweet Jesus Christ" in the same manner that Max in *Light in August* throws in his exclamations obviously intended to point up Joe's role. Then, after the crash, we have the chapter "Lovesong of J. A. Prufrock" and we learn that the reporter is merely the fool, born on All Fools Day, his major motivation having been some vague quest for a "truth" compounded of desire for Laverne and of knowing of the mystique of flight.

The mechanic, Jiggs, is described as a "manpony," a "centaur," and in other respects like a horse, but the effect is merely grotesque and does not carry with it any of Faulkner's habitual overtones of power and force. Once he is described eating a sandwich, holding it like a crucifix (186), but again

---

* Page references are to the Harrison Smith and Robert Haas, Inc. edition of *Pylon* (New York, 1935).

the image does not go beyond the simplest descriptive level. Laverne, one of Faulkner's embodiments of sexuality and desirability, could easily have become a figure of mythic import in her parachute descent from the sky, but this does not happen. Her son, whose paternity cannot be known certainly, calls forth from the reporter an ironic "Talk about your immaculate conceptions" (48).

Of the two pilots killed, the first, Lt. Frank Burnham, has placed beneath his photograph the legend (i n r i) which Waggoner says "measures the distance between the scene being portrayed and the religious meaning of Lent." [20] Schumann goes to his death in the waters of the lake rather than risk the possibility of his disintegrating plane falling in the stands. This is presented to the reader as a true sacrifice but again it is unrelated to the context of any larger pattern suggested by the Mardi Gras season. There will be no resurrection here; the plane cannot be raised.

The disposition of the boy at the end of the novel does not suggest any values by which we may judge the characters involved or society as a whole. The folklore of speed is totally unrelated to any Christian values that might have been suggested by the use of Mardi Gras in "Franciana" and even the description of the Franciana spring "which emerges out of the Indian summer of fall almost, like a mistimed stage resurrection which takes the curtain even before rigor mortis has made its bow" (171) suggests nothing in terms of the novel's action unless we fasten on the adjective *stage* and use it to create a tenuous rationale for an "unreal city." As *Mosquitoes* represents Faulkner's homage to Huxley, so *Pylon* represents his homage to T. S. Eliot, a dependence that has been examined by Hyatt Waggoner. In relation to a study of Faulkner's use of mythic elements, we need only note the waste land theme which is common enough in his view of modern society. The central symbol of the pylons remains largely undeveloped but may be regarded as ironic, displaced phallic symbols promising death more than life in the wasteland soci-

ety with its reversed values. Waggoner concludes his defense
of the novel with the statement that

> *Pylon* is certainly ambiguous and perhaps ambivalent. . . .
> Nevertheless, *Pylon* is both vividly and solidly created.
> To reject it completely as a work of art, as many have
> done, seems to me to imply that clarity of symbolic implica-
> tion in a work of art is all-important. It is important, and *Py-
> lon* falls short of the achievement of Faulkner's very fine
> works. But since the imaginative richness of it never fails,
> even where judgement falters, it deserves and rewards our
> closest attention.[21]

Even if we agree that "clarity of symbolic implication in a
work of art" is not all-important, Faulkner's failure to achieve
any depth of meaning from certain symbols we have seen to
be habitual with him and which at this point in his career
have received full development would argue that *Pylon* is the
most carelessly written of all his novels. From the standpoint
of my examination of mythic content and mythic thought,
the novel never rises above the first level of myth, the level of
allusion without the integration with theme or plot. Its relationship to the other novels of this period is seen most clearly
in the portrayal of a demonic world, a world which is per-
ceived not through the mythic configuration, but through the
despair of the rational empiric mind witnessing a world in
which the machine has corrupted the natural world and is
making it over in its own image. Again Faulkner's sense of
smell is at the center of the imagery and *Pylon* reeks of grease
as a symbol of this new order.

Absalom, Absalom! which has been treated out of chronological order, would normally appear in this place. It is interesting to note that with *Light in August* and *Absalom, Absalom!* each is preceded by a novel that belongs rather clearly
in the realistic mode, its tendency toward myth halted with
some superficial allusions and a concentration on a demonic
world which stops short of any mythic configuration. This

could be adduced as evidence to support Frye's insights in the "Theory of Myths" where he makes the observation that "Ironic literature begins with realism [which has a tendency to "throw the emphasis on content and representation rather than on the shape of the story"] and tends toward myth, its mythical patterns being as a rule more suggestive of the demonic than of the apocalyptic." [22] Faulkner's work shows this rhythm repeated in the chronological succession of these published works.

After *Absalom! Absalom!* Faulkner put together stories previously published and with a new concluding story "Odor of Verbena" published them as *The Unvanquished*. The resulting novel has been unnecessarily belabored by some critics, among them Irving Howe, who himself is so concerned about "the heroic potential of the subject [the Civil War]" that he will not accept the book for what it is, Faulkner's first full examination of the initiation of a young boy. It will become one of Faulkner's favorite themes, repeated in *Go Down, Moses, Intruder in the Dust,* and *The Reivers.* It is only if we approach *The Unvanquished* with the unwarranted presupposition that the author must write about "the South and the Civil War in accents of tragedy or sustained seriousness" that we will be tempted to ask with Howe "was this the war that roused William Tecumseh Sherman to his burst of eloquence?" [23]

Moving the action back in time to the War itself revives many of the mythic elements of the conflict. The demonizing of the Northerners in the South's process of solidification and alienation is evident in Bayard's reaction to his first sight of a Union soldier: "I remember thinking, 'He looks just like a man'" (28). * And this is carried on in Drusilla's morality when she ("the Greek amphora priestess of a succinct and formal violence") (252) justifies the killing of the two carpetbaggers by Colonel Sartoris: "They were Northerners, for-

* Page references are to Random House edition of *The Unvanquished* (New York, 1938).

121

eigners who had no business here" (257). It is in terms of denying this morality that Bayard must achieve his individuality, his new integration as a personality who can live with himself. In the process of doing this, he must evaluate his father's actions, the "mythic" John Sartoris, and deny them too. The daimon of a myth does not undergo such a rational evaluation; belief is either total and mythic in the sense of pre-rational or it does not exist.

The horse is developed more clearly as a symbol of the force, the essence, of the struggle which itself has the ritualistic importance in that on the proper outcome depends the fate of the nation or community. "I heard the general say myself that if we had enough horses, he wouldn't always care whether there was anybody to ride them or not," remarks a Union sergeant (34). The Colonel's horse, Jupiter, is equated with a thunderbolt in the scene that Will Falls will remember so much later. Jane Ellen Harrison, discussing the idea of *tabu* associated with the thunderbolt says, "it is an attitude towards *mana*; something full of *mana*, instinct," [24] and it is in just these moments that Colonel John appears most god-like —in the moments when he is equated with Jupiter, the horse, in the role of master or manipulator of the mana so necessary to the successful completion of the ritual struggle. Granny's trading in horses and mules may also be construed as this kind of manipulation of mana.

But the clearest example of mythic action is that of the Negroes journeying to the promised land. In the story "Raid," Granny, Bayard, and Ringo set out in the wagon to recover the chest of family silver from the Union forces. At evening they camp, having outdistanced a strange dust cloud that had been following them out of the west. In the middle of the night Bayard wakens:

> All of a sudden all three of us were sitting up in the wagon, listening. They were coming up the road. It sounded like about fifty of them; we could hear the feet hurrying, and a kind of panting murmur. It was not singing exactly; it was

not that loud. It was just a sound, a breathing, a kind of gasping, murmuring chant and the feet whispering in the deep dust . . . .

We couldn't see them and they did not see us; maybe they didn't even look, just walking fast in the dark with that panting, hurrying murmuring, going on . . . . That night we waked up three times and sat up in the wagon in the dark and heard niggers pass in the road. The last time it was after dawn and we had already fed the horses. It was a big crowd of them this time, and they sounded like they were running, like they had to keep ahead of daylight. (94-95)

On the road they find a Negress with a few months old baby who had been unable to keep up with the group. " 'Hit's Jordan we coming to,' she said. 'Jesus see me that far' " (96).

When the wagon reaches Hawkhurst, Cousin Drusilla continues the description of the Negroes' exodus:

"They began to pass in the road yonder while the house was still burning. We couldn't count them; men and women carrying children who couldn't walk and carrying old men and women who should have been at home waiting to die. They were singing, walking along the road singing, not even looking to either side. The dust didn't even settle for two days, because all that night they still passed; we sat up listening to them, and the next morning every few yards along the road would be the old ones who couldn't keep up any more, sitting or lying down and even crawling along, calling to the others to help them; and the others—the young strong ones—not stopping, not even looking at them. I don't think they even heard or saw them. 'Going to Jordan,' they told me. 'Going to cross Jordan.' " (103-4)

The idea that has taken possession of their minds is that General Sherman is to lead them all to Jordan, but at the river the Union forces have thrown out a barrier of cavalry to hold them back and intend to blow up their pontoon bridge as soon as the troops have crossed it.

"They are all right until they get up there and see or smell the water. That's when they go mad. Not fighting; it's like they can't even see the horses shoving them back and the

123

scabbards beating them; it's like they can't see anything but the water and the other bank." (104)

Drusilla's account differs from Bayard's description of the Negroes' actions in that it makes a value judgment: the action is irrational, "mad." This is the opposition of rational, analytical thought to the mythic mode of thought and action evidenced by the Negroes. On the mythic level, the word does not signify, it *is* and is *action* in the sense that its power is itself and not the thing it points to. The Yankees have propagandized, used words with the hope of arousing emotional reactions, but they have not counted on the more primitive intelligence of the Negroes and the completely different mode of thought. It is not a case of evaluating the force behind their actions in terms of negative capability to reason. It is not merely simple-mindedness that governs such action; it is a very positive mode of thought: the mythic mode. To the modern scientific mind, out of touch with the power of this kind of thought, the scene has a quality we might inadequately label "haunting," attempting to bridge the gap between the primitive and civilized. It is perhaps Faulkner's use of the mythic mode of perception on the part of some of his characters and the description of this mode of thought as motivation for other characters that led to Sean O'Faolain's rather ridiculous comment that Faulkner "has written best of all when he has written like a Negro." [25]

The Unvanquished is important in the history of Faulkner's publications in that it represents his first attempt to work out a reconciliation with society on the part of his central character. Heretofore, unless we except *As I Lay Dying*, all his novels have presented a form of alienation from society resulting in defeat or a reaffirmation of the stasis of the waste land. In *The Unvanquished* we have the first true initiation pattern, true in the sense that the mythic rites are meant to assure the integration of the subject into adult society. In this sense, the novel points to Faulkner's work in the next decade.

The use of this initiation pattern signals another kind of progression in his work, a movement away from the central device of a mythic consciousness at the center of his four great novels. I contend that much of the acknowledged power of these earlier works is due to the success with which the author has surmounted the bondage of language to a rational-empiric world view and reoriented it to the communication of a world view that is pre-rational or mythic in its configuration.

I would stress the word *movement* here, for myth in the many senses that we acknowledge it is not a static thing. Cassirer examines the dynamic nature of myth as a symbolic mode evolving new conceptual relationships between subject and object, concepts which move toward those of an empiric reality; its essence is the study of a dynamic spiritual power. Frye's theory of modes, examining the content of literature through its history, results in a cyclical pattern descending from myth, stories about gods, through romance and the mimetic modes to the ironic mode where are found reappearing patterns of myth. While Cassirer is concerned with an epistemological theory and Frye with an historical view of literature, both propose patterns of change that move from a pre-rational or supra-rational mode toward a rational empiric mode, although there is in neither case a complete break with the preceding mythic mode and both posit patterns which allow a modified cyclical return to the original.

In studying Faulkner's novels, the chronological approach seems most necessary for my purposes, for there is this kind of movement exhibited in the total body of work. From the early novels with their solid rational-empiric foundation, their acceptance of a traditional narrative form, and a central ironic tone, we can see a movement to a form which seeks to communicate another reality that tends toward the mythic mode. The next movement is that which is signaled in *The Unvanquished* but which will not become clear until *Go Down, Moses*. In the meantime, in *The Wild Palms* and *The*

Hamlet, there is enough distinction from the previous orientation to myth to warrant the use of Frye's phrase, "the area of romance," used to designate that entire area which lies between myth and naturalism as extremes of literary design and which is characterized by the tendency to displace myth in a human direction.[26]

6. Toward Romance

Faulkner's next novel, The Wild Palms, while not rich in ornamental mythical allusion, again illustrates his attempt to arrive at a total expression through an experimental form, this time the juxtaposition of two supposedly unrelated stories. The general statement might be made that when his characters find themselves in conflict with an idea the resolution is tragic in nature; when they find themselves in conflict with natural forces it is comic. Certainly there seems little justification for the critical evaluation of Faulkner's naturalism which insists upon his presentation of nature as essentially inimical. Nature is the norm by which man tests himself, and his triumph (none of his characters falls to nature's forces) is a measure of the man, not an outcry against an inimical force.

Joseph Moldenhauer's admirable analysis of the novel finds

Harry's tragedy (the thesis of the novel) is caused not by the implacable forces of external nature nor by Charlotte's "powerful sexual need," (as Howe has said) but by his own inner weakness. His struggle throughout the story is internal. "Old Man" serves as the antithesis of the novel; the convict succeeds because his struggle is almost purely external.[1]

This analysis is constructed largely in terms of the Protestant conscience of Harry Wilbourne, and while I will agree with the analysis on this level, I believe that it might gain greater depth if viewed in terms of yet another myth, that of Tristan and Iseult:

> There is no need to have read Béroul's *Tristan* or M. Bédier's, and no need to have heard Wagner's opera, in order to undergo in the case of everyday life the nostalgic dominion of such a myth. It is manifested in the majority of novels and films, in the popularity these enjoy with the masses, the acceptance which they meet with in the hearts of middle-class people . . . . The myth operates wherever passion is dreamed of as an ideal instead of being feared like a malignant fever; wherever its fatal character is welcomed, invoked, or imagined as a magnificent and desirable disaster instead of as simply a disaster. It lives upon the lives of people who think that love is their fate (and as unavoidable as the effect of the love-potion is in romance); that it swoops upon powerless and ravished men and women in order to consume them in a pure flame; or that it is stronger and more real than happiness, society, or morality. It lives upon the very life of the romanticism within us; it is the great mystery of that religion of which the poets of the nineteenth century made themselves the priests and the prophets.[2]

It is a commonplace of Faulkner criticism that he was much indebted to the late nineteenth-century poets, and especially to Swinburne who wrote six of a projected ten cantos of a poem on the Tristan legend.

To consider first the "Wild Palms" section of *The Wild Palms*, Faulkner has chosen to construct it beginning with the highest point of the action, Harry and Charlotte waiting for the final transformation, the death that will give their passion its ultimate transcendental form. It is not until the next chapter of "Wild Palms" that we are presented with the genesis of this passion and its normal chronology. Here we discover Harry on his twenty-seventh birthday, an intern, very poor, and who, because of his economic straits, can rationalize for his virginity:

> *I have repudiated money and hence love. Not abjured it, repudiated. I do not need it; by next year or two years or five years I will know to be true what I now believe to be true: I will not even need to want it.* (34) *

If we were to view the novel as a Dionysiac myth, not even Aeschylus could provide us with a more succinct statement of the hero's *hybris* before the fall.

A fellow intern talks him into attending a party "in one of the narrow, dim, balcony-hung one-way streets between Jackson Square and Royal Street in the Vieux Carre" (36) where he meets Charlotte Rittenmeyer (38) and is invited to have dinner with her and her husband (41). After that dinner, Charlotte's husband leaves them and goes to bed:

> Then she crushed out the cigarette and rose and came to where he stood before the cold hearth and stopped, facing him. "What to do about it, Harry?"
> "I don't know. I never was in love before." (42)

I have included the page numbers to emphasize the nature of the mystery of passion Faulkner is suggesting. There is no lover's potion, but the genesis of their passion is treated in as mysterious and abrupt a fashion as if there were. Charlotte and Harry are like Tristan and Iseult, and Tristan and Iseult, says Rougemont, are

> like all other great lovers; they imagine that they have been ravished 'beyond good and evil' into a kind of transcendental state outside ordinary human experience, into an ineffable absolute irreconcilable with the world, but that they feel to be *more real than the world.* Their oppressive fate, even though they yield to it with wailings, obliterates the antithesis of good and evil, and carries them away be-

---

* Page references are to Random House edition of *The Wild Palms* (New York, 1939).

yond the source of moral values, beyond pleasure and pain,
beyond the realm of distinctions—into a realm where oppo-
sites cancel out.[3]

But Rougemont points out for Tristan and Iseult that they
really do not love one another:

> *What they love is love and being in love.* They behave as if
> aware that whatever obstructs love must ensure and consoli-
> date it in the heart of each and intensify it infinitely in the
> moment they reach the absolute obstacle, which is death.
> Tristan loves the awareness that he is loving far more than
> he loves Iseult the Fair. And Iseult does nothing to hold
> Tristan. All she needs is her passionate dream. Their need
> of one another is in order to be aflame, and they do not
> need one another as they are. What they need is not one
> another's presence, but one another's absence. *Thus the
> partings of the lovers are dictated by their passion itself*, and
> by the love they bestow on their passion rather than on its
> satisfaction or on its living object. That is why Romance
> abounds in obstructions, why when mutually encouraging
> their joint dream in which each remains solitary they show
> such astounding indifference, and why events work up in a
> romantic climax to a fatal apotheosis.[4]

Harry and Charlotte, as lovers, create most of their obstacles, although she is more successful in the pursuit of passion than he is. There is, of course, the immediate obstacle of
her husband. He is Catholic, Charlotte explains, and would
fight a divorce, although she has told him everything there is
to tell. The children do not represent an obstacle to her, for
she has accepted them as part of the suffering that passion
must represent:

> "I wasn't thinking of them. I mean, I have already thought
> of them. So now I dont need to think of them any more
> because I know the answer and I dont think I can change
> me because the second time I ever saw you I learned what I
> had read in books but I never had actually believed: that love
> and suffering are the same thing and that the value of love
> is the sum of what you have to pay for it and any time you
> get it cheap you have cheated yourself. So I don't need to

think about the children. I settled that a long time ago."
(48)

Charlotte delivers this explanation in a rented hotel room where they have met to consummate their passion, but Harry's initiation into the mysteries of love is delayed by Charlotte's inability to make love under these conditions. The obstacle is accepted passively by Harry.

The next obstacle that prevents their passion is money. This is removed when Harry finds the billfold in the trash basket containing almost thirteen hundred dollars. They entrain for Chicago, Charlotte's husband riding a short way with them to say good-bye. When he gets off, Charlotte insists that Harry engage an empty drawing room and he is finally initiated into the "mystery" of sex. Later in Chicago, just before they are to leave for Utah, Harry tries to explain to their newspaperman friend McCord the "eclipse" that ensued upon his late initiation:

> "I was outside of time . . . . It was like the instant of virginity, it was the instant of virginity: that condition, fact, that does not actually exist except during the instant you know you are losing it; it lasted as long as it did because I was too old, I waited too long; twenty-seven is too long to wait to get out of your system what you should have rid yourself of at fourteen or fifteen or maybe even younger."
> (137)

This intellectualizing of his position is part of the psychological pattern of obstructions Harry throws up between himself and the passion, obstructions that Moldenhauer has analyzed in terms of a Puritan conscience. Throughout "Wild Palms" the tale of passionate love is developed in terms of those characteristics Rougemont has remarked in the tale of Tristan and Iseult: obstacles which obstruct the free course of passion and the essential isolation of the lovers.

On the train out of New Orleans, Harry had reflected: *"She doesn't love me now . . . . She doesn't love anything now"* (59). On the second morning in Chicago when Charlotte has returned to tell him she has found a studio apartment where she can pursue her work as sculptor, "he thought again, *There's a part of her that doesn't love anybody, anything*" (82). Harry reveals his approach to the relationship to be that of the romancer: "the romance of illicit love . . . the passionate idea of two damned and doomed and isolated forever against the world and God and the irrevocable" (82). Charlotte, whom Harry acknowledges to be "a better man than I am," insists more strongly on the value of passion:

> "Listen: it's got to be all honeymoon, always. Forever and ever, until one of us dies. It cant be anything else. Either heaven, or hell: no comfortable safe peaceful purgatory between for you and me to wait in until good behavior or forbearance or shame or repentance overtakes us . . . . They say love dies between two people. That's wrong. It doesn't die; you're the one that dies." (83)

The obstacle of money is still with them and Charlotte begins to make figures for department stores. "She worked with tense and concentrated fury. She would be at the bench when he went to sleep, he would wake at two or three oclock and find the fierce light above it still burning." (90) When Harry loses his job and their money runs out, they leave for the Wisconsin cottage loaned to them by McCord. Here, with fifty dollars worth of food and absolute solitude, a world in which Charlotte calls him Adam, the conditions for fulfillment would seem to be assured. But again Harry is unable to relax. "*I am bored. I am bored to extinction. There is nothing here that I am needed for. Not even by her*" (112). Losing time, he devises a calendar "by the dates of and intervals between Charlotte's menstrual periods." He discovers that it is later than he thought; he has been misled by Indian summer, "the old weary Lilith of the year." His solution is to wire McCord to come and take Charlotte back while he will remain, the lover arranging the separation that will reinstate the love of love. But Charlotte is the stronger and insists they return to Chicago together.

Chicago the second time around further heightens the paradox of this passion. Charlotte works nights as a department store window dresser and Harry spends the days writing stories for the confession magazines. "Thus he was awake mostly while she slept, and vice versa" (122). He looks upon them as if five years married, and as with the married Tristan, it is a period of celibacy. When Charlotte is offered a permanent job, Harry makes the decision to go to Utah as a mine doctor. Before they again board the train, Harry delivers his lecture to McCord in which he explains that he has come out of his eclipse, that the period of extended initiation is over. During this time the mystic obedience to passion has failed, but now Harry's move is an *avowed* attempt to recapture the "real" world of their passion. At the same time he delivers himself of a denunciation of "They"—society. Moldenhauer points out that the qualities he denounces in society are his own and that "selfishness and self-deception underlie all Wilbourne's declarations." [5]

The Utah episode does not bring fulfillment either. Again there is a period of celibacy to keep the passion an object in itself: Charlotte refuses to make love when they have to share the same sleeping quarters with the mine manager and his wife. When they have left, there is again a period of passionate love, but through a contraceptive accident, Charlotte becomes pregnant and insists that Harry perform the abortion. The various obstacles the lovers have placed between themselves are analogous to the knight's behavior when all external obstacles have been overcome: Tristan's drawn sword lying between him and the sleeping Iseult and now the drawn scalpel.

With Charlotte dying from the infection brought on by the botched abortion, they go to the rented beach house on the gulf and await her death. It is analogous to the moment of the Tristan myth analyzed by Rougemont:

Now it turns out that the ultimate obstacle is death, and at the close of the tale death is revealed as having been the real end, what passion has yearned for from the beginning, the avenging of a fate that, having been suffered, is now at last redeemed.[6]

But death is not the end for Harry Wilbourne. Sentenced to fifty years at hard labor, he refuses the cyanide capsule offered by Charlotte's husband:

> *So it is the old meat after all, no matter how old. Because if memory exists outside of the flesh it wont be memory because it wont know what it remembers so when she became not then half of memory became not and if I become not then all of remembering will cease to be. —Yes, he thought, between grief and nothing I will take grief.* (324)

Faulkner has gone the romancer one better in insisting on the memory of passion after the death of Charlotte, but it emphasizes the true nature of the passion that has been his subject. "Wild Palms" is the presentation of a single action in the strictest Aristotelian sense, the movement of the psyche toward a transformation under passion. The denouement, however, is not like that found by Fergusson in Wagner's romance:

> It is evident that this passion of purgation is quite unlike the luxury of merely yielding to feeling, the gloomy satisfaction which does not look beyond the dissolution of the moral being; and the questions to ask about romantic art are whether dissolution or a new equilibrium is envisaged; and in the latter case, what the "new equilibrium" seems to be.[7]

"Wild Palms" *does* end on the note of merely yielding to feeling. The tragic rhythm does not extend itself to society either as dissolution or a new equilibrium. There is only Harry Wilbourne's "final affirmation of his wish to enjoy the full pain of punishment." [8]

Rougemont defends his designation of the Tristan legend as myth through its expression of the fact that passion is linked with death:

. . . a myth arises whenever it becomes dangerous or impossible to speak plainly about certain social or religious matters, or affective relations, and yet there is a desire to preserve these or else it is impossible to destroy them. There is, for example, no need of myths nowadays in order to set forth scientific truths, which we deal with from an entirely 'lay' standpoint and which therefore have everything to gain from individual criticism. *But a myth is needed to express the dark and unmentionable fact that passion is linked with death,* and involves the destruction of any one yielding himself up to it with all his strength.[9]

Whether we regard it as true myth or as, in Frye's modes, a step removed from myth, it provides us with more evidence of Faulkner's tendency toward mythic forms as analogues for his works.

There is yet, however, the companion piece "Old Man" to be considered. Faulkner has designated the story as secondary to "Wild Palms":

The story I was trying to tell was the story of Charlotte and Harry Wilbourne. I decided that it needed a contrapuntal quality like music. And so I wrote the other story simply to underline the story of Charlotte and Harry.[10]

What is there missing in "Wild Palms" that necessitated this counterpoint? Viewed as romance, it is the quality of adventure. Its remarkable singleness of action, its purity in presentation of the psyche's pursuit of passion leaves no room for the adventures of the hero of romance. "Old Man" is almost as pure in its presentation of this complementary theme. It is also the positive view of man's position which I have been insisting upon as an inescapable part of Faulkner's total vision.

The comedy of "Old Man" is a necessary part of *The Wild Palms* as the Lena Grove episodes are a necessary part of *Light in August*. Both provide "the basic paradox of myth: the paradox of the dual focus." They do not deny the agony of the suffering contained in their companion stories, but "they reveal within, behind, and around it essential peace." [11]

"The standard path of the mythological adventure of the hero," says Campbell,

> is a magnification of the formula represented in the rites of passage: *separation—initiation—return:* which might be named the nuclear unit of the monomyth.
>
> A *hero ventures forth from the world of common day into a region of supernatural wonder: fabulous forces are there encountered and a decisive victory is won: the hero comes back from this mysterious adventure with the power to bestow boons on his fellow man.*
>
> This circular adventure of the hero appears in a negative form in stories of the deluge type, where it is not the hero who goes to the power, but the power that rises against the hero, and again subsides . . . . The deluge hero is a symbol of the germinal vitality of man surviving even the worst tides of catastrophe and sin.[12]

Faulkner's nameless hero of "Old Man" enacts this cycle with a touch of irony that has been noted by criticism. The society he leaves is the self-contained, "safe" society of the prison farm, "safe" in that here the convict is insulated against the many human problems that would face him in a normal society. The deluge rises and he and his fellow convicts are herded out to meet it. He is given his instructions to rescue a woman and a man and sets out with his ineffectual companion to perform this mission. The water-monster upsets the boat, however, and he loses his companion. Righting the boat and getting into it again, he is carried by the current back to the scene of this first encounter and is again dealt a blow. Looking up into the tree, he finds the "maiden" he was to rescue:

> . . . and who to say what Helen, what living Garbo, he had not dreamed of rescuing from what craggy pinnacle or dragoned keep when he and his companion embarked in the skiff. He watched her, he made no further effort to help her beyond holding the skiff savagely steady while she lowered herself from the limb—the entire body, the deformed swell of belly bulging the calico, suspended by its arms, thinking, *And this is what I get. This, out of all the female meat that*

walks, is what I have to be caught in a runaway boat with.
(149–51)

Because of his charge to return with the woman as well
as the boat, the convict endures as much foolishness as the
characters of *As I Lay Dying* who are bound to Addy's request. He is refused aid by the outlaws on the houseboat and
is shot at by the "khaki figures"; he is battered by wave after
wave of flood water and cannot rid himself of the woman who
is about to give birth. Grounded on an old Indian mound, he
manages to throw the woman to land just as the baby comes.
At this point Faulkner interpolates the scene of "Wild
Palms" in which the abortion fails and comes back to "Old
Man" on the note of ironic contrast with the convict presiding at birth with an old tin can to sever the umbilical cord, an
operation which has no ill after effects. The Indian mound
teeming with snakes is reminiscent of the omphalos circled by
the snake daimon, a symbol of fertility. From this point, after
having lost his "lance," the oar, and having fashioned a grotesque substitute, the convict and his charges set out again
and are picked up by a river boat heading south. Set ashore
rather arbitrarily, the convict comes among the Cajuns and
performs the necessary task of the hero, battling monsters: in
this case wrestling alligators and killing them with his knife.
Threatened once again by the water, he takes the boat and his
charges and eventually makes his way back to his society
where, having been given up for dead, he is "reborn" into his
prison society with an added ten years sentence (new life) for
his "attempted escape." This return, coughed up by the
"monster" which has supposedly engulfed him, satisfies one
of the significant adventures of the hero.

"When the hero-quest has been accomplished," says
Campbell, "through penetration to the source, or through the
grace of some male or female, human or animal, personification, the adventurer still must return with his life-transmuting
trophy." [13] The trophy in this case, as is most usual with

Faulkner, is the child, the new life. The convict's "message,"
however, is quite ironic. Summing up his adventures for the
rest of the convicts, the plump convict who started the adventure with him can only bemoan the fact that it means ten
more years without a woman. " 'Women—!' the tall convict
said." It is the last word of the novel. But the irony of this
pronouncement is mitigated, it must be remembered, by the
tale of Charlotte in "Wild Palms," another reason the two
stories should not be separated.

Taken together as they were intended to be, the two stories in counterpoint constitute a modern romance sharply dividing the tragedy of a passion leading to ultimate death and
the adventures of a hero who battles giant forces and returns
with the promise of new life. Each represents a part of Faulkner's polar vision. Juxtaposed, they present a complete vision;
separated, they are merely good stories. *The Wild Palms*
again demonstrates Faulkner's tendency to follow the form of
myth.

> Where the moralist would be filled with indignation and
> the tragic poet with pity and terror, mythology breaks the
> whole of life into a vast, horrendous Divine Comedy. Its
> Olympian laugh is not escapist in the least, but hard, with
> the hardness of life itself—which, we may take it, is the
> hardness of God, the Creator. Mythology, in this respect,
> makes the tragic attitude seem somewhat hysterical, and the
> merely moral judgement shortsighted. Yet the hardness is
> balanced by an assurance that all that we see is but the re-
> flex of a power that endures, untouched by the pain.
> Thus the tales are both pitiless and terrorless—suffused with
> the joy of a transcendent anonymity regarding itself in all of
> the self-centered, battling egos that are born and die in
> time.[14]

The allusive and analogous use of the myths of chivalric
Romance continues in the later novels. It is especially impor-
tant in the creation of the character of Gavin Stevens, who, as
Mrs. Vickery and Cleanth Brooks point out, bears many of

the marks of the chivalric, courtly lover. Northrop Frye's modes distinguish between myth and romance "by the hero's power of action: in the myth proper he is divine, in the romance proper he is human." However, he adds, "This distinction is much sharper theologically than it is poetically, and myth and romance both belong in the general category of mythopoeic literature." [15]

Before proceeding to *The Hamlet*, I should like to step outside of the novels for a moment to make use of William Bysshe Stein's analysis of "Faulkner's Devil," a consideration of the short story "Barn Burning." Here, Stein says, Faulkner's

> rehabilitation of the Adversary, while controlled by traditional iconography, also recognizes the inevitable manifestation of new guises of evil. But whatever the forms of these vile impostures, he carefully integrates them into the main pattern of action—Abner's compulsive infatuation with fire . . . . The Protagonist's enmity toward light and order (anchored ironically in the Hebrew derivation of his name Abner, meaning literally, "Father [God] is light") is figured in his obtrusive and sinister attire . . . . And in line with the old superstition about the Devil's illusory materiality, his body has "more than ever that impervious quality of something cut ruthlessly from tin, depthless, as though, sidewise to the sun, it would cast no shadow."

Stein also cites the " 'hand like a curled claw' " and Abner's limp as characteristics of the "bestial, deformed *diabolus* of the Middle Ages" and the manure stains on de Spain's carpet as "the symbolic stamp of the fires of hell," his tramping through the fresh horse manure betraying "an affinity with the fecal tastes of the Devil (so Luther eloquently attests)."[16]

Much of this imagery is carried on in the first part of *The Hamlet* which recounts the entrance of Ab Snopes and his family into Frenchman's Bend. The dominant image is fire. "You might say that fire seems to follow him around, like dogs follows some people" (13).* The exclamation "Hell fire!" recurs throughout the book, but in the first chapter is reserved for Jody Varner as he is informed of the history of Ab Snopes and is met by Flem's intent to become a clerk in the store. He manages to use it no less than fifteen times (12–24).

Book 2 of *The Hamlet*, "Eula," is Faulkner's creation of the earth goddess, relying heavily on mythical allusion, and, in terms of the plot, presenting the analogy to the Persephone myth again. Eula, who "simply did not move at all of her own volition" (95), is until the age of six carried about by the Negro manservant, "staggering slightly beneath his long, dangling, already indisputably female burden like a bizarre and chaperoned Sabine rape" (96). When she is eight, Jody decides she must attend school, and to get her there, the eventual arangement is for him to carry her behind him on horseback.

> On the first morning Varner had put the horse into a fast trot, to get it over with quick, but almost at once he began to feel the entire body behind him, which even motionless in a chair seemed to postulate an invincible abhorrence of straight lines, jigging its component boneless curves against his back. He had a vision of himself transporting not only across the village's horizon but across the embracing proscenium of the entire inhabited world like the sun itself, a kaleidoscopic convolution of mammalian ellipses. (100)

Jody thus becomes like Phaethon, and like Phaethon is unable to control the forces he has taken under his charge. In an attempt to control Eula's sexuality he insists that she be encased in corsets. "He would grasp her each time he saw her outside the house, in public or alone, and see for himself if she had them on" (131). But of course the energy exuded by Eula's sexuality is too great and Eula eventually does become pregnant. The only injury to Jody, however, is to his name, which he hysterically wishes to defend.

* Page references are to the Modern Library edition of *The Hamlet* (New York, 1956)

When Eula, whose "entire appearance suggested some symbology out of the old Dionysic times—honey in sunlight and bursting grapes, the writhen bleeding of the crushed fecundated vine beneath the hard rapacious trampling goat-hoof" (95), enters the school, her sexuality is described in terms of the effect it has upon the young teacher Labove and the male students who range up to the age of twenty-one. Having taught in the village school for three years while working his way through college, Labove at last has his degree and is admitted to the bar. But

> he must return, drawn back into the radius and impact of an eleven-year-old girl who, even while sitting with veiled eyes against the sun like a cat on the schoolhouse steps at recess and eating a cold potato, postulated that ungirdled quality of the very goddesses in his Homer and Thucydides. (113–14)

He must return to where he had first seen the girl as

> a face eight years old and a body of fourteen with the female shape of twenty, which on the instant of crossing the threshold brought into the bleak, ill-lighted, poorly-heated room dedicated to the harsh functioning of Protestant primary education a moist blast of spring's liquorish corruption, a pagan triumphal prostration before the supreme primal uterus. (114)

> By merely walking down the aisle between them she would transform the very wooden desks and benches themselves into a grove of Venus. (115)

Labove teaches the village school for another three years:

> By then he was the monk indeed, the bleak schoolhouse, the little barren village, was his mountain, his Gethsemane and, he knew it, his Golgotha too. He was the virile anchorite of old time. (118)

It is in his imagination that Faulkner places the mythic analogy for Eula's doom:

> He could almost see the husband which she would someday have. He would be a dwarf, a gnome, without glands or de-

sire, who would be no more a physical factor in her life than the owner's name on the fly-leaf of a book. There it was again, out of the books again, the dead defacement of type which had already betrayed him: the crippled Vulcan to that Venus, who would not possess her but merely own her. (119)

It is the impotent Flem Snopes who is to play the role of Vulcan, the fire-scarred god.

T. Y. Greet notes that under Eula's influence Labove's "transformation into a satyr begins: his legs are described as 'haired-over like those of a faun.' "[17] On the afternoon Eula, now fourteen, is waiting for Jody, "the jealous seething eunuch priest," to fetch her from school, Labove makes his move; Eula is able to defend herself. Labove remains in the school house waiting for the avenging Jody who does not come. As he waits he imagines Eula coming to school again tomorrow morning,

> tranquil, untroubled, not even remembering, carrying the cold potato which at recess she would sit on the sunny steps and eat like one of the unchaste and perhaps even anonymously pregnant immortals eating bread of paradise on a sunwise slope of Olympus. (124)

Finally he goes to the store * where he discovers that "She never told him at all. She didn't even forget to. She doesn't know anything happened that was worth mentioning" (127). He asks Jody for a nail which he uses to fasten the key of the school house to the door and disappears.

From that point Eula is described in terms of her courtship, first by the local boys who on Sunday surrounded this "centrice"—

> the body of which there was simply too much dressed in the clothing of childhood, like a slumberer washed out of Para-

* Cleanth Brooks misreads this passage, having Jody come to the schoolhouse rather than Labove going to the store to force the issue. Since Eula has said nothing, there would be no reason for Jody to come to the schoolhouse. See *William Faulkner, the Yoknapatawpha Country* (New Haven, 1963), pp. 176–77.

dise by a night flood and discovered by chance passers and covered hurriedly with the first garment to hand, still sleeping. (132)

When Hoake McCarron presumes to court her,

the youths of last summer's trace-galled mules rose in embattled concert to defend that in which apparently they and the brother both had no belief, even though they themselves had failed signally to disprove it, as knights before them have probably done. (137)

Finally, pregnant, Eula is delivered up to Flem Snopes to wife. Established as a goddess of fertility, this has the symbolic effect of delivering up the earth to the impotent devil. "This," says Greet, "is the crux of the novel, that the favor of the gods—Love, Fertility—has been sacrificed to rational opportunism." [18] Ratliff, who was in Jefferson at the time of the marriage, reflects on the tragedy of this waste, and his musings carry over into the fantasy in which he sees Flem descending into hell and displacing the Prince of Darkness. Greet remarks that Flem's absence during Book 3 is the absence of the Fisher King and that in this absence life attempts to renew itself. [19] Although Flem is impotent like the Fisher King, it seems more accurate to note Faulkner's juxtaposition of the marriage to Eula and the fantasy in which Flem takes over hell, a combination that points to Flem as Hades and to Eula as Persephone. This mythic factor is reflected in the approaching winter. The marriage evidently took place in July, and Book 3 "The Long Summer," makes much of the weather:

That was the fall before the winter from which the people as they became older were to establish time and date events. The summer's rainless heat—the blazing days beneath which even the oak leaves turned brown and died. (263)

There was snow on Thanksgiving and though it did not remain two days, it was followed early in December by an iron cold which locked the earth in frozen rigidity, so that after a week or so actual dust blew from it. (266)

The freeze could not last forever. On the ninth of March it even snowed again and this snow even went away without turning to ice. (268)

It is at this precise time that Eula returns with her child (268):

Then even that winter was over at last. It ended as it had begun, in rain, not cold rain but loud fierce gusts of warm water washing out of the earth the iron enduring frost, the belated spring hard on its bright heels and all coming at once, pell-mell and disordered, fruit and bloom and leaf, pied meadow and blossoming wood and the long fields shearing dark out of winter's slumber, to the shearing plow. (268–69) *

This much of the pattern is clear. The critical difficulty justifying *The Hamlet* as a unified novel and not merely a collection of stories has come with Book 3. Books 1, 2 and 4 present a coherent and unified story of Flem Snope's rise to local economic power, power over even the life forces of the earth, and then his power over reason simply by allowing the passion of greed in men to manifest itself as in the tale of the spotted horses and the salting of the Old Frenchman Place. The Flem-Satan-Hades and Eula-Persephone analogies support the theme of these three books, but if we seek here to find a rationale for the third book it must be in terms of the suffering and chaos which ensue with the disappearance of Persephone. This is difficult to substantiate largely because of the Ike Snopes-cow episode which expressly begins in April. If the time element were different, there would not be much difficulty in demonstrating that the "stock diddling" and murder of Book 3 were intended to demonstrate just that kind of chaos; however, since Ike's April "love" makes this tenuous, it will not do to push the analogy too far.

Olga Vickery, who always pursues a sane course, finds

---

* Greet, who would elevate the Ike Snopes-cow affair into a great redemptive symbol, says "Rain is described but once in *The Hamlet*; it falls on Ike and his beloved" (342). This is obviously wrong.

"the meaning of the book is established not by the plot but in and through the successive tales of barter and stories of love," [20] a course of analysis followed by Cleanth Brooks as well. Greet's analysis makes much of the quality of medieval romance found in the episode of Ike Snopes and the cow. He points out that Ike saves the cow from the flames of a brush fire only after withstanding the onslaughts of the fear-crazed horse. He might have gone further to point up the parallel to the Siegfried myth with the circle of fire surrounding the maiden. Faulkner even gives the horse a mythic dimension in describing "the fierce dragon-reek of its passage, blasting at Ike's hair and garments." The tale is obviously constructed as a parody of the knight's adventures in saving his beloved. The quality of parody is not found by Greet as he pursues his analysis:

> On his way home Ike loses a coin which Houston has given him, but he refuses to search for it, this un-Snopeslike rejection marking him as a courtly lover who accepts no material compensation. Immediately afterward, however, he returns and leads the cow from her stall. He has braved the dragon and in the idyll which follows he rejoices in his reward.
> Not only do these events suggest the medieval romance but so does the tone in which they are treated. Eula was often described in bovine terms, but the cow is Astarte . . . and Ike, weaving for her clumsy garlands, is devout priest and swain together . . . . The style elevates the lovers again into symbols, encouraging the reader to seek in myth and legend for its rationale." [21]

The point of all this is, for Greet, to elevate this love, by opposing it to the Eula-Flem marriage, to the central position of a redemptive symbol within the novel. Mrs. Vickery is much closer to the truth in acknowledging the excesses of the rhetoric:

> The relationship between legend and reality, each providing an implicit satire of the other, becomes apparent. From the point of view of the legend and tradition, whether economic or romantic, Flem and Ike Snopes represent a complete

degeneration. But confronted with the reality of these two characters, it is the purple rhetoric of the romantic tradition and the heroic trappings of conquest that are suddenly exposed as false or inflated.[22]

Cleanth Brooks is perhaps justified in taking Greet to task for some of his excesses, but his antidote, "common sense," precludes finding almost any significance in what I find to be Faulkner's rather consistent reliance upon myths and the form of myth to inform his work. "Yoknapatawpha County," says Brooks,

> is thought of [by Greet] as a kind of waste land, lying under a curse and waiting for the rain which will restore its fertility. But the country that we are asked to view in Faulkner's novel is not at all the haunted land of the Grail legend. It may be that the fall of rain is described only once in the novel, but water is coming from somewhere: Frenchman's Bend is no desert. There is plenty of reference to rivers and creeks.[23]

Surely this is to go to the other extreme. While Greet *is* wrong about the rainfalls, and while his preoccupation with Faulkner's indebtedness to Eliot misleads him into the waste land, and although I prefer to disagree with the point of his analysis, that is not to say that his suggestions for searching out overtones of Romance and myth should be rejected for a literal reading, for the overtones *are* there; and I believe my analysis of myth in Faulkner's works has already justified the fact that attention must be paid.

Other points of Faulkner's parody might be cited: there is the clarification of the name of Lump Snopes, which we learn is indeed Launcelot. Perhaps even the name Mrs. Littlejohn is to stir up memories of Sherwood Forest; and traveling even farther afield, could Faulkner be playing with the name Io, "the wanderer," pursued by the gadfly of Hera when we find I. O. Snopes run out of town suddenly by what is obviously a victim of his polygamous mating? There is also the solution to Ike's affair: the magical potion suggested by Reverend Whitfield which demands the sacrifice of the cow for a true witch's brew. And finally, remembering the derogatory view of Tennyson expressed by Hightower in *Light in August*, one wonders how much of the *Idylls of the King* was unconsciously absorbed and how much consciously rejected by Faulkner in his own reading of the poet. Perhaps the hollow oak in which Mink Snopes stuffs the body of Houston is even an echo of the hollow oak in which Merlin is encased in "Merlin and Vivien."

The other half of Book 3 is given over to the love story of Houston and his murder by Mink Snopes, with Mink waiting for the help from Flem which is not to come. Both of these loves in Book 3 share an element of romance. The love of Houston for Lucy Pate has many of the qualities of the courtly romance to be found in the love of Wilbourne and Charlotte in *The Wild Palms*. It is mysterious to Houston in its genesis and he attempts, without success, to set up obstacles before this force. "It was a feud, a gage, wordless, uncapitulating, between that unflagging will not for love or passion but for the married state, and that furious and as unbending one for solitariness and freedom" (211). At sixteen he leaves home and is gone for twelve years, seven of them spent with a common law wife taken from a Galveston brothel. At the end of that time, he returns and in the following January they are married. But his capitulation is not complete. The courtly lover pledges his entire self in accepting his lady's gage; Houston fails in this by buying the stallion.

> He bought the stallion too then as if for a wedding present to her, though he never said so. Or if that blood and bone and muscles represented that polygamous and bitless masculinity which he had relinquished, he never said that. And if there were any among his neighbors and acquaintances— Will Varner or Ratliff perhaps—who discerned that this was the actual transference, the deliberate filling of the vacancy of his abdication, they did not say it either. (218)

The horse kills Lucy and Houston kills the horse. He banishes all female life but the cow from his farm and two years later is killed by Mink in the dispute over the pound fee.

The murder by Mink finds its larger justification in the scope of the full trilogy, for it is in the last volume that Mink becomes the agent of vengeance and retribution upon Flem. However, within the context of *The Hamlet,* these three stories of Ike, Houston, and Mink that make up Book 3 still offer a difficulty to those attempting to defend the structural integrity of the novel. If it is not merely a structural flaw, criticism, I believe, has not yet supplied the proper rationale.

The episodes of the spotted ponies and the sale of the Old Frenchman place take up the whole of Book 4. As I have indicated, these episodes fit more easily into the overall pattern suggested by the Flem Snopes-Satan analogy of Books 1 and 2. Having risen to the position of the Prince of Darkness in Ratliff's imagination, Flem need only feed upon the desires of those around him. In the spotted ponies episode I find no need to search in Freudian pastures to account for the symbolism of the horses. The position taken by Phyllis Hershleifer, that horses are characteristically used by Faulkner as objects of abnormal sexual experience,[24] leads to some very intricate constructions based on the novels but nonetheless somewhat removed. It is perhaps paradoxical that I should suggest the concept of *mana* as a simpler approach. Indeed, this approach will not rule out the relation to a sexual force when it is apparent, for *mana* is a concept whose "significance lies . . . in its characteristic 'fluidity,' in its merging of properties which to our way of thinking are clearly distinguished."[25] The Freudians must remember that they too are appealing to a meaning arrived at in a manner other than "our way of thinking," i.e., the rational-empiric mode. However, the spotted ponies become symbols of something larger than abnormal sexual forces. We can easily accept the literal reading that sees the horses as economic factors and, as such, desirable; but there is the reasonable view offered by Ratliff that these particular animals are not of this breed. Nonetheless, an irrational desire seizes the men viewing these animals and their wild force, and I believe this might be explained as a mythic mode of thought which sees itself in control of and manipulating this force to its own end. The stallion of Houston might also be viewed in this manner, but in this case, the force is definitely one with sexual overtones. Yet Faulkner insists that it is not merely sex, and certainly not abnormal sex, but extends it to include a mystique of masculine freedom, of the retention of an individual personality in the face of a relationship that ideally precludes this. The presence of this force seems necessary and desirable to Houston until it results in the death of his wife.

The Hamlet almost gains integrity as a novel through the mythic analogues which suggest the course of Flem Snopes' rise in Frenchman's Bend. It is not so successful as *The Unvanquished* in this respect, but it is certainly richer. Faulkner's next work, *Go Down, Moses*, again presents the challenge of material reworked and offered in a new and larger form.

7. The Ethical Period

With *Go Down, Moses* we come to another significant demarcation in a chronological view of Faulkner's work. In the earliest novels we found him striking the sophomore's sophisticated pose as critic of society, but there was no evidence that he had any valid set of values to offer as a replacement for those he found wanting. There is no indication in those earliest novels that the author would create some of the greatest works of American fiction. Then with *The Sound and the Fury* Faulkner dropped this superficial attitude and concentrated on the direct presentation of characters.

In the four major novels of this middle period we find a balance struck between the sufferings of the individual or group of individuals and an optimistic counterweight stated indirectly through a referent of mythical nature or more directly through a form analogous to myth. With *The Unvanquished*, Faulkner for the first time dealt with a character of intelligence and reason who faced the evil about him and through an intelligent effort worked out a compromise. It is this effort of will directed by intelligence at effecting a socially acceptable compromise with "the center of evil" that marks his work published between *The Hamlet* and *A Fable*.

The pivotal nature of the story of Isaac McCaslin found in the three stories "The Old People," "The Bear," and "Delta Autumn," has been discerned by R. W. B. Lewis, who, however, restricts his analysis to "The Bear" and does not take note of *The Unvanquished:*

> *The Bear* is a pivotal work. Change is of its essence. Our notion about it is reinforced when we encounter the same reanimated human will at work and a still larger conviction of human freedom in the novel which followed it, *Intruder in the Dust.* In both stories, but much more spectacularly and indeed much more visibly in *The Bear*, what is positive in human nature and in the moral structure of the world envelops and surrounds what is evil; which is to say, more significantly, that the corrupting and the destructive and the desperate in human experience become known to us in their opposition and even their subordination to the creative and the soul-preserving.[1]

With *The Unvanquished* and then later with *Go Down, Moses* there is a shifting accent in Faulkner's work from the artist's representation of a more purely mythic *existence* to a search for *meaning* consciously based on experience, a shifting accent that is equivalent to the development of the mythic consciousness into the more specifically religious consciousness. In the world of pure myth, says Cassirer,

> the mythical image is by no means taken as an image, as spiritual expression. Rather, it is so deeply embedded in man's intuition of the world of things, of "objective" reality and the objective process, as to appear an integral part of it. Here again there is originally no division between the real and the ideal, between the sphere of "existence" and that of "meaning," but there is rather a continuous flux between the two spheres, both in man's thought and belief and in his action.[2]

In the great novels of the middle period, Faulkner's esthetic maintains this constant flux between the spheres of meaning and existence so that the "meaning" of the novel is directly apparent through the "existence" of his characters. In the confused realities of Benjy or Quentin Compson, the tortured quest of Joe Christmas, or the grandiose aspirations of Thomas Sutpen there is the quality of directness. Nothing is thought, represented, "supposed" that is not at the same time real and effective. It is this very quality of attempted directness that sets these great novels apart from the historical esthetic of the novel which has always accepted the form as mere representation until the experiments of Joyce denied this limitation and sought, through the stream of consciousness, to destroy the "merely 'aesthetic' " barriers which an art form had developed to mediate between experience and meaning. The very forms of these novels, forms which have aroused so much critical attention, serve the end of destroying the conditioned expectations of readers and eliminating to some extent the acknowledged artificiality of an art form and bringing it closer to the realm of myth.

This study nowhere argues that Faulkner has created myth. Indeed, it argues against the loose use of the word which allows some critics to imply this. It accepts the novel as an art form developed within the rational-empiric mode but attempts to demonstrate that within this form he has succeeded in embodying a world view that bears a significant relation to the world of myth, and that he has endowed many of his most complex characters with configurations of reality that can best be explained through the epistemology of myth.

As ontogeny recapitulates phylogeny, so Faulkner's intellectual history repeats the tendency of the mythic mode of thought to move toward a specifically religious consciousness.

Although the contents of myth and religion are inextricably interwoven, their form is not the same. And the particularity of the religious form is disclosed in the changed attitude which consciousness here assumes toward the mythical image world. It cannot do without this world, it cannot immediately reject it; but seen through the medium of the religious attitude this world gradually takes on new meaning. The new ideality, the new spiritual dimension that is opened up through religion not only lends myth a new signification but actually introduces the opposition between "meaning" and "existence" into the realm of myth. Religion takes the decisive step that is essentially alien to myth: in its use of sensuous images and signs it recognizes them as such —a means of expression which, although they reveal a determinate meaning, must necessarily remain inadequate to it, which "point" to this meaning but never wholly exhaust it.[3]

The movement I am suggesting in Faulkner's intellectual history is something quite other than a positivistic approach to epistemology which posits successive stages in modes of thought, each replacing and doing away with the former. As the center of his interest moves to an ethical solution to the awareness of evil, it remains yet largely within the analogous mythic form of the initiation or employs, as in the intellectual apex of his career, *A Fable*, the strictest relation to a mythic analogue.

It would be of little purpose to my argument to attempt to defend *Go Down, Moses* as a novel, although such attempts have been made; it will be sufficient to regard it as a collection of stories, three of which constitute a single coherent work and with four rather loosely related stories added for the book length Faulkner often mentioned as necessary to insure the purchaser his value on the dollar.

The initiation rites of Isaac McCaslin embodied in "The Old People" and "The Bear" are not merely analogous in form, but most precise in every detail. They have been examined at length and therefore I shall note them but briefly here. At the age of ten, Ike, already trained by Sam Fathers in the rudiments of the hunt, is taken into the big woods, the place of initiation. Sam Fathers' position is that of the priest of the cult of the wilderness, priest by virtue of his mastery of its mysteries and his direct relation to the golden age of the spirit of the wilderness:

> "He was a wild man. When he was born, all his blood on both sides, except the little white part, knew things that had been tamed out of our blood so long ago that we have not only forgotten them, we have to live together in herds to protect ourselves from our own sources." (167) *

He had "taught the boy the woods, to hunt, when to shoot and when not to shoot, when to kill and when not to kill, and better, what to do with it afterward" (170). It is when Ike can write his age in two numbers that he will be ready to *become* a man. In Ike's first and second "moon for hunting" he does not even see a deer, but he is nonetheless being initiated into the mysteries of the wilderness, bringing back with him "even from his first brief sojourn, an unforgettable sense of the big woods" (175). But this is not the equivalent of becoming a member of the cult, for that requires the ceremony of drawing blood, "the big blood which would make him a man, a hunter" (175). Not fully initiated, the boy cannot understand Sam Fathers' decision to live alone in the woods, believing it to be a life of loneliness and solitude. But eventually at the age of twelve he fulfills the requirements of the kill:

> So the instant came. He pulled trigger and Sam Fathers marked his face with the hot blood which he had spilled and he ceased to be a child and became a hunter and a man. (177–78)

It is only now that Sam Fathers can begin to reveal to Ike the deeper mysteries of the big woods. That afternoon as the party is leaving the woods, the other hunters are put off on the trail of a lesser deer while Sam places Isaac on a stand where he will see the big buck:

* Page references are to the Modern Library edition of *Go Down, Moses* (New York, 1955).

Then the boy saw the buck. It was coming down the ridge,
as if it were walking out of the very sound of the horn
which related its death . . . . Then it saw them. And still
it did not begin to run. It just stopped for an instant . . . ;
then its muscles suppled, gathered. It did not even alter its
course, not fleeing, not even running . . . , passing within
twenty feet of them, its head high and the eye not proud and
not haughty but just full and wild and unafraid, and Sam
standing beside the boy now, his right arm raised at full
length, palm-outward, speaking in that tongue which the
boy had learned from listening to him and Joe Baker in the
blacksmith shop, while up the ridge Walter Ewell's horn
was still blowing them in to a dead buck.
    "Oleh, Chief," Sam said. "Grandfather." (183–84)

It is not until they are home and McCaslin tires of teasing Ike
with pretended doubt about his story of having seen the deer
that McCaslin reveals to him that "Sam took me in there
once after I killed my first deer" (187).

"The Old People" takes Ike's initiation through to his
acceptance into the society of hunters, but it is in "The Bear"
that he is fully initiated into the cult of the wilderness. "The
Bear" recapitulates the rites set forth in "The Old People"
with an even more explicit awareness of myth: his initiation is
a rebirth in the true mythic sense:

He entered his novitiate to the true wilderness with Sam beside him . . . . It seemed to him that at the age of ten he
was witnessing his own birth. It was not even strange to
him. He had experienced it all before, and not merely in
dreams . . . . Then for two weeks he ate the coarse rapid
food—the shapeless sour bread, the wild strange meat,
venison and bear and turkey and coon which he had never
tasted before—which men ate, cooked by men who were
hunters first and cooks afterward . . . . (195–96)

These are the standard elements of the initiation rites analyzed by the anthropologists: the boy separated from society
as a whole, taken to a secret place where there are no women,
existing on a special diet, learning the mysteries of the cult,
and thereby being reborn into adult society. It is these mys-

teries of the wilderness that "The Bear" enlarges upon, differing from "The Old People" in that the boy is allowed these insights before the big kill. In his tenth year, with Sam beside him, the boy has his first experience of the bear, "the old bear, solitary, indomitable, and alone; widowered childless and absolved of mortality—old Priam reft of his old wife and outlived all his sons" (193–94). The bear, the totem spirit of the wilderness, has "come to see who's here, who's new in camp this year, whether he can shoot or not, can stay or not" (198). The ultimate test of excellence in the cult will be to prove worthy of this spirit.

It is in June of the following year, not the moon of the hunt, that Ike seeks out his direct experience of the bear. The rites of initiation, says Cassirer, are at first purely egocentric, their purpose being to strengthen the individual's mana:

> Thus we are still entirely within the world of magical thought and feeling; but in the midst of this world a new motif makes its appearance. A man's sensory wishes and desires do not flow equally in all directions; he no longer seeks to transpose them immediately and unrestrictedly into reality; rather he limits them at certain points in order to make them withheld and, one might say, stored-up power free for other purposes. Through this narrowing of the scope of desire, expressed in the negative acts of asceticism and sacrifice, the content of the desire is raised to its highest concentration and thus to a new form of consciousness.[4]

Ike's first sacrifice before this power of the wilderness, the land in its still primordial form, is the relinquishment of gun, compass, and watch, which he must abandon before the bear will appear to him. He cannot compel the bear; he must forego the symbols of man's egocentric power by which he feels himself to have mastered life, time, and space, for the aim of this hunt is not merely tracking and killing game, but to create a magical relation between the hunter and his quarry.

It is this very element of Ike's experience of the divine power which allows him to transcend the limitations of the

mere hunters, and it is through the acknowledgment of the
ethical virtues of courage, humility, bravery, and pride, a pride
within the boundries of the *I* as opposed to the *thou*, that
Ike becomes differentiated from the other hunters in that he
is truly at one with the wilderness. It is Boon who kills the
bear finally, not Ike, although the opportunity had presented
itself to him. Ike is the true initiate of the cult, the purpose of
which is to transcend the separation of the I from the absolute. It is the freedom gained by this discovery of selflessness
that contrasts Ike to Boon in the close of the story where we
have Boon hammering at his gun beneath the gum tree,

> hammering the disjointed barrel against the gun-breech with
> the frantic abandon of a madman. He didn't even look up
> to see who it was. Still hammering, he merely shouted back
> at the boy in a hoarse strangled voice: "Get out of here!
> Dont touch them! Dont touch a one of them! They're
> mine!" (331)

On his way to the gum tree, Ike had made a detour to visit
the graves in the plot Major de Spain had reserved out of the
sale of the land to the lumbering company. There are features
of an ancestor cult in Ike's gifts to the dead. The souls of the
ancestors are not dead, but exist and *are*. Part of the sense of
presence is demonstrated by the gifts to the dead, for although dead, they retain their pleasures and their needs. Ike
goes directly to the tree with

> the other axel-grease tin nailed to the trunk, . . . long since
> empty of the food and tobacco he had put into it that day,
> as empty of that as it would presently be of this which he
> drew from his pocket—the twist of tobacco, the new ban-
> danna handkerchief, the small paper sack of the peppermint
> candy which Sam had used to love; that gone too, almost
> before he had turned his back, not vanished but merely
> translated into the myriad life which printed the dark mold
> of these secret and sunless places with delicate fairy
> tracks . . . ; he had not stopped, he had only paused, quit-
> ting the knoll which was no abode of the dead because
> there was not death, not Lion and not Sam: not held fast in

earth but free in earth and not in earth but of earth, myriad
yet undiffused of every myriad part, leaf and twig and particle, air and sun and rain and dew and night. (328)

Then, one leg frozen in the act of stepping forward, he becomes aware of the great snake which glides away harmlessly,
Ike saluting it as Sam Fathers had saluted the great buck:
" 'Chief,' he said: 'Grandfather' " (330). The spirit of the
wilderness has manifested itself to him once again as it had in
the great buck and in Ben.

The fourth part of "The Bear" gives us, out of chronological order, the true freedom gained by Ike's experience of the
wilderness, a freedom that manifests itself in the sacrifice of
his inheritance. Ike is the opposite of Sutpen in this respect,
for Sutpen's dream lies still within the sphere of the magical
world view.

> Fundamentally, every sacrifice implies a negative factor: a
> limitation of sensory desire, a renunciation which the I
> imposes on itself. Here lies an essential trait of sacrifice,
> which raises it from the very outset above the level of the
> magical world view . . . which is based on belief in the
> omnipotence of human desires.[5]

On his twenty-first birthday, Isaac McCaslin faces his cousin
Carothers McCaslin Edmonds in the commissary of the plantation with his decision to relinquish his inheritance and attempts to explain the basis of his decision. It is not a repudiation, he explains, since the land has never belonged to any of
those who have called themselves the owners of it:

> 'Because He told in the Book how He created the earth,
> made it and looked at it and said it was all right, and then
> He made man. He made the earth first and peopled it with
> dumb creatures, and then he created man to be His overseer
> on the earth and to hold suzerainty over the earth and the
> animals on it in His name, not to hold for himself and his
> descendants inviolable title forever, generation after genera-
> tion.' (257)

But, argues McCaslin, even the Bible chronicles the ownership of the land through the generations sprung from Abraham, and history records

> the next thousand years while men fought over the fragments . . . until at last even the fragments were exhausted and men snarled over the gnawed bones of the old world's worthless evening until an accidental egg discovered to them a new hemisphere.' (258)

The New World offered to man the promise of a new golden age. All of this, Ike argues, was a part of God's plan. His argument takes an intricate turn as he explains his vision of the curse on the land, the vision which he is using as his rationale for relinquishment. The blood of the white man was to purge the land of the curse of the Indian blood, but at the same time the white man brought in the curse of slavery which must also be purged. " 'He used the blood which had brought in the evil to destroy the evil as doctors use fever to burn up fever, poison to slay poison' " (259). From out of all the white blood, God evidently chose that of Lucius Quintus Carothers McCaslin, not only in his own person, but in the generations of his get. God created them

> 'and knew them capable of all things because he had shaped them out of the primal Absolute which contained all and had watched them since in their individual exaltation and baseness and they themselves not knowing why nor how nor even when: until at last He saw that they were all Grandfather all of them and that even from them the elected and chosen the best he could expect . . . would be Bucks and Buddies and not even enough of them . . . . He must have seen me too. —an Isaac born into a later life than Abraham's and repudiating immolation: fatherless and therefore safe declining the altar because maybe this time the exasperated Hand might not supply the kid—' (283)

Then came the time that God said *This is enough* and was evidently prepared to turn His face away. But in the same moment there arose John Brown who astonished God with his direct action, abjuring the delaying tactics which were holding back His plan:

> '. . . *Then where are you going with that gun?* and the other told him in one sentence one word and He: amazed: Who knew neither hope nor pride nor grief *But your Association, your Committee, your Officers. Where are your Minutes, your Motions, your Preliminary Procedures?* and the other *I ain't against them. They are all right I reckon for them that have the time. I am just against the weak because they are niggers being held in bondage by the strong just because they are white.'* (285)

So God turned his face once again *toward* the South, because within the system of slavery there still existed certain kindnesses and virtues which held promise, and perhaps through the suffering of the Civil War these virtues would become dominant. Now, "twenty-three years after surrender and twenty-four from emancipation," Ike announces his relinquishment of the land.

The land is still cursed by ownership. That curse is compounded by the miscegenation and incest of his grandfather who has mixed the white blood and Negro blood which is to surround Ike all of his days. This latter curse Ike will attempt to deal with as did his father and uncle through the distribution of money and attempts at guidance. But the former curse calls for the renunciation of his birthright. While his cousin attempts to argue with him in legalistic terms, Ike serenely insists that he is free. " 'Yes. Sam Fathers set me free' " (300). His initiation into the mysteries of the wilderness have become equated with knowledge of the Absolute and its relation to the land expressed in biblical terms. Ike has discovered in himself "a fixed center, a unity of will, over against the dispersal and diversity of his sensory drives," a center that sustains him even in the face of his wife's rejection of him after he refuses to claim his birthright, the price she demands for herself.

But this is not to make of Isaac McCaslin Faulkner's

saint. Faulkner has given us a character who has found an individual peace only, and he is far from so simple minded as to suggest that Ike has succeeded in any social sense. In contrast to previous novels in which a rational-empiric view of the world has proven incomplete, requiring the balance of a more optimistic view supplied in the mythic vein, the story of Isaac McCaslin, dominantly mythic in mode and providing a character who transcends the problem of evil as he finds it, requires of Faulkner a rational-empiric balance. This is found in the final story, "Delta Autumn." While Ike's actions governed by the mythic-religious directness of the individual's relation to the absolute might seem noble to the romantic primitivist, it is not consistent with Faulkner's vision. If one man has found peace, this is not the solution to the "curse" which engendered that search. The problem was and is a social one and the solution must be in terms of society, not in terms of a single individual. What might have appeared to be a victory is proved to be an ironic defeat, a sterile abnegation of social responsibility.

"Delta Autumn" takes us fifty years and more beyond Ike's original renunciation of the land. He has lived since his twenty-first year as a carpenter,

> not in mere static and hopeful emulation of the Nazarene
> . . . but . . . because if the Nazarene had found carpenter-
> ing good for the life and ends He had assumed and elected
> to serve, it would be all right too for Isaac McCaslin even
> though Isaac McCaslin's ends, although simple enough in
> their apparent motivation, were and would be always in-
> comprehensible to him. ("The Bear," 310)

Evidently whatever insight Isaac gained through his mythic initiation cannot be translated into the rational-empiric mode although Ike had made the attempt in his argument with Mc-Caslin: " 'I'm trying to explain to the head of my family something which I have got to do which I dont quite understand myself' " ("The Bear," p. 288). His "truth" is one which must be espoused in the terms of the romantic transcendentalist. Since he had been using the Bible in an attempt to explain his position and since McCaslin employs the same text to contradict him. Isaac calls for an intuitive understanding:

'There are some things He said in the Book, and some things reported of Him that He did not say. And I know what you will say now: that if truth is one thing to me and another thing to you, how will we choose which is truth? You dont need to choose. The heart already knows.' ("The Bear," 260)

In his old age, Isaac still partakes of the hunt although the wilderness has retreated two hundred miles from Jefferson "and now those who accompanied him were the sons and even grandsons of the men who had ridden for twenty-four hours in the rain or sleet behind the steaming mules" (336). His sacrifice has had no effect within the natural or social order. The land is not only yet owned, but nature, the wilderness, has been destroyed for commercial ends. The other curse, related to the land, is also present. Roth Edmonds, the grandson of McCaslin Edmonds, involves Ike in his sexual misalliance that will bring his mistress into camp with the child she has borne him. This is obviously not the same kind of hunting camp that could provide the ritual initiation of a youth. Nor is Ike the priest of any cult as Sam Fathers had been. The younger men treat him with condescension and even mild contempt although he has been their mentor in the lore of the hunt. His stories of the past arouse not the vision that Sam Fathers' stories had given Ike as a boy but only resentment. As Ike talks of long ago hunts, Roth Edmonds reads into his words the implication that the men were better in the past too:

"I didn't say that," the old man said. "There are good men everywhere, at all times. Most men are. Some are just unlucky, because most men are a little better than their circumstances give them a chance to be. And I've known some that even circumstances couldn't stop."

"So you've lived almost eighty years," Edmonds said. "And that's what you finally learned about the other animals you lived among. I suppose the question to ask you is, where have you been all the time you were dead?" (345)

The insult does not particularly disturb Ike. As he continues in his attempt to communicate with the younger men, he falls back once again upon the necessity for an intuitive understanding of "truth," the understanding of the heart. But he fails to communicate and even his personal security which he has gained through his reliance upon the truth of the heart is shaken finally by the mistress of Roth Edmonds who appears the next morning.

The others have left for the hunt, leaving Ike alone in the camp. Roth has left with him an envelope containing money for the girl who will come and a one word message: "No." When the girl comes, Ike learns that for all his years and his sacrifice, nothing has changed since his grandfather's miscegenation and incest. Further, she is aware of this and yet it has not stopped her from becoming involved in an affair that she knew could come to nothing. As Ike listens to all this there is a quality, a factor, of the story that he cannot quite grasp and which causes something akin to panic in him:

"Yes," he said, harshly, rapidly, but not so harsh now and soon not harsh at all but just rapid, urgent, until he knew that his voice was running away with him and he had neither intended it nor could stop it: "That's right. Go back North. Marry: a man in your own race. That's the only salvation for you—for a while yet, maybe a long while yet. We will have to wait. Marry a black man. You are young, handsome, almost white; you could find a black man who would see in you what it was you saw in him, who would ask nothing of you and expect less and get even still less than that, if it's revenge you want. Then you will forget all this, forget it ever happened, that he ever existed—" until he could stop it at last and did, sitting there in his huddle of blankets during the instant, when, without moving at all, she blazed silently down at him. Then that was gone too. She stood in the

163

gleaming and still dripping slicker, looking quietly down at him from under the sodden hat.

"Old man," she said, "have you lived so long and forgotten so much that you dont remember anything you ever knew or felt or even heard about love?" (363)

This is the ultimate judgment upon Ike's own "sin." In his attempt to find personal peace he has not only divorced himself from society and any effective role within it, but he has divorced himself from the human condition. Our final view of him is not that of a noble, transcendent philosopher, but a superannuated, pathetic old man. This need not be construed as a negative judgment of the wilderness cult nor of the initiation rites it once provided. The failure of Isaac McCaslin is the failure of a man, not the failure of the wilderness. And with Ike's failure, with the inward turning of his religious spirit, mankind in general fails the land:

> No wonder the ruined woods I used to know dont cry for retribution! he thought: The people who have destroyed it will accomplish its revenge. (364)

While Abraham was willing to sacrifice Isaac to demonstrate his obedience to God's will, Isaac's sacrifice of the land has had no such denouement. What Isaac learned in the wilderness has given him a prophetic insight into God's plan. Unlike the prophet, however, he has not sought to spread the word of God but to use it to gain his personal peace. " '—an Issac born into a later life than Abraham's and repudiating immolation . . . declining the altar because maybe this time the exasperated Hand might not supply the kid' " (283). God called for Isaac's very life as a sacrifice, but this Isaac tenders up the land as a substitute and has only deceived himself.

The greatness of *Go Down, Moses* is not that it offers a solution, for it does not. We can neither condemn the mysteries of the wilderness nor the society which renders these teachings inoperative within it. Nor need we test Isaac's reading of God's plan to make a judgment upon it, although we can and must judge Isaac's use of his knowledge within his own society. Faulkner's greatness is in his very attempt to deal with the insoluble, to offer up the contents of a still swirling solution and to capture its very instability as it remains in solution. This is unsettling for those critics who expect the writer to wait until the maelstrom of particles in suspension can be separated from their context into a recognizable and easily describable sediment. It is the penchant of the rational-empiric mind to demand from *Go Down, Moses* an answer to the racial problems of the South, even if it is only Faulkner's answer, but I believe it cannot be done. Nor is it what he was trying to do. We might find a better explanation of his efforts in Isaac's words about the biblical writers:

> 'They were trying to write down the heart's truth out of the heart's driving complexity, for all the complex and troubled hearts which would beat after them. What they were trying to tell, what He wanted said, was too simple. Those for whom they transcribed His words could not have believed them. It had to be expounded in the everyday terms which they were familiar with and could comprehend, not only those who listened but those who told it too, because if they who were that near to Him as to have been elected from among all who breathed and spoke language to transcribe and relay His words, could comprehend truth only through the complexity of passion and lust and hate and fear which drives the heart, what distance back to truth must they traverse whom truth could only reach by word-of-mouth?' (260–61)

Or more directly, we can turn to Faulkner's words at the University of Virginia:

> You write a story to tell about people, man in constant struggle with his own heart, with the hearts of others, or with his environment. It's man in the ageless, eternal struggles which we inherit and we go through as though they'd never happened before, shown for a moment in a dramatic instant of the furious motion of being alive, that's all any story is. You catch this fluidity which is human life and you focus a light on it and you stop it long enough for people to be able to see it.[6]

In *Go Down, Moses* among other things, Faulkner has captured the psyche in its turn to the religious-ethical mode of consciousness with its consequent transcendence of the world of material values. While the laws of mythic thought eliminate the distance between the object and the subject, the religious consciousness presupposes a definite *I-thou* relationship and leads to an ethical code, a formulation of the laws of that relationship. In the transcendental mode of thought, a further progression of the religious mode, we find an attempt to surmount the I-thou relationship and an attempt to merge the *self*, the limited, with the *other*, the unlimited, the infinite. In this respect the transcendentalist is seeking out the condition of the mystic who has succeeded in surmounting the *I-thou* distinction. Mysticism, which represents the ultimate progression of the religious consciousness, thus comes in a circular fashion near to the laws of the mythic mode in its elimination of the distance between subject and object. This might help to explain the sympathy of the transcendentalists for the myths of the East. And, as Faulkner is demonstrably taken with the mythic mode and with the large body of myths, so we should not be surprised to find in this final period during which his work assumes an ethical intent overtones of the American tradition of Transcendentalism.

Irving D. Blum has noted the parallelisms between Faulkner's ideas about nature and those of Emerson. Quoting from "Nature" and "Self Reliance," Blum draws the conclusion that "Ike McCaslin, Faulkner's hero, has more than 'wisdom alone.' His is the insight into the universal. To him 'nature is the symbol of spirit.' " [7] One might also draw a more general parallel to Thoreau who announced his intent

> to drive life into a corner, and reduce it to its lowest terms, and, if it proved mean, why then to get the whole and genuine meanness of it, and publish its meanness to the world; or if it were sublime, to know it by experience, and be able to give a true account of it in my next excursion.[8]

Thoreau, however, remains largely the artist of the "how," while Faulkner attempts to communicate the meanness and sublimity directly.

Before leaving *Go Down, Moses,* I should like to note elements of two of the so loosely related stories. In "Pantaloon in Black," Rider, the virile young Negro who has just buried his wife, is counseled not to return to his home: "You dont wants ter go back dar. She be wawkin yit' " (136). But he does want to go back and evidently for that very reason. Sitting in the house with his dog, he is aware of the dog's departure and then, as the dog begins to howl outside,

> he saw her too. She was standing in the kitchen door, looking at him. He didn't move. He didn't breathe nor speak until he knew his voice would be all right, his face fixed not to alarm her. "Mannie," he said. "Hit's awright. Ah aint afraid." Then he took a step toward her, slow, not even raising his hand yet, and stopped. Then he took another step. But this time as soon as he moved she began to fade. He stopped at once, not breathing again, motionless, willing his eyes to see that she had stopped too. But she had not stopped. She was fading, going. (140)

This manifestation has many parallels in the documentation of myths, the wandering soul occupying much of Frazer's attention in *Taboo and the Perils of the Soul,* the third volume of *The Golden Bough.* For the mythic mind, death does not constitute an annihilation of existence, but a translation into another form of existence.

Another example of Faulkner's use of the Negro consciousness in the mythic mode is found in the concluding story, "Go Down, Moses." Here Mollie Beauchamp, the old Negress, has an extrasensory awareness of danger to her grandson who is about to be electrocuted in an Illinois prison and enlists Gavin Stevens' aid. Her construction of the situation is in biblical terms: "Roth Edmonds sold my Benjamin. Sold him in Egypt. Pharaoh got him—.' " This is not so specifically mythic in its construction, but it again illustrates his use of the Negro consciousness operating in terms of the strong hold of myth. Sean O'Faolin is right in his general observation of Faulkner's strength in capturing this mode of thought, although his manner of putting it is unfortunate. I believe his reading of Faulkner is among the most sensitive on record; however, it suffers from his own failure to find an adequate statement for the strength of his style. Obviously, when he says that Faulkner writes best when he writes like a Negro, he is attempting to make a distinction between modes of perception—a distinction which unfortunately comes out as a distinction between Negro and white.

Intruder in the Dust presents us with a modern ethical initiation of a young boy. The initiation is, however, far removed from the realm of myth and one must extend himself to speak of the "rites" involved. Andrew Lytle, in a review of the book, says that the point of view in the novel "rests at last not upon the boy's coming into manhood, but upon manhood, or its essence: The Man." [9] Giving the novel the benefit of his own Southern heritage, Lytle says,

> The South's hope for regeneration lies in its struggle itself to restore, not from outside pressure, to that part of its population the rights of manhood of which it is deprived. Understanding of this is proof of the boy's initiation and his right to the toga virilis.[10]

For him, Lucas Beauchamp occupies the position of "basic symbol of the Southern predicament," and the boy's initiation is to be viewed in terms of "the boy's active identity with the basic symbol":

> At the opening of the book on a hunting trip to the plantation he falls into a creek of icy water, in November, goes under three times and comes up to confront Lucas: the first encounter. The shock of the experience and the sight of Lucas immediately afterwards . . . is a kind of baptism from which he will forevermore be changed. Even the time of the year marks it, the dead season which always precedes regeneration.[11]

This is as far as one can safely go in describing the action in terms of ritual.

Compared to the story of Isaac McCaslin, *Intruder in the Dust* again offers Faulkner's tendency to offer us one story going "downward" and one story going "upward." In Isaac McCaslin we had the young initiate whose knowledge of the "mysteries" of his society led him to a repudiation and divorcement from that society; in the story of Chick Mallison we have the story of a young boy who learns of his society but takes action within that society and does not repudiate it. Chick, at the age of twelve, has fallen through the ice while hunting. Lucas appears on the scene and herds Chick and the two Negro boys who are with him to his own house where his clothes are dried and he is fed. Mrs. Vickery has observed that at this point Chick accepts, without thinking, the differences between the white and black worlds; that having been fed and sheltered, his attempt at payment is a perversion of the host-guest relationship into that of a Negro-white relationship.[12] The money falls to the floor and Lucas commands one of the Negro boys to pick it up and return it to Chick. After that he lives with the necessity of redeeming his social error and of freeing himself of his obligation to Lucas. He sends the gift of the dress to Molly, Lucas' wife, but the gift is cancelled out when Lucas sends him the gallon of molasses. Then three years later, he passes Lucas on the street and Lucas makes no sign of recognition; and Chick thinks,

> He didn't even fail to remember me this time. He didn't even know me. He hasn't even bothered to forget me: thinking in a sort of peace even: *It's over. That was all* because he was free, the man who for three years had obsessed his life waking and sleeping too had walked out of it. (25–26) *

But when Lucas is picked up for the murder of a white man and a lynching seems inevitable, Chick knows he has not

---

* Page references are to the Random House edition of *Intruder in the Dust* (New York, 1948).

been free, that Lucas' hospitality has bound him in something more than a social obligation. His first impulse is to saddle his horse and ride out of town, ride so far that by the time he returns it will be all over. But where Isaac had sacrificed the land to gain his peace, Chick knows that it is irresponsibility that he must sacrifice to gain *his* peace and he does not ride away but instead goes to the graveyard with Miss Habersham and Aleck Sander to dig up the corpse, an action that proves Lucas' innocence.

The larger part of the novel, divorced from the frequent grave openings, is given over to the understanding Chick gains from his experience. Faulkner insists on the distinction between two kinds of knowledge or belief, that of rational empiricism which he repeatedly attributes to the world of men and that of simple intuition which he equally often attributes to women and children. While women and children may act wisely in terms of their special kind of knowledge, it is necessary, however, that this knowledge be translated into the realm of the rational-empiric if it is to be socially effective.

> The problem of the child emerging into manhood is, in a sense, a verbal one, for he is compelled to reconcile language with experience and in the light of their significant interaction to accept, reject, or redefine his tradition. In such a situation there is room not only for the revivifying action of Chick but for the verbal readjustments of Gavin Stevens.[13]

The role of Gavin Stevens in the novel has been attacked primarily on the basis of his verbosity. Cleanth Brooks effectively refutes the position that Stevens should be regarded as Faulkner's spokesman:

> Doubtless, what he says often represents what many Southerners think and what Faulkner himself—at one time or another—has thought. But Gavin is not presented as the sage and wise counselor of the community. His notions have to take their chances along with those of less "intellectual" characters.[14]

But while Stevens may be discarded as Faulkner's spokesman, it should be noted that the political views he expresses in this novel are quite similar to those Faulkner himself will reiterate in *Requiem for a Nun* where the prose sections attack the concept of a political order imposing social order upon the individual, relieving the individual of the necessity or right of formulating his own ethical principles. Even if that social order is a desirable one, as an equality among the races is, it must be arrived at through an ethical judgment on the part of the individual, not legislated by the body politic. It is Gavin's role to orient Chick's knowledge based on experience to an effective social understanding.

> Gavin Stevens concerns himself with fostering Chick's intellectual comprehension of public morality and social relationships. Chick's venture into Beat Four to open a Gowrie grave, despite his knowledge that even his uncle would not understand or approve, constitutes his excursion into the wilderness. On his return, he, like Isaac, is ready to repudiate society and to isolate himself from it. Because of Stevens' efforts, he does not do so; he returns into history and time, a step that Isaac never took. In so doing he . . . establishes once more the identification of the individual's interests with those of the community even as he affirms the responsibility of the individual not only for his own conduct but for the conduct of all men.[15]

The greatest reconciliation Chick must make as a result of his experience is with the community as a whole. After the sheriff returns to town with the evidence that proves Lucas' innocence, Chick, through the car window, sees the face of the mob gathered to be present at the Gowries' vengeance:

> . . . not faces, but a face, not a mass nor even a mosaic of them but a Face: not even ravening nor uninsatiate but just in motion, insensate, vacant of thought or even passion: an Expression significantless and without past . . . without dignity and not even evocative horror: just neckless slack-muscled and asleep, hanging suspended face to face with him just beyond the glass of the back window. (182)

As soon as the news spreads that Lucas is not guilty, the mob evaporates. Chick, giddy with sleeplessness, can hang on only to the fact that "They ran." This refrain recurs throughout his musings. The source of his contempt for the mob is that at this moment they made no gesture toward Lucas to absolve themselves of their guilt. It is Chick's disgust that Gavin Stevens must attempt to mitigate:

> ". . . there is a simple numerical point [Stevens tells him] at which a mob cancels and abolishes itself, maybe because it has finally got too big for darkness, the cave it was spawned in is no longer big enough to conceal it from light and so at last whether it will or not it has to look at itself. . . . Or maybe it's because man having passed into mob passes then into mass which abolishes mob by absorption, metabolism, then having got too large even for mass becomes man again conceptible of pity and justice and conscience even if only in the recollection of his long painful aspiration toward them, toward that something anyway of one serene universal light."
> "So man is always right," he [Chick] said.
> "No," his uncle said. "He tries to be if they who use him for their own power and aggrandisement let him alone. Pity and justice and conscience too—that belief in more than the divinity of individual man . . . but in the divinity of his continuity as Man." (201-2)

This theme will become central in *A Fable* where Faulkner offers the apotheosis of his transcendental vision. Here we find Faulkner reaching back behind the crystallized forces of law to the spirit of the community, creating that force of myth Jane Ellen Harrison discovers in the concept of Themis:

> The Greek word *Themis* and the English word *Doom* [one of Faulkner's favorite words] are, philology tells us, one and the same; and it is curious to note that their development moves on exactly parallel lines. *Doom* is the thing set, fixed, settled; it begins in convention, the stress of public opinion; it ends in statutory judgement. Your private doom is your private opinion, but that is weak and ineffective. It is the collective doom, public opinion, that, for man's common convenience, crystallizes into Law. . . . Here the social fact is trembling on the very verge of godhead. [Themis] is the force that brings and binds men together, she is 'herd instinct,' the collective conscience, the social sanction. She is

fas, the social imperative. This social imperative is among a primitive group diffuse, vague, inchoate, yet absolutely binding. Later it crystallizes into fixed conventions, regular tribal customs; finally in the *polis* it takes shape as Law and Justice.[16]

In the ethical period, this searching for the relationship of the individual to the forms of society and the transcendence of these forms to once again recreate the community of man, to discover "the divinity of his continuity," is central to Faulkner's writing.

Intruder in the Dust constitutes one of Faulkner's unusual experiments in that here his vision is presented largely in the rational-empiric mode. The entire meaning of Chick's experience is handled in terms of a rational consideration. Faulkner does not employ his usual technique of presenting this resolution and reconciliation through action. There is no sacrificial figure through whom we witness man's transcendence of social forms. Whether he, like his critics, felt this presentation to be a "talky" failure or not, it is interesting to note that in his next novel, *Requiem for a Nun,* he once again deals with this problem in terms of a sacrificial figure, Nancy.

Gavin Stevens, Faulkner's voice of the rational-empiric, continues to play an important role in *Requiem for a Nun.* The redemption of Temple Drake after so many years offers once again his characteristic balance between the negative part of his vision and the optimistic, hopeful part. And once again, Faulkner employs a highly experimental form: three acts of a drama, each prefaced by a long prose section. The first of these introduces the courthouse of Jefferson as a symbol, telling of the foundation of the town and how it was named. Reaching back to the original state of the wilderness, he traces the historical process by which social forms were established and their perverting effect on individual initiative and ethics. In the chaos over the disappearance of the massive lock that had been taken from the mail bag and placed on the door of the jail, Pettigrew, the express rider, stands apart from the confusion but complicates it by intruding into the situation the letter of the law of the United States which he represents. The others turn their attention to Pettigrew, attempting to determine his aim in adding to their problem:

> 'Hell,' Compson said. 'Everybody knows what's wrong with him. It's ethics. He's a damned moralist.'
> 'Ethics?' Peabody said. He sounded almost startled. He said quickly: 'That's bad. How can we corrupt an ethical man?' (26) *

The way to corrupt an ethical man is to build a courthouse, thereby establishing a city, and to name that city after the man. Thomas Jefferson Pettigrew is informed that the town is to be named Jefferson; he pauses in his grooming of his horse and after a moment of silence suggests that the cost of the lock could be entered on the Indian Account, charged to Washington, as "axle grease."

This solution had presented itself earlier, allowing Faulkner to express his contempt for the economic system developed by society that would free men of individual responsibility:

> . . . a solution so simple, so limitless in retroact, that they didn't even wonder why nobody had thought of it before; which not only solved the problem but abolished it; and not just that one, but all problems, from now on into perpetuity, opening to their vision like the rending of a veil, like a glorious prophecy, the vast splendid limitless panorama of America: that land of boundless opportunity, that bourne, created not by or of the people, as was the heavenly manna of old, with no return demand on man save the chewing and swallowing since out of its own matchless Allgood it would create produce train support and perpetuate a race of laborers dedicated to the single purpose of picking the manna up and putting it into his lax hand or even between his jaws—illimitable, vast, without beginning or end, not even a trade or a craft but a beneficence as are sunlight and rain and air, inalienable and immutable.
> 'Put it on the Book,' Ratcliffe said. (20)

* Page references are to the Random House edition of *Requiem for a Nun* (New York, 1951).

The corruption of Pettigrew establishes at its very foundation the moral contradiction represented by the courthouse, which, observes Mrs. Vickery,

> is at once the symbol of man's dream of moral perfection and the cause of its destruction. Having housed their hopes and aspirations not only decently but magnificently, men freed themselves of responsibility for making their dreams a reality. The subsequent confusion of morality and legality was inevitable; appropriately, the temple of justice serves as the guardian of all the old, accumulated legal documents which are a constant reminder of legalized injustice, of men's exploitation of the land and other men.[17]

The second of these prose sections deals with the State Capitol at Jackson: "The Golden Dome (Beginning was the Word)." As the concept of a state emerged,

> men's mouths were full of law and order, all men's mouths were round with the sound of money; one unanimous golden affirmation ululated the nation's boundless immeasurable forenoon: profit plus regimen equals security. (104)

And a desire for security within a regimented society leads to a consequent loss of human dignity and freedom. Mrs. Vickery also deals with the symbolic value of the jail which is presented in the third of these prose sections:

> While the courthouse and the capitol suggest the fusion and confusion of ethics with law and the surrender of individual responsibility, the jail serves at once as an extension of and a departure from this position. In a sense, punishment has become as abstract and arbitrary as the law it purports to implement . . . . Paradoxically, however, the jail is also the one place which isolates the individual from the masses, thereby returning him to self-awareness, stripping him of all pretense and leaving him at last face to face with his own humanity.[18]

Ultimately, however, the jail becomes a symbol of transcendence. It is not through the isolation and alienation of any prisoner that Faulkner chooses to present its meaning, but through its presence in the historical consciousness of the citizens—and here he distinguishes between the "new people in the town" and "old citizens . . . , not old people but old citizens." It is in their consciousness that the jail reveals its meaningful tradition. The area of symbolic reference narrows down to the single pane of old glass, diamond-scratched by the "frail anemic" daughter of the one-time jailer: *"Cecilia Farmer April 16th 1861"* (229). The scratched signature and date become the focus of imagination recreating the life of the girl, in the process destroying the distance of time, transcending time:

> And again one sense assumes the office of two or three; not only hearing, listening and seeing too, but you are even standing on the same spot, the same boards she did that day she wrote her name into the window. (256)

And the stranger who has been led to this spot by an "old citizen" suddenly realizes, in an epiphany worthy of Whitman,

> that there is no time: no space: no distance: a fragile and workless scratching almost depthless in a sheet of old barely transparent glass, and (all you had to do was look at it a while; all you have to do now is remember it) . . . across the vast instantaneous intervention from the long long time ago: *'Listen stranger; this was myself: this was I.'* (261–62)

In this conclusion to the prose sections, the jail achieves its final separation from the other public buildings in its symbolic meaning. The court house and State Capitol remain symbols of abstract social forces; only the jail exists as a repository of individual human drama, drama which through its countless manifestations is raised to a transcendent level of meaning.

In counterpart to these sections are the three acts of Temple's drama. I find it impossible to accept Waggoner's evaluation of the resultant form:

> *Requiem* is the sort of thing an artist of Faulkner's kind does for the fun of it, and because its easy. A by-product of a rich imagination, it is casual, almost playful in its recapitulation of the major themes of the earlier works.

Formally, it is a daring experiment. . . . One can imagine Faulkner saying to himself that he would try uniting in this work both of the two great styles of our time, his own and Hemingway's; that he would really give the critics something to puzzle over and misunderstand this time, writing like himself and like the artistic opposite of himself, alternating a sensuous, lyric, evocative style in which character and plot disappear in an excruciating awareness of time and place, with a bare, direct, behavioristic style in which facts—words and actions—make their own poetry.[19]

The form is not really new to Faulkner. He has employed it several times in the past in an attempt to bring together within the covers of one volume the opposing poles of his vision of human existence. It is not "easy" or "playful," but a strained and forced juxtaposition of a harsh view of human society and a hopeful, optimistic view of individual potential within this society. This latter view has consistently been presented with overtones of myth and it is not surprising that sooner or later Faulkner should have attempted this in the form of a drama, for the dramatic form is the closest approximation to the direct sense of myth which has at its center the mime. We are asked for the moment to forego the conventions of the novel and to share in the actor's direct representation of the redemption of Temple Drake.

As the sections devoted to the buildings as symbols develop the idea of a social-political order that has absolved men of the necessity of making individual ethical decisions, so the acts of the drama present the immediacy of one individual forced out of the protective confines of this artificial order, forced to abandon the *persona* which has allowed her to exist in this society, forced to admit the reality of her existence and to come to terms with it as she may.

Temple Drake's story is picked up eight years after the events related in *Sanctuary*. She has been married to Gowan Stevens for these seven years, married at the Embassy in Paris the winter after the trial. The marriage has not been particularly successful. Gowan has married primarily to vindicate his honor and has since held Temple in the position of being grateful for his gentlemanly conduct. They returned to Jefferson to face down the shame and assumed their position as

> the Gowan Stevenses, young, popular: a new bungalow on the right street to start the Saturday-night hangovers in, a country club with a country-club younger set of rallying friends to make it a Saturday-night hangover worthy the name of a Saturday-night country-club hangover, a pew in the right church to recover from it in, provided of course they were not too hungover even to get to church. Then the son and heir came; and now we have Nancy. (157)

Nancy Mannigoe, the Negro nurse hired to care for the child, brings to focus the two personalities of Temple: Temple Drake and Mrs. Gowan Stevens:

> . . . the Gowan Stevenses are young and modern. so young and modern that all the other young country-club set applauded when they took an ex-dopefiend nigger whore out of the gutter to nurse their children, because the rest of the young country-club set didn't know that it wasn't the Gowan Stevenses but Temple Drake who had chosen the ex-dopefiend nigger whore for the reason that an ex-dopefiend nigger whore was the only animal in Jefferson that spoke Temple Drake's language—(157–58)

This is the situation that might go on indefinitely but for the intrusion of the past. While Popeye's captive in the Memphis brothel, Temple had written letters to her lover Red. Now Red's younger brother turns up with the letters to blackmail Mrs. Gowan Stevens. Instead he meets Temple Drake, restless and willing to abandon her life as Mrs. Gowan Stevens. The two plan to run away taking with them the younger child. When all else fails, Nancy, to prevent their running off, smothers the child in its crib and is arrested and tried for the murder.

The drama part of *Requiem for a Nun* begins with the sentencing of Nancy whose only response to the sentence of death is "Yes, Lord." At the beginning of the trial, Nancy had been rehearsed by her attorney, Gavin Stevens, to respond to the charge with "Not Guilty":

Except that she didn't say it: just raising her head enough to be heard plain—not loud: just plain—and said, 'Guilty, Lord'—like that, disrupting and confounding and dispersing and flinging back two thousand years, the whole edifice of corpus juris and rules of evidence we have been working to make stand up by itself ever since Caesar. (200)

Throughout the trial, nothing of Temple Drake's actions has come out; Mrs. Gowan Stevens is the aggrieved mother in the eyes of the community and Nancy's act is that of an "ex-dopefiend nigger whore." Although Temple attempts to escape the entire situation by traveling, she returns to Jefferson just before Nancy's scheduled execution and agrees to go with Gavin Stevens to see the Governor and to tell her story in a last ditch attempt to save Nancy's life.

The sacrifice demanded of Temple does not come easily. She attempts to put it off by interceding with the Governor as Mrs. Gowan Stevens, but Gavin Stevens insists that it must be as Temple Drake. Gavin arranges to have his nephew Gowan secreted in the Governor's chambers and Temple's confession is finished with Gowan sitting in the Governor's place. As Mrs. Vickery says,

The Governor's symbolic abdication of the seat of judgement . . . hurls back the years of blind confusion of justice and law, the years of irresponsible dependence on abstract authority. In one moment, it shatters the three symbolic edifices of the prose chapters and the whole intricate system of delegating responsibility that they represented. All the Governor can do is determine legal guilt to which neither Temple nor Gowan are subject. He can prescribe no punishment and no absolution for them because they have not sinned against the State or its law but against each other, against their children, and their own humanity.[20]

Temple's confession is not equivalent to redemption, however. Forced by Gavin Stevens, it is as far as the rational-empiric mode can take her, stripping off the mask but leaving her with doubts as to its efficacy. Whatever positive is to come now must come through another mode of knowledge and it is in the final interview with Nancy in the jail that we are allowed a glimpse of this.

Nancy's killing of the child was, in her mind, not to prevent Temple running away with Pete, but to save the child. She has not attempted to escape her punishment but faces it with equanimity and faith in a greater order than the mere legal order that has sentenced her to death. As Gavin Stevens and Temple face her in the prison, their attempts to understand her come as questions calling for answers that can be understood rationally, a program that is inherently absurd and which threatens to become mawkish. Nowhere are the limitations of Gavin Stevens exposed more clearly than in his attempts to translate Nancy's knowledge into rational terms. Faulkner is clearly aware of this and saves the entire scene from the very brink of disaster by introducing the subject of Nancy's child, lost when she was kicked in the stomach by a man. Stevens is outraged by the idea that she should have no idea who the father of the child was. Nancy's answer, "If you backed your behind into a buzz-saw, could you tell which tooth hit you first?" completely silences Stevens. To all their questions she can only reply, "I don't know. I believes." And her only advice is "Believe." When the mythic-religious consciousness faces the rational-empiric world, Faulkner faces the fact that there is no other structure than faith to bridge the distance between the two.

Waggoner's thesis that Faulkner's "imagination works effectively only when it works in Biblical terms," [21] has the limitation that it recognizes only a limited manifestation of the mythical-religious spirit, a limitation that Faulkner's works do not suffer. To test them against this narrowed field of reference is to miss the greater part of Faulkner's vision, the inescapable hope and optimism that is present. If this hope is to be found only in the scheme of Christianity, it is no wonder Waggoner must say:

> In Faulkner's greatest works the tragedy seems final, unrelieved, inescapable in any dimension. This is very nearly

the same as saying that when he writes at his best we find all the categories of Christian thought and feeling except faith and hope in the classic, and Pauline, sense. . . .

Faulkner's fiction is best understood in Biblical categories. It proceeds from piety and is conducive to piety. If we would go beyond some such statements as these, we must be content to leave clarity behind.[22]

I must argue that it is absolutely necessary to go beyond "some such statements as these," beyond merely biblical categories to the categories of the mythical mode of thought in order to understand even the biblical references adequately, indeed, to *gain* clarity.

While Waggoner accepts Nancy's "outline of orthodox belief," this does not in any way help us to understand the murder of the child, the motivating act of the novel. His "Biblical categories" do not allow him to "see in her action enough to understand why she felt driven to murder the child to prevent suffering. We suspect her of being a little mad." [23] Nancy's killing of the child is a complex thing. There is at once the sacrifice of the child and the sacrifice of herself. As much of the rationale as she is able to offer is found in her denial of the life Temple threatens to create for herself and for the child whom she loved, in Temple's words, at the very moment she raised her hand against it. But it is primarily for the children: "I aint talking about your husband. I aint even talking about you. I'm talking about two little children" (184). And by extension, perhaps all children as such.

It is fundamentally a religious act. The "ex-dopefiend nigger whore" has become the protectress of the children. There is implicitly the rejection of her former life; we hear nothing of any continuation after she has taken the position in the Stevens' household. And Nancy is a deeply religious woman. I believe, therefore that we should examine the killing of the child in terms of sacrifice rooted in the mythic-religious consciousness. Sacrifice, says Evelyn Underhill, is a positive act:

Its essence is something given; not something given up. It is a freewill offering, a humble gesture which embodies and expresses with more or less completeness the living heart of religion; the self-giving of the creature to its God. By this self-giving action, man takes his conscious part in the response of the universe to the Source of its being; and unites the small movements of his childish soul to the eternal sacrifice of the Son.[24]

The sacrifice contains the three elements Miss Underhill finds in her examination:

For in sacrifice something is given voluntarily and unconditionally to God, in defiance of the inveterate possessiveness and claimfulness of man; and this gesture of generosity is felt to be the best that we can do (a) to atone for our shortcomings in other respects, (b) as a means of that approach to God which is an essential element in worship, (c) as an earnest of devotedness. From the point of view of primitive thought, this gift could not fully be made without the death of the victim; for its life—the essence of the offering, and token of the offerer's own life—must be released and handed over to the supernatural powers . . . . Here, then, we have an explanation of some of the more terrible aspects of sacrifice; even including those human sacrifices in which, with a dreadful logic, the awakening soul of the primitive acknowledges the absolute priority of the Unseen.[25]

We must remember that Nancy is giving not only the child to God, but giving herself as well. The redemption of Temple Drake is an uncertain thing which the novel does not explore fully; the redemption of Nancy is a fully accomplished thing as she awaits her execution. She believes. There is, for her, the absolute priority of the Unseen. The sacrificer has intuited "the costly paradox of life surrendered that life may be achieved." [26] And the sacrifice for the believer is not life destroyed, but life transformed, for it is essentially a belief in the mythic domain where death is not acknowledged as an end but merely a transformation. If we view Nancy's logic in terms of a rational-empiric system, we must, perhaps, conclude that she is "a little mad." But if we attempt to view the act in terms of her own logic, we find that it has a coherence of its own, and I believe this is what Faulkner intended us to see.

Requiem for a Nun is not an easy book. It is another of Faulkner's many attempts to present his faith in the potential of human life against the background of the many forces, natural and social, that threaten this potential. Once again he relies for this expression of hope on the presentation of a character who operates in terms of a mythic directness.

In *A Fable*, Faulkner again explores the theme of the individual's redemption in the face of social forms which would relieve him of any necessity for individual responsibility. However, the scope of the action is enlarged to epic proportions and the number of heroes in their various quests serves to present Faulkner's most complex vision of man's condition. As Andrew Lytle observes,

> In *A Fable* all Faulkner's heroes, and everybody is a hero there, suffer the deliberate loss either of rank or life. Each protagonist and antagonist, and each is protagonist-antagonist, is a criminal. Each violates in varying degree the civil or military code. Each kills that of himself which he values most; or upon his quest he kills his fellow man. But if he is a murderer, he is a sacred criminal, somewhat like the priest-murderer at Nemi. Lose life to save it; suffer little children to come unto me, for such is the kingdom of Heaven: paradoxes interpreted in terms of the quest mean that man must plunge himself into degradation to be reborn out of the perfect knowledge of and triumph over himself; and sometimes he can only find life through physical death; and always at the risk of the loss of himself.[27]

Lytle's analysis breaks down, however, when it falls into one of the standard traps of myth criticism: the introduction of the tarot deck. This serves but to muddy up the waters, for the analogies to the cards are neither coherent nor is there any pertinence in their application to *A Fable*. I believe it is far better to remain within the realm of the archetype of the scapegoat, a mythic pattern that is demonstrably present throughout Faulkner's works.

The scope of the novel embraces half of Europe and the United States and focuses the debilitating forces of society into the single demonic image of war controlled by the hierarchy of militarism. For the protagonist of the thematic action, Faulkner dares to offer nothing less than the spirit of Man. It is perhaps this fact that leads Lytle to call the novel a morality, a work outside the bounds of fiction as understood today. In an age of belief, he says,

> A man witnessing a morality would, in the action dealing with the drama of the soul, automatically specify whatever was unique and personal in himself. But today where we have conventions empty of belief and institutions being reduced to organizations and forms which have lost the natural object, a morality lacks authority. It is why fiction as a literary form appears now and not in the fourteenth century. Everyman now must first become unique man.[28]

Lytle's objections are valid and point the way to the various other objections raised by the critics. This is but to say that *A Fable* is a difficult book for readers because they do not share the author's ideas or, perhaps even, his mode of thought. *A Fable* calls upon the reader, more than any other of Faulkner's books, for an awareness of the mythic-religious mode of thought, because it is a religious expression not of Christianity, not of Christ, but of the cult of man; and the rejection of the fictional focus on the uniqueness of man is the espousal of an approximation of ritualistic form. The various sacrifices of the various heroes are ritualistic sacrifices reaffirming the strength by which man endures and even prevails. Of this cultic process, Cassirer says,

> It can be clearly shown that a vast number of mythical motifs had their origin in the intuition of a cultic rather than natural process. They go back not to any physical thing or event but to an activity of man, and it is this activity that is explicitly represented in them. A particular process that is

repeated over and over in the cult is mythically interpreted and understood by being linked to a unique temporal event and viewed as its reflection.[29]

Thus the various sacrifices partake of that unique sacrifice of the Son of Man, Christ, who in Faulkner's theology assumes that role in which is mirrored all the struggling and suffering of man; and in the death of Christ is mirrored the transcendence of man, a transcendence which in Faulkner's maturity supplants the earlier groping for the metaphoric significance in the image of the resurrection. It is a highly religious statement in which he once again infuses belief, vital and mythic, into "conventions empty of belief."

The action that A *Fable* offers is that of a regiment's rebellion. An attack is ordered and the troops refuse to leave the trenches. The entire regiment is spirited away to barbed wire imprisonment while the military authorities determine what is to be done. The leaders of the mutiny are thirteen: the corporal and his twelve "disciples." The first character introduced is the division commander, Gragnon, who like the mythic hero is an orphan of mysterious parentage, but whose primary role is that of a scapegoat to a rigid, abstract, military code of honor. The military is, in its own right, a secret cult with its own mysteries. Rank is dwelt upon a great deal. The mysterious fraternal secrets of the corporal who leads the mutiny that will once again allow man to stand erect do not penetrate even the ranks of the non-commissioned officers: "the thirteen men in French uniforms who had been known for a year now among all combat troops below the grade of sergeant in the British forces and obviously in the French too" (66).* Gragnon, the lowest in the hierarchy of generals, still subscribes to the published code of honor and war and because of the mutiny demands his own arrest and the execution of the entire regiment. It is the corps commander, Lallemont, who attempts to make him see the reality of the military.

* Page references are to the Random House edition of A *Fable* (New York, 1954).

'Bah,' the corps commander said again. 'It is man who is our enemy: the vast seething moiling spiritless mass of him. Once to each period of his inglorious history, one of us appears with the stature of a giant, suddenly and without warning in the middle of a nation as a dairymaid enters a buttery, and with his sword for paddle he heaps and pounds and stiffens the malleable mass and even holds it cohered and purposeful for a time. But never for always, nor even for very long: sometimes before he can even turn his back it has relinquished, dis-cohered, faster and faster flowing and seeking back to its own base anonymity. . . . We hauled them up out of their ignominious mud by their bootstraps; in one more little instant they might have changed the world's face. But they never do. They collapse, as yours did this morning. They always will. But not us. We will even drag them willy-nilly up again, in time, and they will collapse again. But not us. It wont be us.' (30)

The attack assigned to Gragnon was designed in the greater plan to be a failure. He had accepted this; but to fail in this particular manner demands the full sacrifice of the scapegoat. It is too late for him to accept the knowledge Lallemont has offered him; to him, the officers are still those " 'who not only went where they went, but led them, went first, in front, who desired for them nothing but glory, demanded of them nothing but courage' " (41). Gragnon, deluded by his code of honor, sees the mutiny as a personal insult, and his failure demands an ignominious death. At the end, he refuses the fiction of a bullet in the front that will allow him to be passed off as a hero, demanding the bullet in the back and struggling against his assassins until the bullet enters just behind his ear. Ironically, that hole is plugged up with wax and another bullet is placed in the proper position.

The mutiny is known to be wider than this one regiment and the military suspends the war while the generals meet to decide how to cope with it, for there are rules that must be followed to end wars: " 'But not this way. Not like a group of peasants in a half-mown field suddenly shouldering their scythes and lunch-pails and walking off' " (53). Dummy ammunition is supplied the anti-aircraft units and three planes with dummy ammunition are sent up for appearances as a German general is flown in to confer with the allied generals. One of the flyers, a very young lieutenant named Levine, discovers the mockery in which he has taken part. He, like Gragnon, is committed to the externals of war—the glory and honor of dying in defense of his country. His disillusionment leads to his suicide.

It is these men of the military hierarchy who represent the sleepers of Thoreau's transcendental vision. And it is the men of the ranks who rebel under the corporal and the runner who are the railroad ties of Thoreau's metaphor, rising out of their imposed place and necessitating the activity connected with putting them down again.

The mutiny to this point has been a merely negative act. The troops had refused to leave the trenches at the specified command. There is yet another act to be performed and at the center of this is the runner, a one time British officer who has forced his demotion to the ranks to be free of "having to perform forever at inescapable intervals that sort of masturbation about the human race people call hoping" (62). Symbolically he has rejected the code and the area of knowledge of the officer class, but the taint of his former class prevents him for some time from learning of what is going on in the ranks. His informant is "an A.S.C. private more than sixty years old" who makes the first equation of the corporal with Christ and his teachings with those of Christ (67–68).

But there is another kind of activity that is being carried on in the ranks and kept from the officer class. This centers around the sentry-groom who has been loaning money to the troops at exorbitant interest rates in what amounts to a gambling agreement in which the troops bet against the sentry that they will not be alive to pay their debts. The runner learns that the interest rates are lower if one is a Mason. He learns nothing from the sentry himself, but, taking some money on loan, he goes to Paris where he discovers the Negro lay-preacher Sutterfield, now known as Tooleyman from the name of the association he heads: *Les Amis Myriades et Anonymes à la France de Tout le Monde.* From him he learns about the sentry-groom and the horse.

The groom had been the inseparable companion of the racing horse, a champion runner, crippled in a train wreck and then kept secret by the groom and the Negro hostler and the Negro's twelve-year-old grandson who rides the crippled horse in the races they run as they spirit the horse around the country keeping one jump ahead of the various pursuers who would return the horse to stud:

> not a theft, but a passion, an immolation, an apotheosis—no gang of opportunists fleeing with a crippled horse whose value, even whole, has ceased weeks back to equal the sum spent on its pursuit, but the immortal pageant-piece of the tender legend which was the crowning glory of man's own legend beginning when his first paired children lost well the world and from which paired prototypes they still challenged paradise, still paired and still immortal against the chronicle's grimed and blood-stained pages: Adam and Lilith and Paris and Helen and Pyramus and Thisbe and all the other recordless Romeos and their Juliets, the world's oldest and most shining tale limning in his brief turn the warp-legged foul-mouthed English horse-groom as ever Paris or Lochinvar or any else of earth's splendid rapers. (153–54)

I believe this is Faulkner's most explicit use of the horse as representing a kind of mana. The imagery dealing with the relationship to this spirit of not only the sentry-groom and the two Negroes but everyone who sees the horse run is presented in terms of passion, imagery sustained by the deputy who relinquishes the chase as he senses the meaning of the horse:

> thinking how it was no wonder that man had never been able to solve the problems of his span upon earth, since he has taken no steps whatever to educate himself, not in how to manage his lusts and follies; they harm him only in sporadic, almost individual instances; but in how to cope with his own blind mass and weight: seeing them—the man and the horse and the two Negroes whom they had snatched as

it were willy nilly into that fierce and radiant orbit—
doomed not at all because passion is ephemeral (which was
why they had never found any better name for it, which was
why Eve and the Snake and Mary and the Lamb and Ahab
and the Whale and Androcles and Balzac's African deserter,
and all the celestial zoology of horse and goat and swan and
bull, were the firmament of man's history instead of the
mere rubble of his past. . . . (161)

The central focus of this horse episode is not, however,
on the sentry-groom but on the simple people of the central
southern states and the survival of traces of the golden age of
individuality that was associated with the frontier. The great
rewards offered for information about the horse bring no betrayal. As the System closes in on the group the defections are
not *to* the System, but *from* it. When the pursuers finally
catch up with the group and the sentry-groom kills the horse
to save it from the ignominious fate of a stud, the people of
the little Missouri town rise up against their own system of
law, again symbolized by the courtroom:

> . . . the lawyer watched Man pouring steadily into the
> tabernacle, the shrine itself, of his last tribal mysteries, en-
> tering it without temerity or challenge, because why not? it
> was his, he had decreed it, built it, sweated it up . . . and
> the floor was his because he had built it, paid for it, and
> who could spit on it if not he. (172–73)

The sentry-groom has already disappeared, back to the Tennessee valley where he had received a kind of initiation and
from whence he will make his way back to England where he
will be enlisted in the war. It is the old Negro and his grandson the "mob" free from the law in its unanimous gesture of
freedom from the very institutions it has built up around itself.

The story the runner hears from the old Negro does not
give us the sentry-groom as any truly initiated person. The
groom had undergone two ritual initiations during the course
of his wanderings with the horse: acceptance into the order of
the Masons and baptism by the old Negro into the Baptist

church. But he is still the unregenerate foul mouthed being described as "Darkness' emissary" (158), a centaur-like figure, and a "moloch-effigy of self-sustenance" (196). The old Negro has found him out in the war to offer him aid but has been summarily rejected. " 'He aint ready yet,' " he says of him (202). There is no moral regeneration evidenced by the religious initiation and the only effect of the initiation into the fraternal organization is a reduction in interest rates for the other members of the order; and what can be measured in money is, for Faulkner, debased.

It is the old Negro Sutterfield, now known as "all the world" who has the insight denied the sentry-groom. He too shared in the passion for what the horse represented:

> —a minister, a man of God, sworn and dedicated enemy of man's lusts and follies, yet who from that first moment had not only abetted theft and gambling, but had given to the same cause the tender virgin years of his own child as ever of old had Samuel's father or Abraham his Isaac. (159)

When the pursuit is over, the lawyer hired by the converted deputy to represent the trio (a duty rendered impossible in view of man's denial of the forms of law) questions the old man:

> 'Are you an ordained minister?'
> 'I dont know. I bears witness.'
> 'To what? God?'
> 'To man. God dont need me. I bears witness to Him of course, but my main witness is to man.' (180)

When he has finished telling the runner his story and the runner questions him, he, like Nancy, simply responds: " 'I can believe' " (201). Now the Negro simply waits for the moment when he will be needed. " 'Send for me,' " he says to the runner (204).

All of this information precedes the mutiny by more than a year. The mutiny takes place on a Monday. On Tuesday night, the runner is trying to convince the sentry to use his power over the men, power he holds by virtue of his Masonic fraternity and his financial hold over them, to perform the next act, the positive act after the merely negative act of mutiny: to lead the troops, weaponless, out into no man's land:

> 'You can do it. You own the whole battalion, every man in it under corporal, beneficiary of every man's insurance in it who hasn't got a wife and I. O. U.'s for their next month's pay of all the rest of them in that belt around your waist. All you'll need is just to tell them to when you say, Follow me.' (84)

The sentry's answer is a violent attack, kicking at the runner's face until restrained.

The old A.S.C. private has told the runner of the dummy anti-aircraft shells, calling them the signal, the announcement: "To let the whole world know that He has risen" (81). The runner understands that it is to allow a German emissary to enter the lines for a conference and that the next action must take place before the combined military hierarchy can agree on a course of action. When he regains consciousness after his beating, he escapes and makes his way to Paris to once again see the Reverend Toolcyman. Together they return to the trenches and the runner attempts to force the sentry to make the sign, but he struggles against them until, without the sign, the troops begin to rise out of the trenches,

> crawling on their hands and knees through the gaps in the wire as though up out of hell itself . . . not only the battalion but the German one or regiment or whatever it was, the two of them running toward each other now, emptyhanded, approaching until he could see, distinguish the individual faces but still all one face. (321)

Then begins the barrage laid down on the troops by both sides. In that moment the sentry achieves a momentary initiation in the brotherhood of man:

> 'No!' he cried, 'no! Not to us!' not even realizing that he had said 'we' and not 'I' for the first time in his life probably, certainly for the first time in four years. (321)

The last thing heard of the barrage is the runner's voice "crying out of the soundless rush of flame which enveloped half his body neatly from heel through navel through chin: 'They can't kill us! They cant! Not dare not: they cant!' " (321–22).

Meanwhile, the military is dealing with the mutiny in its own way. In the figure of the chief of staff, the old Marshal, are mixed many of the qualities of God the Father, Satan, the questing hero, Caesar, and even Christ. He too is an orphan, reared by his aunt who is married to a Cabinet Minister and has as his godfather the board chairman of "that gigantic international federation producing munitions" (246). Upon graduation from the military academy he assumes African duty at a post "famous in its circles as the Black Hole of Calcutta" where he serves for six years during which time the only action we learn of is his prevention of a war with the natives by sending out the trooper whose life has been demanded by the natives in payment for his crimes. At the end of that time he is replaced by the figure who will become his Quartermaster General in a scene in which the Quartermaster's role is that of a John the Baptist welcoming the Christ.

The Quartermaster's approach to the fort in the desert is to "not Golgotha of course but Gethsemane," to replace the man " 'who sought a desert not as Simeon did but as Anthony, using Mithridates and Heliogabalus not merely to acquire a roosting-place for contempt and scorn, but for fee to the cave where the lion itself lay down' " (258–59). The Quartermaster's vision of the past and future of the General's life sees the six years in the desert as a testing of

'all of them, the trinity [nephew, uncle, godfather] still intact because it had never been otherwise, testing as one the fragility's capacity for the destiny and the consecration, using the desert for yardstick as when in the old days the cadet would spend that last night of his maiden squiredom on his knees on the lonely chapel's stone floor before the cushion bearing the virgin spurs of his tomorrow's knighthood.' (261)

It will take time, he clairvoyantly tells him, for the world to understand him truly.

> 'It will need a new time, a new age, a new century . . . ; it will be more than twenty years even before the day, the moment when you will appear again, without past, as if you had never been. Because by that time you will no longer exist for them except in mutual remembering: a lay figure not only without life but integrated as myth only in mutual confederation.' (262)

He does not ask where he is going, but knows he will return "in the shape of man's living hope" when his time is come (263). He bows to kiss his hand and gives him a benediction:

> 'With Christ in God,' he said. 'Go now.'
> 'So I'm to save France,' the other said.
> 'France,' he said, not even brusquely, not even contemptuously. 'You will save man. Farewell.' (264)

The only other parts of the General's history we know are that he secluded himself in a Tibetan lamasery and that thirty-three or thirty-four years ago he had an adulterous love affair which begot the son who is the Corporal of the mutineers.

In the week of the mutiny, on Thursday night, the Quartermaster General has another private interview with the Marshal. He faces him with the fact of the German general's arrival and the barrage laid down by both sides on the unarmed British battalion and the unarmed German forces coming to meet them. "We" did this, he says, assuming the full responsibility for the betrayal of man by the military hierarchy. He tenders his resignation to the Marshal and rejects the vision he had posited forty-seven years ago of the Marshal as man's savior, accusing him of fearing man:

> 'I am not afraid of man,' the old general said. 'Fear implies ignorance. Where ignorance is not, you do not need to fear: only respect. I dont fear man's capacities, I merely respect them.'
> 'And use them,' the Quartermaster General said.
> 'Beware of them,' the old general said. (329)

Ironically, the Marshal proceeds to "use" the Quartermaster General in terms of his knowledge of the man's moral conscience. He immediately points out that the betrayal is not to be attributed to the military hierarchy, but to man himself, since it was one of the Corporal's own men who had betrayed him, the Judas-figure Polchek. He refuses the resignation of the Quartermaster General, pointing out that he has failed in his attempted gesture, for the Corporal will die for his principles whereas he himself makes only the futile gesture of resigning his commission, not even asking that the life of the Corporal be spared:

> 'He wont accept that life!' the other cried. 'If he does—'
> stopped, amazed, aghast, foreknowing and despaired while
> the gentle voice went on:
> 'If he does, if he accepts his life, keeps his life, he will
> have abrogated his own gesture and martyrdom. If I gave
> him his life tonight, I myself could render null and void
> what you call the hope and the dream of his sacrifice. By
> destroying his life tomorrow morning, I will establish forever
> that he didn't even live in vain, let alone die so.' (332)

The Quartermaster, forced to acknowledge his continuing responsibility within the hierarchy in the death of the Corporal, picks up his commission once again and leaves.

Although the Corporal's delineation offers many parallels to the life of Christ, it is not a slavish imitation. His first appearance is not calculated to present him as a second Christ but concentrates upon his transcendent identity with man. The corporal is called before a British colonel, a French major, and an American captain in the Marshal's rooms to be identified. The colonel identifies him as a man killed at Mons four years ago; the captain identifies him as a man buried at sea the previous October. "So all that remains for us is to witness to his resurrection," says the old general (279). The French major contributes his knowledge of this "ubiquitous corporal": his collection taken up for a little girl going blind to send her to Paris for an operation, certainly a displaced version of the healing of the blind; another collection for the "wedding and the wine" when a young couple were without the wherewithal to marry; and another collection levied on the regiment to find a home for an old man driven beyond sanity by the war around him.

The Marshal leaves this scene to talk to Magda-Marthe, the Corporal's older half sister, who retells the story of the Corporal's birth "in a cow-byre behind a roadside inn" on Christmas thirty-three years ago, a birth that was "to create a son for one of you to condemn to death as though to save the earth, save the world, save man's history, save mankind" (287). She brings with her the locket the Marshal had given her mother as a sign, the typical sign to identify the quester to the father in the pattern of myth, and asks not for the Corporal's life but for his body after the execution.

The role of the Marshal is the most complex in the book. His views of man become explicit in the temptation scene in which he takes the corporal out of the town to a high hill top where he offers him progressively more and more if he will deny his ideas by taking the freedom he offers him. Mrs. Vickery, examining his role, calls him a false savior. She suggests that his view of man's lot stops short with Faulkner's famed quality of endurance and says that he in his Nobel prize speech goes beyond this. [30] But it is the Marshal, not the Corporal who ends the scene with the proud statement that man will prevail (354). The Marshal, as Mrs. Vickery points out, acts always in terms of the greatest good for the greatest number, and he informs the Corporal that he will give him up for execution on these terms:

> Because I believe in man within his capacities and limitations. I not only believe he is capable of enduring and will endure, but that he must endure, at least until he himself invents evolves produces a better tool than he to substitute for himself. (347)

He suggests to his son the dichotomy between their two world views:

> . . . we are two articulations, self-elected possibly, anyway
> elected, anyway postulated, not so much to defend as to test
> two inimical conditions which, through no fault of ours but
> through the simple paucity and restrictions of the arena
> where they meet, must contend and—one of them—perish:
> I Champion of this mundane earth which, whether I like it
> or not, is, and to which I did not ask to come, yet since I
> am here, not only must stop but intend to stop during my
> allotted while; you champion of an esoteric realm of man's
> baseless hopes and his infinite capacity—no: passion—for
> unfact. No, they are not inimical really, there is no contest
> actually; they can even exist side by side together in this one
> restricted arena, and could and would, had yours not inter-
> fered with mine. So once more: take the earth. (347–48)

The Marshal is the voice of the rational-empiric view. He
himself recognizes the possibility of his world existing side by
side with the "esoteric" mythic world postulated by his son's
view. His limitation, insofar as we may cite one, is that he
cannot conceive of the possibility that when the two come
into conflict with one another that his son's view should become the victor. It is life itself that he holds out to his son as
the single priceless thing and it is life he urges him to take.

Faulkner has complicated the reader's task greatly, for,
having identified the conflict between the forms of society
(the military) and man's indomitable spirit, he is led to expect
an equally distinct conflict between the views of the military's
highest commander and the Corporal. Furthermore, conditioned as he is by the Christian analogue, he is prepared to reject the Marshal's views out of hand. The consternation
which the book has aroused is due to the fact that the reader,
conditioned to the rational-empiric view, is forced to agree
with the Marshal throughout his argument. Among the critics
of the novel, it is again Mrs. Vickery who most clearly senses
the nature of the problem. But her approach is to attempt to
demonstrate the inadequacies of the Marshal's world view
and at times this results in a hair splitting logic I find unsatis-
factory.[31] Her conclusion, that the Marshal's view of man "is

incomplete rather than false," is, of course, the right one. It is the rational-empiric view, thoroughly logical and with room even for a kind of idealism, but yet inadequate. As in almost all Faulkner's other works, the mythic counterbalance to this view of life is not presented in terms of words—there is nothing like an argument between the Marshal and the Corporal —it is beyond words. It is through the Corporal's life that we find Faulkner's criticism of the rational-empiric mode. Whether it is regarded as a transcendence of, or a reaching behind, the crystalized institutions of man, Faulkner is here "trembling on the very verge" of a mythical godhead within the cult of man. It is the spirit of man that asserts itself in the face of the limitations imposed upon it by the rational-empiric forces seeking to manipulate it to its own ends. When the corporal rejects the offer of his life and the world, it is in terms of the ten followers who still remain faithful, they who represent the community of man. This he cannot betray.

> The instinct of those who, in framing the old definitions of religion, included 'mystery' and 'the infinite' was right— though their explanations wrong. The mystery, the thing greater than man, is potent, not only or chiefly because it is unintelligible and calls for explanation, not because it stimulates a baffled understanding, but because it is *felt* as an obligation. The thing greater than man, the 'power not himself that makes for righteousness,' is, in the main, not the mystery of the universe to which as yet he is not awake, but the pressure of that unknown ever incumbent force, herd instinct, the social conscience.[32]

The old Marshal who has been presented with parallels to Caesar (the recurring phrase "Render unto Chaulnes-mont"), God the Father, Satan, the questing hero, and Christ is nonetheless denied the one simple act in his life that is reserved for the Corporal: a sacrificial death as man. All the parallels remain in the rational-empiric realm, divorcing even God the Father, except as agent, from the apotheosis of man. Faulkner's reading of Christianity has not changed: Christ's divinity lay totally in his sacrificial death as a man.

Perhaps, in view of this, Faulkner has belabored the Christ parallels. On the Thursday night before the execution, there is a last supper at which Polchek, the Judas figure, betrays his uneasiness; one of his men, Pierre, denies him to save himself; there follows then the summons to his father and the temptation scene. Returned to the prison, they find that Pierre has returned to the fold. But the Corporal is not returned to his cell with the others; instead he is put in with a thief and a murderer who are to die with him on the morrow. Horse, the feeble minded murderer, can only approximate one word, Paris, and this becomes the equivalent of Paradise as a destination to be gained through death.

The Corporal is summoned out once again, this time to the office of the prison commandant where the priest waits for him with the utensils of the Last Sacrament arranged on the desk. The priest, however, is also acting as the agent of the Marshal, offering the Corporal one more chance to choose life. The Corporal again refuses and the priest goes down on his knees before him asking the Corporal to save him, the priest. Helping him to his feet, the Corporal then goes to the door "to strike two or three rapping blows with his knuckles on the wood" (367), the signal from the priest in the confessional to dismiss the confessor. The roles have been reversed. The priest facing the true essence of his religion finds all else meaningless in comparison and, borrowing a bayonet, suicides in the Roman manner.

The execution the next morning finds the Corporal at the stake between the thief and the murderer. When his body topples over, a loop of barbed wire tangles around the post and the Corporal's head. His body is carried away for burial by his sister and interred in a hillside. That night a barrage falls on the area and in the morning the women returning to the site find it blasted. Marthe runs ahead:

> When they overtook her, she was holding in her hand a shard of the pale new unpainted wood which had been the coffin. . . . That was Sunday. When the girl returned with

the shovel, still running, they took turns with it, all that day until it was too dark to see. They found a few more shards and fragments of the coffin, but the body itself was gone. (401)

After the peace, there is a descent into hell as the twelve men are sent out to bring back the remains of an unknown soldier. The ravages of the land are

already beginning to vanish beneath a fierce rank colorless growth of nourishmentless grass coming not tenderly out of the earth's surface but as though miles and leagues up from Hell itself, as if the Devil himself were trying to hide what man had done to the earth which was his mother. (407)

Their orders read:

"Proceed to Verdun and thence with expedition and despatch to the catacombs beneath the Fort of Valaumont and extricate therefrom one complete cadaver of one French soldier." (409)

The sergeant, "an office man, meticulous and reliable," armed with his orders like Aeneas with the golden bough, herds his men "one by one into the stone tunnel, to drop, plunge in their turn down the steep pitch of the stone stairs as though into the bowels of the earth" (409). Unnerved by their experience in this hell, the men want brandy. In Verdun an old woman believing the body they have brought back to be her son buys the corpse from the men and they get their brandy. But they are now faced with the problem of finding another body to fill the coffin. The body they find is presumably that of the Corporal and it is that body that is taken to rest in the tomb of the unknown soldier.

Two short scenes complete the novel. In the first, two men appear at the home of the Corporal's sisters: they are the runner, half man, half scar and the Judas figure, Polchek. His parallels are completed by the thirty pieces of silver he attempts to give to the sisters and his exit from the house which forsehadows his suicide:

199

. . . the tall feather in the hat which he had never removed breaking into the line of the lintel as if he actually were hanging on a cord from it against the vacant shape of the spring darkness. Then he was gone too. (432–33)

The runner, the St. Paul to the Corporal's Christ, has come to get the medal given to the Corporal, an external sign of the disciple. In the last scene, the funeral cortege of the Marshal pauses at the tomb of the unknown soldier. At that moment the runner breaks out of the crowd, interrupting the eulogy. He throws the medal at the caisson,

his voice ringing again in the aghast air as the crowd rushed down upon him: 'You too helped carry the torch of man into that twilight where he shall be no more; these are his epitaphs: They shall not pass. My country right or wrong. Here is a spot which is forever England—' (346)

The crowd beats him and leaves him lying in the gutter. Over him bends the Quartermaster General weeping:

'That's right,' the runner said: Tremble. I'm not going to die. Never.'
'I am not laughing,' the old man bending over him said. 'What you see are tears.' (437)

Faulkner has, in the past, insisted with equal vigor that the spirit of man cannot be quenched. However, in A *Fable* he makes his most universal statement of this thesis. Whether he has overdone the Christian allusions is a moot question. Unless we understand the intent of these allusions, unless we see him following his habitual pattern of using the sacrifice of Christ as a man as the rationale of his divinity, we are likely to find, as have some critics, that the novel is a meaningless mishmash.

8. Yoknapatawpha Revisited

*I*n *The Town* Faulkner makes a pronounced shift from the mythic import of the Flem-Eula relationship in *The Hamlet* to the realm of Romance. Many critics have felt the novel to be falling off from *The Hamlet* but as a novel it is much more tightly conceived. *The Hamlet* ended with Flem in control of everything: "Snopes turned his head and spat over the wagon wheel. He jerked the reins slightly. 'Come up,' he said" (373). Snopesism is established there as the ultimate form of the acquisitive instinct. But, as we have seen, it is not Faulkner's bent to leave the world in the powers of any evil force without suggesting a hopeful antithesis. *The Town* and *The Mansion* together offer us this optimism in the eventual reassertion of the good.

But it is not Flem and not merely Snopesism that is at the center of this novel; it is Gavin Stevens. Cleanth Brooks has dealt with this most admirably, noting the Don Quixote element in his characterization but not pursuing the characterization of Ratliff as a Sancho Panza, the rational voice trying to tell Gavin Stevens what the truth is only to despair repeatedly, "He missed it," "And still he missed it." Until finally Ratliff must tell us *why* he missed it:

> No no, no no, no no. He was wrong. He's a lawyer, and to a lawyer, if it aint complicated it dont matter whether it works or not because if it aint complicated up enough it aint right and so even if it works, you dont believe it. (296)*

While Ratliff will agree with Gavin Stevens that Snopesism is something to fear and to combat, it is remarkable that none of Stevens' efforts do anything to defeat the enemy; indeed, his blunderings simply complicate the natural process by which Snopesism is undone. This natural process of defeating Snopesism is first made manifest in Faulkner's retelling of the short story "Centaur in Brass," where Flem's acquisitiveness is directed at the scrapped and not-yet-scrapped brass lying around the powerhouse. His attempts to work the two Negroes against each other to further his own ends is defeated when Tom Tom and Turl finally pause long enough to talk to each other in the ditch where they have landed: "a sanctuary, a rationality of perspective" (27). Defeating Snopesism is as simple as this, but not for the complicating powers of a Gavin Stevens.

Eula Varner Snopes' emanations of sex help Stevens to complicate his existence immensely. Whereas de Spain meets the force represented by Eula on the basic level of becoming her lover, Stevens must build around her a chivalric tower of unblemished honor in terms of which he can offer combat to de Spain. Stevens' meetings with de Spain all end in his own frustration and defeat, the "fated lust" of the lovers proving stronger than any artificial conventions Stevens can affix to his standard. When he attempts to unseat de Spain as mayor through a suit involving the missing brass from the city powerhouse, Eula offers her body to him, believing simply

---

* Page references are to the Vintage edition of *The Town* (New York, 1957).

that since his actions are due to a kind of sexual frustration, that frustration is hardly worth perpetuating when the solution is so simple. His rejection of her is shocked and frightened. He is, like Harry Wilborne of *The Wild Palms*, another Tristan, or as Cleanth Brooks puts it, "a countrified descendant of Sir Tristan.'" Brooks then introduces Rougemont's analysis of romantic love in terms of the Tristan legend and concludes that

> Gavin, of course, is something more than a belated Tristan. His motivation is complicated. It includes a fierce resentment of Eula . . . . It also includes hurt pride, for he is stung by the fact that Eula is offering herself to him in pity —"because you are unhappy." Gavin furiously resents the condescension, but, as Rougemont would suggest, he may unconsciously be hugging to himself his unhappiness. For Gavin is thoroughly orthodox in insisting that love—at least the passionate, bewildering, romantic love that he craves—is necessarily unhappy.

There is no question of Flem in this passion, for he is impotent. And as for Manfred, Brooks points out that he is merely the "cheerful, fleshly lover" who enjoys Eula without the necessity of bringing the soul into it. "But Gavin cannot contemplate marrying his Iseult; when, much later, he does marry Melisandre, his marriage involves friendship and even affection, but presumably not much passion." [1]

Bloodied up by de Spain and withdrawing his missing brass suit against him, Stevens retires to Heidelberg to take another degree. As he leaves, he turns over to Ratliff the responsibility of warding off Snopesism. But the next example of Snopesism we encounter is an indirect result of Stevens' actions. When the war broke out and Gavin returned to work in the Y.M.C.A., he took with him Montgomery Ward Snopes who saw this as a likely way of evading the draft. Upon his return, Montgomery Ward brings with him the stock of pornographic pictures with which he builds his little peep show business behind the facade of the "Atelier Monty," supposedly a photographic studio. It is time and circumstance that destroy this little business, not the crusading Stevens. In fact, it is Flem who arranges that even after serving a prison term Montgomery Ward will not return to Jefferson, for Flem has discovered that he must have respectability as a complement to his goal of financial power.

It is at this time that Stevens turns his attention to Eula's daughter, Linda, determined to save her from Snopesism and from Jefferson, the bastion of the plague. He begins to "form her mind," giving her books to read and preparing her with dreams of the outside world—eastern colleges and then Greenwich Village. Again, by indirection, his meddling is to result in more disaster, for it is the situation he builds around Linda that results in Eula's suicide.

With the completion of Eula's monument, Linda is free to go to New York to seek the dreams Gavin Stevens has given to her. The story that rounds out the novel is that of the four children of Byron Snopes, the bank robber who disappeared in Texas. The four children are animalistic reversions of Snopesism sent back to Jefferson but who prove too much even for the Snopes clan and they are sent back with shipping tags around their necks. It is now the Snopes who are cleaning the town of their own kind who fail to appreciate the necessity of respectability, the complement Flem seeks to his financial power. As the novel opened with Chick Mallison's pronouncement of the idea of community—"So when I say 'we' and 'we thought' what I mean is Jefferson and what Jefferson thought"—(3) so it ends with the same pronouncement upon the departure of the half-breed Snopes children: ". . . and we—all of us; we represented Jefferson—watched them mount and vanish one by one into that iron impatient maw" (371). Within this framework of the community watching the progress and evolution of Snopesism, Faulkner has followed two closely related stories: that of the comic knight errantry of Gavin Stevens, and the various stories which show the evil influence of Snopesism being frustrated and driven out of the community by much simpler methods than Stevens could conceive. The material reworked from the short stories "Centaur in Brass" and "Mule in the Yard," material that has brought charges that the novel is episodic in construction, is in reality carefully chosen and included for its integral part in illustrating the simplicity by which Snopesism can be countered.

There is very little influence of myth to be found in *The Town*. The shift from the Devil-Hades motif for Flem has the effect of making Flem "humanly wicked" as Brooks puts it and the impact of his evil is consequently diminished. As Eula explains to Stevens after she tells him of Flem's impotence, "You see? You've got to be careful or you'll have to pity him" (331). The evil force which in *The Hamlet* seemed omnipotent is, in *The Town*, not only dealt with capably by simple individuals, but is explicitly impotent.

However, the imagery associated with Eula continues in *The Town*. She is

> that Frenchman's Bend Helen, Semiramis—no: not Helen nor Semiramis: Lilith: the one before Eve herself whom earth's Creator had perforce in desperate and amazed alarm in person to efface, remove, obliterate, that Adam might create a progeny to populate it. (44)

To Gavin's sister she is Semiramis: " 'You don't marry Semiramis: you just commit some form of suicide for her' " (50). To Ratliff, Stevens is like one of the anonymous figures who must have surrounded the famous lovers of legend, "Because there was more folks among the Helens and Juliets and Isoldes and Guineveres than jest the Launcelots and Tristrams and Romeos and Parises" (101). And when Stevens is leaving for Heidelberg, Ratliff comments to himself that "one dont really ever lose Helen, because for the rest of her life she dont never actively get rid of him" (102). Chick Mallison immediately repeats this: "I remember how Ratliff once said that the world's Helens never lose forever the men who once loved and lost them; probably because they—the Helens

—dont want to" (103), and then rephrases it three more times (104, 105, 114). Gavin Stevens repeats his sister's comment, " 'You dont marry Helen and Semiramis; you just commit suicide for her' " (133), and then just before Eula's death he muses about the community's belated reaction to the love affair of Eula and de Spain: "eighteen years ago when Manfred de Spain thought he was just bedding another loose-girdled bucolic Lilith, he was actually creating a piece of buffoon's folklore" (319).

Certainly Faulkner's conscious control of his mythic allusions is demonstrated here. When his purpose is to humanize and minimize the scope of Flem's evil, the mythic allusions disappear; however, to maintain the mythic amplitude of Eula's sexual attractions, he retains and emphasizes the mythic allusions already established.

In *The Mansion* Faulkner continues his account of the downfall of the Snopes, ending with the death of Flem. It is as if his monumental effort of *A Fable* had proved to him that the transcendence of man's spirit really does negate the force of evil and he had set out to witness this by destroying his most effectively evil character. In case anyone would care to put forward Jason Compson as a candidate for this honor, Faulkner includes him too. Jason attempts to outwit Flem in the sale of the Compson pasture, but Flem turns the deal to his favor, holding the land for a postwar housing project. Both Flem and Jason are yoked in service, to "their mutual master, the Devil" (326).*

This constant diminishment of Snopesism as consummate evil, the process of putting it in a new perspective, is continued with Montgomery Ward's reflections after he has succeeded in executing Flem's plan to have Mink caught in an attempted jailbreak, thereby adding another twenty years to his sentence:

* Page references are to the Random House edition of *The Mansion* (New York, 1959).

I dont remember just when it was, I was probably pretty young, when I realised that I had come from what you might call a family, a clan, a race, maybe even a species, of pure sons of bitches. So I said, *Okay, okay, if that's the way it is, we'll just show them. They call the best of lawyers, lawyer's lawyers and the best of actors an actor's actor and the best of athletes a ballplayer's ballplayer. All right, that's what we'll do: every Snopes will make it his private and personal aim to have the whole world recognize him as THE son of a bitch's son of a bitch.*

But we never do it. We never make it. The best we ever do is to be just another Snopes son of a bitch. (86–87)

Ratliff, the most rational and calm evaluator of Snopesism, is the spokesman of the idea Faulkner seems to be advancing. Chick, speaking to his uncle, quotes Ratliff:

"I know, I know, you and Ratliff both have told me often enough; if I've heard Ratliff one time I've heard him a hundred: 'Man aint really evil, he jest aint got any sense.'" (230)

The frustration of Snopesism accounts for two of the interpolated stories which Brooks calls episodic. Clarence Snopes is eliminated from political power by Ratliff's simple expedient of having his pants brushed with twigs from the dogs' thicket which results in a certain state of excitement among the dogs attendant upon the political rally. Uncle Billy Varner, the political boss, is outraged at the three-legged activity of the dogs and summarily withdraws his support of Clarence: "I aint going to have Beat Two and Frenchman's Bend represented nowhere by nobody that ere a son-a-bitching dog that happens by cant tell from a fence post'" (319).

The honor of frustrating Orestes Snopes belongs to Gavin Stevens. In the dispute over the strip of land between the Meadowfill property and the former Compson property now becoming a housing tract, Orestes is finally reduced to an attempt upon Meadowfill's life with a booby trap rigged in such a way as to throw the suspicion on McKinley, an ex-marine. The plan fails and Stevens is able to use the booby trap as blackmail to make Orestes give up title to his part of the land. To Stevens, Snopesism is still a consummate evil; it is Ratliff who tells us what stage we've reached in a true evaluation of the Snopeses:

> "You see?" he [Stevens] said. "It's hopeless. Even when you get rid of one Snopes, there's already another one behind you even before you can turn around."
>
> "That's right," Ratliff said serenely. "As soon as you look, you see right away it aint nothing but just another Snopes." (349)

But of course the major action of the novel is Mink's revenge upon Flem. The novel begins with a retelling of the dispute between Mink and Houston which leads to the ambush murder of Houston. Faulkner gives greater depth to Mink's act, adding an element of injured honor in Mink's avowal that

> "I aint shooting you because of them thirty-seven and a half four-bit days. That's all right; I done long ago forgot and forgive that . . . . That aint why I shot you. I killed you because of that-ere extry one-dollar pound fee." (39)

The shooting of Houston is an un-Snopeslike act in that it is not properly calculated. Mink should have waited for Flem's return from his Texas honeymoon in the belief that Flem could get him off, but his injured honor will not allow this and he is faced with the necessity of placing his trust in *"them"*:

> He simply couldn't wait any longer. He had simply had to trust *them*—the *Them* of whom it was promised that not even a sparrow should fall unmarked. By *them* he didn't mean that whatever-it-was that folks referred to as Old Moster. He didn't believe in any Old Moster. Had seen too much in his time that, if any Old Moster existed, with eyes as sharp and power as strong as was claimed He had, He would have done something about. Besides, he, Mink, wasn't religious . . . . He meant, simply, *them*—they—it, whichever and whatever you wanted to call it, who repre-

sented a simple fundamental justice and equity in human affairs. (5–6)

Throughout his trial, Mink waits for Flem's return and his failure to show up registers with Mink as a complete betrayal. Sentenced to life imprisonment, he fastens on the date twenty years in the future when he will be eligible for parole and freed to enact his vengeance on Flem.

Through Flem's direction, Montgomery Ward is sentenced to Parchman and inveigles Mink into the attempted escape that adds another twenty years to his sentence and another twenty years to Flem's life expectancy. Mink accepts the extended sentence patiently and years later when another escape is planned that will involve him he refuses to participate. The one successful escapee waits outside to kill Mink, but Mink expresses a new kind of faith going beyond the *"they"* or *"them"* of his earlier life. " 'Maybe He will kill them there' " (99). The warden wants to know how Mink has made his peace with God since he has never attended the chapel:

> "I didn't need no church," he said. "I done it in confidence."
> "In confidence?" the Warden said.
> "Yes," he said, almost impatiently. "You dont need to write God a letter. . . ."
> "So He will take care of Stilwell for you," the Warden said.
> "Why not? What's He got against me?" (100)

And evidently God has nothing against Mink, for Stilwell, the escapee, dies when an abandoned, "deconsecrated" church in which he has been hiding falls in on him. Freed earlier than he might have been through the efforts of Linda, Mink makes his way to Memphis to buy a gun, but is delayed for a few days during which he is involved in the building of a church led by the ex-marine who has had a vision of Christ. What Faulkner intended with this incident is uncertain. Christ appeared to the marine as another soldier ordering him to "Fall in"—to resist death. Twice the marine denied the order, saying that as long as he remained still everything would be all right, but Christ demanded movement and life. Faulkner does not tell us of any impact the narration of this vision might have had on Mink. In fact, it seems only to stress his alienation. "He, Mink, watching them all, himself alien, not only unreconciled but irreconcilable: not contemptuous, because he was just waiting" (281). Since Faulkner uses Christ as a symbol of the brotherhood of man we might assume that this episode offers Mink an opportunity to give up his plan of vengeance and to join with this group in a new integrated life. But if this is the intent, it seems to fall flat. The story is not developed adequately in relation to any character's consciousness for it to have sufficient meaning. Mink does, in fact, leave the group, go to Memphis, get his gun, make his way to Jefferson, and kill Flem.

There is a far more mythic factor offered in relation to Mink's life. That is the relation to the land. Faulkner has from the first displayed an interest in the relation between the land and his characters, the close bond between those who lived on and off the land. For Mink, as he contemplates a crop he has labored on in prison, the relationship is understood as one of bondage:

> It was a fine crop, one of the best he remembered, as though everything had been exactly right . . . . As though back there in the spring the ground itself had said, *All right, for once let's confederate instead of fighting*—the ground, the dirt which any and every tenant farmer and sharecropper knew to be his sworn foe and mortal enemy—the hard implacable land which wore out his youth and his tools and then his body itself . . . . *And not just me, but all my tenant and cropper kind that have immolated youth and hope on thirty or forty or fifty acres of dirt that wouldn't nobody but our kind work because you're all our kind have.* (90)

Mink's long prison sentence has let him think out this relationship and he discovers that "people of his kind never had owned even temporarily the land which they believed they had rented between one New Year's and the next one. It was the land itself which owned them . . . in perpetuity" (91). But Mink is now exempt from this thralldom; he is not owned by the land but by the state.

When Mink is freed from prison, Faulkner echoes Wordsworth's "Intimations Ode" to explain further his orientation to nature: "When suddenly, somewhere deep in memory, there was a tree, a single tree" (104). The memory stirred by this remembered tree is of his ill mother for whom he killed a squirrel and he discovers in terms of the tree, "unaxed in memory and unaxeable," that *"it aint a place a man wants to go back to; the place dont even need to be there no more. What aches a man to go back to is what he remembers"* (106).

Mink's problem is that earth represents to him a force seeking to reclaim him, something he cannot allow until he has completed his revenge upon Flem. On his way to Jefferson with the gun, he stops and works in a Negro's cotton field, sleeping that night in a cotton truck:

> He was quite comfortable. But mainly he was off the ground. That was the danger, what a man had to watch against: once you laid flat on the ground, right away the earth started in to draw you back down into it. (402)

Having killed Flem, Mink returns to what once was his home. It is there that Stevens and Ratliff find him and give him money to complete his escape:

> Then the time came to go on. He was glad of it in a way; a man can get tired, burnt out on resting like on anything else. Outside it was dark, cool and pleasant for walking, empty except for the old ground. But then a man didn't need to have to keep his mind steadily on the ground after sixty-three years. In fact, the ground itself never let a man forget it was there waiting, pulling gently and without no hurry at him between every step, saying, Come on, lay down; I aint going to hurt you. Jest lay down. (434)

Now Mink is free of his obligation, free to lie down if he wants, and he arranges himself carefully to face the east. ". . . walk west but when you lay down, face the exact east. So he moved, shifted a little, and now he was exactly right and he was free now, he could afford to risk it" (435). Mink's assimilation into the earth ends the novel with a passage of poetic transcendence:

> . . . it seemed to him that he could feel the Mink Snopes
> that had had to spend so much of his life just having un-
> necessary bother and trouble, beginning to creep, seep, flow
> easy as sleeping; he could almost watch it, following all the
> little grass blades and tiny roots, the little holes the worms
> made, down and down into the ground already full of the
> folks that had the trouble but were free now . . . , all
> mixed and jumbled up comfortable and easy so wouldn't
> nobody even know or even care who was which any more,
> himself among them, equal to any, good as any, brave as
> any, being inextricable from, anonymous with all of them:
> the beautiful, the splendid, the proud and the brave, right
> on up to the very top itself among the shining phantoms
> and dreams which are the milestones of the long human re-
> cording—Helen and the bishops, the kings and the un-
> homed angels, the scornful and graceless seraphim. (435–36)

This concept of the earth as womb of life is not divorced from myth by the emphasis on the hardness of life and the struggle to wrest life from it. Earth remains the seedbed of all life, the true mother, and Mink's intuition of himself becoming one with the earth, although it posits no reincarnation of life, is still a truly mythic intuition.

On the simplest level of allusion, Faulkner again embroiders his text with images intended to convey the sexuality of Eula. The sexual force exerted by her becomes "one strand of Lilith's hair" (111); later she is metaphorically Venus (211); and once again she is equated frequently with Helen. Ratliff, tirelessly recapitulating Stevens' brush with Eula, expands his use of the Helen metaphor:

. . . he had done been disenchanted for good at last of Helen, and so now all he had to worry about was what them Menelaus-Snopeses might be up to in the Yoknapatawpha-Argive community while he had his back turned . . . . He would have plenty of time after he come back to find out that aint nobody yet ever lost Helen. (130)

And when Stevens does come back from Europe and becomes involved in the training of Eula's daughter Linda, he and Ratliff engage in a conversation in which evil is equated with darkness and the glories of man's life with light. Ratliff is talking:

"Helen walked in light." And he says,

"Helen was light. That's why we can still see her, not changed, not even dimmer, from five thousand years away." And I says,

"What about all them others you talk about? Semiramises and Judiths and Liliths and Francescas and Isoldes?" And he says,

"But not like Helen . . . . It's because the others all talked . . . . Do you know there is not one recorded word of hers anywhere in existence, other than that one presumable Yes she must have said that time to Paris?" (133)

Presumably Stevens and Faulkner choose to forget Helen's appearance before Telemachos in *The Odyssey* where she is quite voluble. The Paris-Helen image is invoked twice more for Eula (139 and 360). Helen, Eve, and Lilith are summoned up in relation to Mink's initiation into the sexuality of Memphis (290) and Semiramis and Messalina become a simile for the seductive wonders of the free world upon his release from prison (262).

There is a spattering of biblical imagery also. The judge's dais at Mink's trial might be his Golgotha (41); Ratliff wrestles with his conscience like Jacob (164); the community has only the Galilean with which to battle the amoral life force represented by Eula and de Spain (212); and the young folk attending Wednesday night prayer meeting need never to have heard of the Samson and Delilah euphemism to support their instinctive tendencies toward sex (121).

There is still the role of Linda to be considered. In this novel she is a widow returned from the Spanish Civil War deafened by an explosion. Her return to Jefferson seems unaccountable to the narrators, for there is nothing to hold her here. (In *The Town*, Stevens had arranged to have Hoak McCarron, Linda's real father, at her wedding and therefore Linda is finally aware that Flem is not her true father.) Cleanth Brooks says that

> Linda has in fact come back to see justice executed on Flem. In this novel she becomes a sort of Medea, an implacable avenging spirit, biding her own time, giving no hint of what she actually means to do, making use of Gavin Stevens, and, as part of her scheme, willing to live in the same household with the hated Flem Snopes as she coolly plans his execution.[2]

The imagery from Romance reserved for Stevens in the previous novel, in this novel belongs to Linda, who, after the war during which she worked as a riveter in a shipyard, is now marked with "a really splendid dramatic white streak in her hair running along the top of her skull almost like a plume." To Charles she is one of the "knights-errant liberal reformers," the "white plume collapsed in gallantry across her skull, with all the dragons dead" (350–51). But all the dragons are not yet dead. Linda initiates Mink's release from prison two years ahead of time, knowing that he will kill Flem. Through the Jaguar automobile delivered promptly after Flem's death she manages to communicate to Stevens that the death was truly an execution directed by herself. Thus Stevens discovers that he has been instrumental in the war on Snopesism, but only indirectly and as a tool of another.

This, then is Faulkner's diminution and defeat of Snopesism. The very real evil it once represented evidently could not be sustained in the face of the transcendence of man's spirit expressed in *A Fable*. But this does not mean that

Faulkner was finished with the problem of evil. Nor does the relative absence of mythic influences in these two novels mean that Faulkner was abandoning his penchant for mythic analogues. Indeed, it would appear that the rigorous plan for eliminating Snopesism prevented him from indulging in the mythic analogues he has so often woven into his plots. With this work finished, Faulkner turned in his most relaxed manner to a sentimental "reminiscence" and playfully dealt with not the problem of evil, but with young Lucius Priest's initiation into "un-virtue."

In *The Reivers*, Faulkner introduces Boon, the livery business, and the new consuming passion for automobiles and then dismisses authority from the scene through the device of sending Lucius' parents off to a funeral. Immediately Boon communicates to Lucius by indirection the two of them will take the automobile to Memphis. Lucius' last defenses are gone when Boon offers to teach him how to drive. Lucius immediately slips into the metaphor of the fall as he tells the story: "I know better now of course, and I even knew better then: that Boon's fall and mine were not only instantaneous but simultaneous too" (50).* Throughout the narrative, Lucius will maintain a running commentary on the nature of virtue and non-virtue in an attempt to communicate his evaluation of his loss of innocence:

> So you see what I mean about Virtue? You have heard—or anyway you will—people talk about evil times or an evil generation. There are no such things. No epoch of history nor generation of human beings either ever was or is or will be big enough to hold the un-virtue of any given moment . . . ; all they can do is hope to be as little soiled as possible during their passage through it. Because what pity that Virtue does not—possibly cannot—take care of its own as Non-Virtue does. (52)

* Page references are to the Random House edition of *The Reivers* (New York, 1962).

His realization that he, smarter than Boon, is to be the leader of this excursion hits him with "that same exultant fever-flash which Faustus himself must have experienced" (53). The eleven-year-old Lucius is amazed at the opportunities opened to him by his initiation into deceit, the basest being the simplest:

> . . . so why didn't I take it [the simple, base way of deceit], who was already a lost liar, already damned by deceit; why didn't I go the whole hog and be a coward too; he irrevocable and irremediable like Faustus became? glory in baseness, make, compel my new Master to respect me for my completeness even if he did scorn my size? Only I didn't. It wouldn't have worked, one of us anyway had to be practical. (60–61)

So Lucius is practical and discovers that Non-virtue cooperates with her adherents, all things falling in place to further their plot. This is almost too much for his accustomed innocence:

> I wanted no more of this, no more of free will; I wanted to return, relinquish, be secure, safe from the sort of decisions and deciding whose foster twin was this having to steal an automobile. But it was too late now; I had already chosen, elected; if I had sold my soul to Satan for a mess of pottage, at least I would damn well collect the pottage and eat it too. (66)

As the acknowledged leader of the two, Lucius knows he can demand that they give up the theft of his father's automobile and the trip to Memphis, knows that Boon would concur with his decision; but he does not make the demand:

> . . . I said *All right then. Here I come.* Maybe Boon heard it, since I was still boss. Anyway, he put Jefferson behind us; Satan would at least defend his faithful from the first one or two tomorrows; he said: "We aint really got anything to worry about but Hell Creek bottom tomorrow." (68)

Before they reach Hell Creek bottom, Ned, the Negro, is discovered by his flatulence hidden under a tarpaulin in the back seat. At Hell Creek bottom which must be crossed on their way to the Memphis underworld which is Boon's destination there is a Charon who must aid them across. The old woodsman has plowed up the approaches to the creek to create a sea of mud and charges exorbitantly to ease travelers across with his span of mules. As in the first Yoknapatawpha novel, *Sartoris*, there is a dichotomy between the rural, horse-drawn society and the mechanized, modern society here represented by Memphis and equated with the underworld:

> Boon had told Ned and me that, once we had conquered Hell Creek bottom, we would be in civilisation; he drew a picture of all the roads from there on cluttered thick as fleas with automobiles. Though maybe it was necessary first to put Hell Creek as far behind us as limbo, or forgetfulness, or at least out of sight; maybe we would not be worthy of civilization until we got the Hell Creek mud off. (92)

Hell Creek and the mention of forgetfulness obviously are meant to give us the true name of Hell Creek—Lethe. Hell Creek is the point of no return. ‧

> [Having] conquered Hell Creek we locked the portcullis and set the bridge on fire. And it did seem as though we had won to reprieve as a reward for invincible determination, or refusal to recognize defeat when we faced it or it faced us. Or maybe it was just Virtue who had given up, relinquished us to Non-virtue to cherish and nurture and coddle in the style whose right we had won with the now irrevocable barter of our souls. (93–94)

In Memphis, Boon drops Ned off to pursue his own pleasures and he and Lucius go to Miss Reba's establishment. It is there Ned brings the stolen horse for which he has traded Mr. Priest's automobile. His assurance that he can make the horse run immediately seduces the entire company, again to the amazement of Lucius who had at first believed that his fall had been due to being "so puny a foeman" to Non-virtue. By this time he regards himself as a sophisticate—"not a connoisseur of course"—in the ways of Non-virtue. Suddenly everyone is contributing to the plan to take the horse to Parsham to race, and Lucius observes: "who serves Virtue works alone, unaided, in a chilly vacuum of reserved judgement; where, pledge yourself to Non-virtue and the whole countryside boils with volunteers to help you." (143).

Corrie (or Everbe), the whore Boon has come to visit, is putting up her fifteeen-year-old nephew Otis in Miss Reba's establishment with the intent of teaching him civilized manners. It is Otis who informs Lucius about sex, promising to arrange some kind of peephole to observe the business of the establishment. Lucius is still innocent:

> "What for?" I said. You see, I had to ask it. Because what I wanted was to be back home. I wanted my mother. Because you should be prepared for experience, knowledge, knowing: not bludgeoned unaware in the dark as by a highwayman or footpad. I was just eleven, remember. There are things, circumstances, conditions in the world which should not be there but are, and you cant escape them and indeed, you would not escape them even if you had the choice, since they too are a part of Motion, of participating in life, being alive. But they should arrive with grace, decency, I was having to learn too much too fast, unassisted. (155)

Lucius fights Otis, the "demon child," and when Everbe discovers the cause of his fighting, she makes a pledge to him to give up the business at once and entirely.

The entire company removes to Parsham to race the horse Lightning (or Coppermine) against Acheron. There the truly evil sheriff's deputy Butch threatens to prevent the race as a means of getting what he wants—Everbe. In order to gain the release of the horse for the race Everbe breaks her pledge and contributes her talents. Even now, before the race, Lucius thinks of breaking away from the pattern of Non-virtue, but "It was too late. Maybe yesterday, while I was still a child, but not now. I knew too much, had seen too much. I was a child no longer now; innocence and childhood were forever lost, forever gone from me" (175).

The race against Acheron is run in three heats over two days and Lucius rides Coppermine to victory, thanks to the sardine which Ned is holding for the horse as a reward at the end of the track. When Lucius finishes the race he looks up to find his grandfather there. Returned home, Lucius awaits his punishment; but his grandfather only talks to him, telling him he must learn to live with his knowledge:

> "Live with it? You mean, forever? For the rest of my life? Not ever to get rid of it? Never? I cant. Dont you see I cant?"
> "Yes you can," he said. "You will. A gentleman always does. A gentleman can live through anything. He faces anything. A gentleman accepts the responsibility of his actions and bears their consequences, even when he did not himself instigate them but only acquiesced to them, didn't say No though he knew he should." (302)

There is only one loose end to wrap up: Boon marries Everbe and the last line of the novel reveals that their first child is named Lucius Priest Hogganbeck.

This sentimental close to the novel is not out of order. *The Reivers* is essentially a "shaggy dog" story played as sentimental farce. Non-virtue is not really the equivalent of evil; it is a concept like Emerson's absence of good, something toward which Faulkner has had an emotional leaning for some time. It is evidence of his indebtedness to myth and mythic analogues that he could make of such a story the tale of a young boy's initiation into adulthood. Even the horse is once again used for the force it exerts upon the community, welding the most disparate persons together into a conspiracy to allow the horse to display its ultimate powers. The novel is a fitting climax to Faulkner's consideration of evil, showing him at the point where evil is part of even a gentleman's education but minimizing the force of that evil in men's lives.

Conclusion

Although naturalism has frequently been accepted to mean little more than pessimistic determinism, American literary naturalism, as Walcutt has shown, has always balanced this pessimism with a strong traditional sense of optimistic idealism. It is no different with Faulkner. As an artist, his intuitions of man's condition led him to seek forms which could present the very hardness of life and yet not succumb to the pessimism latent within that view. As a rational-empiricist, his presentation of man's estate is famous enough; and superficially attended to led to the misreadings that produced the near vilification attendant upon his early career. But this reading must always be balanced by his communication of a transcendent ideal. This dichotomy has been firmly entrenched in American critical thought since the Transcendentalists overcame the cultural lag in the United States and introduced the Romantic emphasis on the twofold modes of knowledge. The eighteenth century *Reason* is appropriated in the Emersonian vocabulary for that superior mode we today are likely to call intuition, and the way is then open for the punning designation of the rational-empiric mode as the understanding. The burgeoning lore of psychology has enforced this dichotomy with analyses of conscious and "unconscious" thought.

Accepting this distinction between the rational-empiric and the intuitive modes of thought, what application can be made to Faulkner's work? In an analysis of the novels, the simple dichotomy of the divided stream will not suffice, for in Walcutt's analysis the antithesis of "pure" naturalism is no more than a lingering moral idealism. For Faulkner, the other branch of the stream is a transcendent vision of man's spiritual power to create conceptual reality and, as such, approaches the symbolic mode of myth. In my examination of the novels I have been concerned with distinguishing between modes of knowledge in order to understand many of the points of the novels that have resisted analysis in rational-empiric terms. In his earliest novels, myth serves largely as rhetorical embellishment; but already, in the resurrection image, it portends his later use of myth as *mythos,* analogues which inform theme and structure. In the middle novels, where he displays an intuitive understanding of the true force of myth, this is supplemented by the creation of characters whose configuration of reality bears great correlation with that of the mythic consciousness. At the same time it reveals the necessity, the creative drive he often referred to as his "demon," which drove Faulkner to employ the forces inherent in myths and the mythic consciousness. This "necessity," I suggest, lies in his polar vision of man's estate. As a rational-empiricist, Faulkner has a view of man which embraces the folly, misery, and corruption denying the ideal of man. On the other hand, he cannot and will not surrender his view of man as a being capable of an ideal—that ideal often presented as a transcendental unification with the spirit of man. While in the great middle period Faulkner makes no attempt to present this conflict in any rationalized form, the novels following *Absalom, Absalom!* reveal a change in emphasis, a change that is roughly correlative to the epistemological progress from mythical consciousness to the religious consciousness. In this ethical period, there is a greater development of the rational-empiric attempt to resolve the distance between the poles of man's existence. That this was not a satisfactory resolution is indicated by Faulkner's abandonment of the approach in his magnum opus, *A Fable.* There is no attempt to mitigate the transcendental theme of this novel with any rational-empiric voice. And, if we are to adduce the last three novels as evidence, we must conclude that *A Fable* succeeded in laying to rest Faulkner's "demon," for these last three communicate none of the great tension of their predecessors. Myth as a factor in these novels is a consciously controlled tool subordinated to a vision already realized, the problem of evil no longer endangering the survival of the "veri-ties."

The use of the word *myth* in relation to the series of Yoknapatawpha novels is unwarranted. What myth is present there can largely be accounted for in terms of a mythical consciousness on the part of certain characters who interpret their regional inheritance in mythic terms. If we are to persist in the use of the term, it must be only after a careful redefinition of the word, a procedure which is largely unnecessary in view of the fact that the word *saga* already exists and would serve the same purpose better. The usual approach to the body of Faulkner's work, that of dividing the novels into those with a Yoknapatawpha background and those with other backgrounds, is also misleading. A consideration of the novels in the chronology of their publication is more revealing of the author's intellectual growth, if not of his artistic success.

Faulkner's period of artistic greatness manifested in the middle period and to a lesser degree in *Go Down, Moses* and *A Fable* is that of the poet of creative intuition. Here we have the "poetry" which Maritain says "obliges us to consider the intellect both in its wellsprings inside the human soul and as functioning in a nonrational . . . or nonlogical way." [3] Faulkner's distrust of language, his constant distortion of words and syntax, reveals what Maritain calls the "process of liberation from conceptual, logical, discursive reason," a process intended to allow scope for "intuitive reason," which is prior to logical reason.[4] The modern artist, says Maritain, frees himself from logical reason not by abolishing it, but by transforming it to make it serve the needs of his intuition. The essence of Faulkner's intuition is in that realm of mythic thought which is prior to logical reason.

His work stands as one of the finest examples of American literary naturalism. The term naturalism however, still remains as unsettled in our critical vocabulary as *myth*. Even Walcutt must use two meanings for the word: "pure" naturalism which is closer to the popular meaning of the term, signifying what in Faulkner I have labeled his rational-empiric vision concentrating on a demonic world; and the larger meaning of naturalism as a divided stream of "pure" naturalism and idealism. In Faulkner's work the antithesis to the "pure" naturalism exists in close relation to the forms of myth. There does not seem to be any immediate and direct relationship in Faulkner's intellectual history to the Transcendentalists, but the path of myth takes him independently to the same spot. Where the problem of evil constitutes the focal point of his rational-empiric vision, an ultimate transcendence enables him to accept the dominance of the spirit of man behind these appearances and to laugh the Olympian laugh.

Notes

Chapter 1

1. Ernst Cassirer, *The Philosophy of Symbolic Forms*, Vol. II: *Mythical Thought*, trans. Ralph Manheim (New Haven, 1955), pp. 11–12, 13.
2. Ibid., p. 29.
3. Benedetto Croce, *Aesthetic*, trans. Douglas Ainslie (London, 1909), p. 13.
4. *Myth and Mythmaking*, ed. Henry A. Murray (New York, 1960), p. 301.
5. *William Faulkner: Three Decades of Criticism*, ed. Frederick Hoffman and Olga Vickery (East Lansing, 1960), p. 281.
6. Lind, p. 297.
7. *Anatomy of Criticism* (Princeton, 1957), p. 33.
8. Ibid., pp. 33–34.
9. Ibid., p. 42.
10. Ibid., p. 41.
11. Cassirer, pp. 73–74.
12. Ibid., pp. 11–12.
13. Ibid., p. 156.
14. Ibid., pp. 157–58.
15. Ibid., p. 158.
16. Ibid., p. 108.
17. Ibid., p. 111.
18. *Cosmos and History: The Myth of the Eternal Return*, trans. Willard Trask (New York, 1959), p. 95.
19. Ibid., pp. 96–98.

Notes

Chapter 2

1. Olga Vickery, *The Novels of William Faulkner* (Baton Rouge, 1964), p. 1.
2. Ovid, *Metamorphoses*, trans. Rolfe Humphries (Bloomington, 1955), p. 109.
3. Vickery, p. 8.
4. Vickery, p. 23.
5. Quoted by Robert Cantwell, Introduction to *Sartoris*, Signet edition (New York, 1953), p. viii.

Chapter 3

1. Irving Howe, *William Faulkner*, 2nd ed. (New York, 1962), pp. 20–21.
2. Introduction to Faulkner's *New Orleans Sketches* (New Brunswick, 1958), pp. 27–29.
3. *Faulkner in the University*, ed. Frederick L. Gwynn and Joseph L. Blotner (Charlottesville, 1959), p. 253.
4. Ibid., p. 1.
5. Ibid., p. 31.
6. Ibid., p. 267.
7. *Modern Fiction Studies*, II (Autumn 1956), 143.
8. Ibid., p. 141.
9. *Faulkner in the University*, p. 5.
10. "The Interior Monologues of *The Sound and The Fury*," *English Institute Essays, 1952*, ed. Alan S. Downer (New York, 1954).
11. *The Philosophy of Symbolic Forms*, II, 29.
12. Ibid., p. 31.
13. Ibid., pp. 32–34.
14. Ibid., pp. 35–36.
15. Ibid., p. 74.
16. Ibid., pp. 110–11.
17. "The Working Novelist and the Mythmaking Process," *Myth and Mythmaking*, pp. 146–47, 151.
18. Cassirer, p. 42.
19. *The Novels of William Faulkner*, p. 8.
20. "Faulkner: The Word as Principle and Power," *Three Decades of Criticism*, pp. 199–200.
21. *Faulkner at Nagano*, ed. Robert A. Jelliffe (Tokyo, 1956), p. 104.
22. *The Golden Bough*, 3rd ed. (New York, 1935), IV, 137.
23. *Faulkner at Nagano*, p. 183.
24. *Perelandra* (New York, 1946), p. 215.

Notes

Chapter 4

1. *The Golden Bough*, 3rd ed. (New York, 1935), V, 95–96.
2. *The Philosophy of Symbolic Forms*, II, 37.
3. Ibid., p. 45.
4. Ibid., p. 194.
5. Ibid., p. 184.
6. Hyatt Waggoner, *William Faulkner, From Jefferson to the World* (Lexington, 1959), p. 66.
7. *University of Kansas City Review*, XXI (Summer 1955), 287.
8. Cassirer, pp. 77–78.

Chapter 5

1. Sherwood Anderson, *A Story Teller's Story* (New York, 1927), pp. 184–97.
2. *Anatomy of Criticism*, p. 134.
3. Ibid., pp. 139–40.
4. Ibid., p. 137.
5. Ibid., p. 147.
6. Ibid., p. 149.
7. Ibid., p. 147.
8. Ibid., p. 149.
9. Ibid., p. 223.
10. *Faulkner in the University*, p. 86.
11. John L. Longley, Jr., *The Tragic Mask* (Chapel Hill, 1963), pp. 194–95.
12. *The Hero with a Thousand Faces* (New York, 1956), p. 259.
13. *The Philosophy of Symbolic Forms*, II, 74.
14. Campbell, pp. 54–55.
15. Cassirer, p. 190.
16. Frye, p. 202.
17. Cassirer, p. 119.
18. Frye, p. 148.
19. Frye, pp. 202–3.
20. *William Faulkner, From Jefferson to the World*, p. 131.
21. Ibid., pp. 131–32.
22. Frye, p. 140.
23. Howe, *William Faulkner*, p. 45.
24. *Themis: A Study of the Social Origins of Greek Religion* (New York, 1962), p. 91.

25. *The Vanishing Hero: Studies of the Hero in the Modern Novel*, (New York, 1958), p. 107.
26. Frye, pp. 136–37.

Chapter 6

1. "Unity of Theme and Structure in *The Wild Palms*," *Three Decades of Criticism*, p. 321.
2. Denis de Rougemont, *Love in the Western World* (New York, 1957), p. 11.
3. Rougemont, p. 29.
4. Ibid., pp. 31–32.
5. Moldenhauer, p. 312.
6. Rougemont, p. 45.
7. Francis Fergusson, *The Idea of a Theater* (New York, 1953), p. 83.
8. Moldenhauer, p. 313.
9. Rougemont, p. 8.
10. *Faulkner in the University*, p. 171.
11. Campbell, *The Hero with a Thousand Faces*, p. 288.
12. Ibid., pp. 30, 37.
13. Ibid., p. 193.
14. Ibid., pp. 45–46.
15. Frye, *Anatomy of Criticism*, p. 188.
16. *Modern Language Notes*, LXXVI (December 1961), 731–32.
17. "The Theme and Structure of Faulkner's *The Hamlet*," *Three Decades of Criticism*, p. 337.
18. Greet, p. 338.
19. Ibid., p. 339.
20. Vickery, *The Novels of William Faulkner*, p. 167.
21. Greet, p. 340.
22. Vickery, pp. 179–80.
23. Brooks, p. 408.
24. "As Whirlwinds in the South: *Light in August*," *Perspective*, II (Summer 1949), 225–38.
25. Cassirer, *The Philosophy of Symbolic Forms*, II, 77.

Chapter 7

1. "The Hero in the New World: William Faulkner's *The Bear*," *Kenyon Review*, XIII (Autumn 1951), 642.
2. Cassirer, *The Philosophy of Symbolic Forms*, II, 238.
3. Ibid., p. 239.

4. Cassirer, pp. 222–23.
5. Ibid., p. 221.
6. *Faulkner in the University*, p. 239.
7. "The Parallel Philosophy of Emerson's *Nature* and Faulkner's *The Bear*," *The Emerson Society Quarterly* (IV Quarter 1958), 22–25.
8. *Walden* (New York, 1950), p. 82.
9. "Regeneration for the Man," *William Faulkner: Two Decades of Criticism*, ed. Frederick Hoffman and Olga Vickery (East Lansing, 1954), p. 256.
10. Ibid., p. 257.
11. Ibid., p. 258.
12. *The Novels of William Faulkner*, pp. 140–41.
13. Vickery, p. 144.
14. *The Yoknapatawpha Country*, pp. 279–80.
15. Vickery, p. 144.
16. *Themis*, pp. 483, 485.
17. Vickery, p. 116.
18. Ibid., p. 117.
19. *William Faulkner, From Jefferson to the World*, pp. 219–20.
20. Vickery, p. 122.
21. Waggoner, p. 244.
22. Ibid., pp. 247–48, 249.
23. Ibid., p. 225.
24. *Worship* (New York, 1957), p. 48.
25. Ibid., p. 50.
26. Ibid., p. 58.
27. "The Son of Man: He Will Prevail," *Sewanee Review*, LXIII (Winter 1955), 116.
28. Ibid., pp. 134–35.
29. Cassirer, p. 219.
30. Vickery, pp. 207–8.
31. Ibid., pp. 207–9.
32. Harrison, *Themis*, p. 490.

Chapter 8

1. *The Yoknapatawpha Country*, pp. 199–200.
2. Brooks, p. 227.
3. Jacques Maritain, *Creative Intuition in Art and Poetry* (New York, 1954), p. 4.
4. Ibid., p. 55.

Bibliography of Works Cited

Anderson, Sherwood. *A Story Teller's Story.* New York, 1927.

Blum, Irving D. "The Parallel Philosophy of Emerson's *Nature* and Faulkner's *The Bear*," *The Emerson Society Quarterly* (IV Quarter 1958), 22–25.

Brooks, Cleanth. *William Faulkner, the Yoknapatawpha Country.* New Haven, 1963.

Campbell, Joseph. *The Hero with a Thousand Faces.* New York, 1956.

Cantwell, Robert. Introduction to Faulkner's *Sartoris.* New York, 1953.

Cassirer, Ernst. *The Philosophy of Symbolic Forms,* Vol. II: *Mythical Thought,* trans. Ralph Manheim. New Haven, 1955.

Collins, Carvel. "A Conscious Literary Use of Freud?" *Literature and Psychology,* III (June 1953), 2–3.

———— "The Interior Monologues of *The Sound and The Fury*," *English Institute Essays,* 1952, ed. Alan S. Downer. New York, 1954.

———— Introduction to Faulkner's *New Orleans Sketches.* New Brunswick, 1958.

Croce, Benedetto. *Aesthetic,* trans. Douglas Ainslie. London, 1909.

Eliade, Mircea. *Cosmos and History: The Myth of the Eternal Return,* trans. Willard Trask. New York, 1959.

Faulkner, William. *Absalom, Absalom!* New York, 1951.

———— *As I Lay Dying.* New York, 1930.

———— *A Fable.* New York, 1954.

———— *Go Down, Moses.* New York, 1955.

Bibliography

Faulkner. *The Hamlet*. New York, 1956.

———— *Intruder in the Dust*. New York, 1948.

———— *Light in August*. New York, 1932.

———— *The Mansion*. New York, 1959.

———— *Mosquitoes*. New York, 1927.

———— *Pylon*. New York, 1935.

———— *The Reivers*. New York, 1962.

———— *Requiem for a Nun*. New York, 1951.

———— *Sanctuary*. New York, 1932.

———— *Sartoris*. New York, 1951.

———— *Soldiers' Pay*. New York, 1926.

———— *The Sound and the Fury*. New York, 1929.

———— *The Town*. New York, 1957.

———— *The Unvanquished*. New York, 1938.

———— *The Wild Palms*. New York, 1939.

Fergusson, Francis. *The Idea of a Theater*. New York, 1953.

Frazer, Sir James G. *The Golden Bough*. New York, 1927.

———— *The Golden Bough*, 3rd ed. 13 vols. New York, 1935.

Frye, Northrop. *Anatomy of Criticism*. Princeton, 1957.

Greet, T. Y. "The Theme and Structure of Faulkner's *The Hamlet*," *PMLA*, LXXII (September 1957), 775–90—reprinted in *William Faulkner: Three Decades of Criticism*, ed. Frederick J. Hoffman and Olga W. Vickery. East Lansing, 1960, pp. 330–47.

Gwynn, Frederick L. and Joseph L. Blotner (eds.). *Faulkner in the University*. Charlottesville, 1959.

Harrison, Jane Ellen. *Themis: A Study of the Social Origins of Greek Religion*. New York, 1962.

Hershleifer, Phyllis. "As Whirlwinds in the South: *Light in August*," *Perspective*, II (Summer 1949), 225–38.

Howe, Irving. *William Faulkner*, 2nd ed. revised. New York, 1962.

Jelliffe, Robert A. (ed.). *Faulkner at Nagano*. Tokyo, 1956.

King, Roma, Jr. "The Janus Symbol in *As I Lay Dying*," *University of Kansas City Review*, XXI (Summer 1955), 287–90.

Leaver, Florence. "Faulkner: The Word as Principle and Power," *South Atlantic Quarterly*, LVII (Autumn 1958), 464–76—reprinted in *Three Decades of Criticism*, pp. 199–209.

Lewis, C. S. *Perelandra*. New York, 1946.

Lewis, R. W. B. "The Hero in the New World: William Faulkner's *The Bear*," *Kenyon Review*, XIII (Autumn 1951), 642.

Lind, Ilse Dusoir. "The Design and Meaning of *Absalom, Absalom!*" *PMLA*,

Bibliography

LXX (December 1955), 887–912—reprinted in *Three Decades of Criticism*, pp. 278–304.

Longley, John L., Jr. *The Tragic Mask*. Chapel Hill, 1963.

Lytle, Andrew. "Regeneration for the Man," *Sewanee Review*, LVII (Winter 1949), 120–27—reprinted in *William Faulkner: Two Decades of Criticism*, ed. Frederick J. Hoffman and Olga W. Vickery. East Lansing, 1954, pp. 251–59.

——— "The Son of Man: He Will Prevail," *Sewanee Review*, LXIII (Winter 1955), 114–37.

——— "The Working Novelist and the Mythmaking Process," *Myth and Mythmaking*, ed. H. A. Murray. New York, 1960, pp. 141–56.

Maritain, Jacques. *Creative Intuition in Art and Poetry*. New York, 1954.

Moldenhauer, Joseph J. "Unity of Theme and Structure in *The Wild Palms*," *Three Decades of Criticism*, pp. 305–22.

Murray, H. A. "The Possible Nature of a 'Mythology' to Come," *Myth and Mythmaking*, pp. 300–52.

O'Faolain, Sean. *The Vanishing Hero: Studies of the Hero in the Modern Novel*. New York, 1958.

Ovid. *Metamorphoses*, trans. Rolfe Humphries. Bloomington, 1955.

Rougemont, Denis de. *Love in the Western World*. New York, 1957.

Stein, Bysshe. "Faulkner's Devil," *Modern Language Notes*, LXXVI (December 1961), 731–32.

Thoreau, Henry D. *Walden*. New York, 1950.

Underhill, Evelyn. *Worship*. New York, 1957.

Vickery, Olga. *The Novels of William Faulkner*. 2nd ed. revised. Baton Rouge, 1964.

Waggoner, Hyatt. *William Faulkner, From Jefferson to the World*. Lexington, 1959.

Wheelwright, Philip. *The Burning Fountain*. Bloomington, 1954.

Zink, Karl. "Faulkner's Garden: Woman and the Immemorial Earth," *Modern Fiction Studies*, II (Autumn 1956), 139–49.

Index

Index

The manuscript was edited by Robert H. Tennenhouse; the book was designed by Richard Kinney. The typeface for the text is linotype Electra designed by W. A. Dwiggins in 1935. The display face is Deepdene designed by Frederic Goudy for the Lanston Monotype Corporation.

The book is printed on S. D. Warren's Olde Style Antique paper and bound in Bancroft's Kennett cloth over boards. Manufactured in the United States of America.

Walter Brylowski is associate professor of English at Eastern Michigan University. He received his B.A. from Kalamazoo College, his M.A. from the University of Connecticut, and his Ph.D. from Michigan State University.

Faulkner's Olympian Laugh is the first extended study of myth in the novels, from *Soldier's Pay* to *The Reivers*. Accepting the position of many critics that Faulkner's work concerns the potentialities of the human spirit for finding meaning, Professor Brylowski concentrates on an analysis of the forms through which such conceptual meaning comes about. His approach is through the primitive configurations of reality manifested by many of the characters, configurations that approximate myth. Faulkner is thus placed among the young writers who followed eagerly upon the work of the Cambridge anthropologists. The new vocabulary of mythic images, most obviously that of the waste land, became a standard image for the writers of the twenties who envisioned their society as morally sterile. Only Faulkner among them transcended the mere vocabulary, intuited the form of myth, and recaptured the primitive view of the world that was created out of a magical, ritual encounter with environment.

After *Sartoris*, Faulkner creates characters that possess our imagination; heretofore they have been accepted as naturalistic aberrations, but viewed from the perspective of mythical thought as a symbolic form they now take on new dimensions. The form of the novels also mirrors the form of myth in that the basic conflict between life-destroying forces and man's ability to transcend the immediate agonies of his existence is reconciled in the realm of the spirit where lies a conceptual peace.

Faulkner's writing of the forties concentrates on the more advanced ethical and social engagement with society, although he continues work on *A Fable*, in which he directly communicates his vision of man's estate. The transcendence of human spirit explicitly stated through the Christ analogue quieted his daemon, for the remainder of his career is devoted to disposing of the evil of Snopesism that threatened his world. And then, having come to the Emersonian position that evil is the absence of good, Faulkner relaxes in a playful coda to his lifelong engagement with myth in *The Reivers*.